Colorado
a manual
for newcomers
and residents

What Others Are Saying About Previous Editions of
Colorado: A Manual for Newcomers and Residents

"[This] book out to be part of any home reference library…For someone just moving here with kids, the list of all the state school systems—public, private, college—is particularly useful. There's also advice on how to live at high altitude, the ins-and-outs of car registration, driver's licenses, insurance and emissions."

—*The Denver Post*

"This book can save you countless hours of frustration…Highly recommended!"

—*Welcome Home Magazine*

"T.J. Walker's compilation of lists and figures of things people need to know about living in Colorado, possibly one of the most comprehensive of its kind, can be a great resource of information for potential, recent or life-long residents."

—*The Four Corners Business Journal*

"…[A] concise, comprehensive and easy to get around book…. The section on schools and libraries is superb. You'll be guaranteed a good time if you take off with a copy of Chapter Nine [State-Wide Recreation & Entertainment] under your arm…. Good time are all around you and Walker can help you find them."

—*Ten Mile Times (Frisco CO)*

"….[A]n impressive amount of basic information on many aspects of our state…a valuable reference book for anyone living in this state—not only new immigrants."

—*Cortez Sentinel (Cortez CO)*

"…[A] timely compendium of facts and figures about the state…an excellent reference… a lot of interesting things within the covers….makes this state simple and easy to understand…"

—*Crestone Eagle (Crestone CO)*

"…[A] book full of helpful hints to help with just about every question a new resident could have. In fact, this useful little book will probably come in handy even for those who have called Colorado home for a number of years."

—*Glenwood Post (Glenwood Springs CO)*

THIRD EDITION

*Everything you need
to know about
living in Colorado*

Colorado
a manual
for newcomers
and residents

T.J. Walker

Publisher's Cataloging-in-Publication
(Prepared by Quality Books, Inc.)

Walker, T. J., 1956-
    Colorado : a manual for residents and newcomers :
everything you need to know about living in Colorado /
T.J. Walker. -- 3rd ed.
    p. cm.
    Includes bibliographical references and index.
    ISBN 1-883726-64-6

    1. Colorado--Guidebooks.   2. Moving, Household--
Colorado--Handbooks, manuals, etc.   I. Title

F774.3.W35 2001   917.8804'34
                           QBI01-201259

Cover design by Ann Douden
Interior design by Pauline Brown of pebble graphics, and
Christine Chambers

Third Edition
ISBN 1-883726-64-6

Published by Bradford Publishing Company
1743 Wazee St., Denver, CO
Copyright © 2001 by Bradford Publishing Company
Printed in the U.S.A.

Contents

1. Once Upon a Time in the West *(Dire Straits, 1979)* 1
   The State of Colorado

2. The Powers that Be *(Roger Waters, 1987)* 15
   Colorado's Government

3. School's Out Forever *(Alice Cooper, 1972)* 51
   State School Systems

4. This Must be the Place *(Talking Heads, 1983)* 81
   State Statistics

5. Behind the Wheel *(Depeche Mode, 1987)* 93
   Registration, Insurance, and Drivers Licenses

6. Send Lawyers, Guns, and Money *(Warren Zevon, 1978)* 113
   Laws, Rules, and Regulations

7. Changes in Latitudes, Changes in Attitudes *(Jimmy Buffet, 1977)* ... 121
   The Ten Fastest Growing Counties in Colorado

8. Money for Nothing *(Dire Straits, 1985)* 149
   Small and Home-Based Business Startup

9. Get Out of Denver *(Bob Seger, 1974)* 183
   Recreation, Entertainment, and Culture

10. Eight Miles High *(The Byrds, 1966)* 207
    High Altitude Living

11. So Far Away *(Dire Straits, 1985)* 221
    Getting from There to Here

12. New Kid in Town *(The Eagles, 1976)* 227
    Resources

Appendix A — Recommended Reading 259

Appendix B — Maps 269

Appendix C — Regional Transportation 273

Bibliography 281

Index 287

Preface to the Third Edition

Colorado has experienced enormous growth in the past decade and and much has changed since the second edition of the *Newcomer's Manual* was published just three years ago. The information in this book is compiled from over 100 government, business, and private resources. Colorado publishers contributed a wealth of information and Appendix A contains descriptions of their many books.

Every effort has been made to update the facts, figures, statistics and phone numbers as accurately as possible. Where possible, the data from the 2000 census reflects the most current information available. However, there may be unintentional mistakes, both typographical and in content. This text should be used only as a general guide.

To expand its usefulness, this new edition includes as many website addresses as we could find. If you don't have a computer, you can use one at your local library to do more research. Have fun following the incredible trail of links you'll find. Keep checking the Internet because thousands of new sites are added and changed daily. If you discover new sites, new information, or errors, let us know. Contact us by email at *www.editor@bradfordpublishing.com*. Thank you!

Once Upon a Time in the West

1

THE STATE OF COLORADO

Colorado Facts at a Glance

History

Geography/Topography

Weather

I moved to Colorado more than a decade ago. I fell in love with the breathtaking beauty of the mountains and the easy-going manner of the people I met while visiting my sister who had moved here exactly one year before. To this day, the new sights, sounds, smells, and discoveries the state offers on a seemingly unlimited basis amaze me. Also, to this day, I still have to ask my wife or sister where this town or that city is located, how to dress for mountain ventures, or about the history of a pile of sawdust that used to be a mining town.

I never bothered to learn much about this state. Trying to put a limit on the number of facts, figures, data, maps, and stories I seem to constantly cram into my head, I acquired new knowledge about Colorado only on a need-to-know basis. Being a self-employed entrepreneur, I quickly learned almost everything about conducting business here. Yet, before researching the material for this book, I couldn't tell you much about Colorado's history (weren't there cowboys and Indians here?), geography (the mountains are west of Denver), weather (it can rain in December and snow in July), unique laws (you can be fined three times the amount of a bad check), or high-altitude living (things just don't cook the same this high up).

In fact, while gathering information for this chapter from other Colorado publishers, one asked me if I planned to include a section on the state's pre-history. My first thought was "If something is pre-history, how do we know anything about it?" Allowing for the non-literal meaning of the word, I soon discovered this state has a very rich and interesting pre-history. Moving forward from there, I found the modern, high school type of history (which previously bored me to tears) to be full of wonderment. Since completing this chapter, I can proudly say "I know about the cliff dwellings in Mesa Verde, I know the location of Montrose, I know Colorado gets an average of 300 days of sunshine a year, and I can even tell you Colorado has 35 registered motorcycles per 1,000 residents!"

That being said, I still have this thing for learning a new subject in two stages. First, I want to see the bare-bones facts—statistics that give me an outline understanding. Then, at my leisure, I go back and fill in the blanks with dialog, prose and explanations. In keeping with this tradition, the first section of this chapter contains some bare-bones facts about Colorado, followed by some fascinating lessons on the pre-history, modern history, geography, topography, and weather of the most beautiful state in the country.

Colorado Facts At A Glance

Most demographic information about population is from the 2000 census. However, Colorado's incredible growth should be considered when evaluating this data.

People Of Colorado

Population, 2000. 4,301,261
Projected population, year 2005. 4,629,421
Population density, 2000 . . . . 41.5 persons per square mile

Population, 1990-2000 . . . . +30.6% change
Population over 18 years, 2000 3,200,466
Population under 18 years, 2000 1,100,795
Population 65 years old and over 9.7%
Asian/Pacific Islander
     population/rate, 2000 . . . . 99,834/2.2%
Black population/rate, 2000 . . . . 165,063/3.8%
Hispanic population/rate, 2000 . . . . 765,386/17.1%
Native American population/rate, 2000. . 44,2410/1.0%
White population/rate, 2000 . . . . 3,560,005/82.8%
Metropolitan area population. 84.0%
Metropolitan area
     population, since 1990 . . . . +30.6% change
Housing units, 2000 1,808,037
Households, 1990-1998 . . . . 21.7% change
Birth rate . . . . 14.7 per 1,000 population
Births to teenage mothers. . . . . 11.9% of total
Life expectancy . . . . 76.96 years
Death rate . . . . 6.6 deaths per 1,000 population
Marriage rate . . . . 8.3 marriages per 1,000 pop.
Divorce rate . . . . 4.8 divorces per 1,000 pop.

Geography In Colorado

Total area . . . . 104,100 square miles
Land area . . . . 103,718 square miles
Water area . . . . 371 square miles
Average elevation . . . . 6,800 feet
Highest point . . . . Mt. Elbert, at 14,433 feet
Lowest point . . . . Arkansas river, at 3,350 feet
Highest temperature . . . . 118° F
Lowest temperature . . . . -61° F
Natural resources . . . . Petroleum, natural gas, coal
Land in national parks . . . . 588,200 acres
Area in state parks . . . . 211,974 acres
Federal lands . . . . 36.3% owned by
                                          Federal Government
Hazardous waste sites . . . . 17 sites on national priority list

Education In Colorado

Public school expenditures . . . . $7,063 per student
Student/teacher ratio . . . . 18.2 students per teacher
Spending, public higher education . $2,780 per student
Tuition revenues, higher education . $2,013 per student
College enrollment, total . . . . 243,000 students

Government Of Colorado

Official name . . . . State of Colorado
Capital . . . . Denver
Admitted to Union . . . . August 1, 1876
Order of Statehood 38
Electoral votes 8
Executive term . . . . 4 years
Governor . . . . Bill Owens (R)
Senators . . . . Wayne Allard (R)
                                             Ben Nighthorse Campbell (R)
Number of U.S. Representatives . . 7 in 2002

Flag: Three alternating horizontal stripes of blue, white and blue
       with a large red "C" containing a gold disk in the center.

Motto: Nil Sine Numine (Nothing without Providence)

State Symbols

Animal . . . . Rocky Mountain Bighorn Sheep
Bird . . . . Lark Bunting
Flower . . . . White and lavender Columbine
Gem . . . . Aquamarine
Song . . . . Where the Columbines Grow
Tree . . . . Blue Spruce

Miscellaneous

Age of buying alcohol 21
Age of leaving school . . . . after age 16
Age of majority (full civil rights) . . 18
Age of marriage with consent 16
Age of marriage without consent . . 18

Economy Of Colorado
Income per capita 31,533
State Funding for Art . . . . $ 0.44 per capita

1999 Gross State Product (in millions)
Total $153,728
Agricultural 2,261
Construction 9,233
Manufacturing 15,622
Mining 462
Transportation and Utilities 18,740
Retail Trade 15,127
Wholesale 9,644
Oil and Gas 1,808
Real Estate 26,869

Communications In Colorado
Television stations 19
AM radio stations 55
FM radio stations 94
Daily newspapers 29

Travel In Colorado
Interstate highways . . . . 952.8 miles
Registered automobiles . . . . 675 per 1,000 population
Registered motorcycles . . . . 35 per 1,000 population

History Of Colorado
In the beginning was the Word, or maybe the Big Bang, or perhaps
both (maybe the sound of the Big Bang was the Word). Regardless,
we can jump ahead a few billion years to only 300 million years ago.
This was the time of the Ancestral Rockies, a vast mountain range
that eventually washed away and became part of a great ocean.
Fossil evidence of this can be found near the town of Lyons in deposits of sandstone that provided material for Denver's sidewalks as
the city grew. Shells of billions of sea creatures turned into the

Colorado limestone used to produce concrete for many of the state's highways and buildings.

Between the Ancestral Rockies and the beginnings of the modern Rockies (about 70 million years ago), what became Colorado was home to such dinosaurs as the bony-backed Stegosaurus, the three-horned Triceratops, and the 85-foot-long Diplodocus. In fact, Colorado has produced some of the richest fossil finds in the country. Also, during this period, much of this region was swampland, leaving behind debris that eventually became vast deposits of coal and natural gas. Volcanoes were not uncommon and their lava flows created many geological features of Colorado including the Table Mountains near Golden.

Skipping ahead to more recent pre-history, we can look at the nomadic tribes of the first Americans who lived here for more than 10,000 years before the first frontier city was built.

At one site, 40 miles north of Denver, artifacts have been carbon-dated to at least 11,250 years ago. Artifacts dating back over 10,000 years have also been found in another site 25 miles southeast of Denver. The origin of the first humans in the southwest is still debated; however, it is generally agreed that some 15-20 thousand years ago, nomadic hunters followed herds of prey across a temporary land bridge that is now the Bering Strait between Alaska and Siberia. Dependent on traveling with their food source, these Asian visitors eventually migrated south. As these tribes evolved from nomadic hunters into agricultural farmers, they laid down roots in places such as Mesa Verde, Colorado some 2,000 years ago.

Mesa Verde is located in Four Corners, the place where Arizona, Colorado, New Mexico, and Utah meet. This entire area was home to early tribes collectively known as the Anasazi. During the 13th century the Anasazi numbered more than 50,000. Yet a half-century later there were none. They didn't die out; their descendants still live in New Mexico and Arizona. For some unknown reason, they simply abandoned the area. We are not talking about leaving some tents or caves here. By the 13th century, Mesa Verde was filled with over 500 cliff dwellings, from one-room houses to large communal structures three or four stories high containing more than 200 rooms.

Between the 14th and 19th centuries, other more familiar tribes including the Ute, Comanche, Navajo, Apache, Kiowa and Shoshoni inhabited Colorado. Numerous wars and slaughters took place between various tribes, the Spanish, French and finally "American" pioneers. This is really becoming reminiscent of high school history class so I believe it's time to move on. For those closet archaeologists, great delight will be found in several of the books mentioned at the beginning of this chapter. A couple are coffee table books, full of fantastic full-color photos of ancient ruins and, while the others may not be able to compete with a rainbow, they are loaded with black and white photos and unlimited details about every major archaeological site in Colorado.

After the end of the Mexican-American War in 1848, farmers from New Mexico settled large portions of Colorado. This slow migration and settlement increased dramatically with the discovery of gold. Virtually all the older towns and cities of Colorado have their origins in mining and prospecting. In 1858, the Green-Russel party found gold along Little Dry Creek near the junction of the South Platte River and Cherry Creek. Exaggerated accounts of the discovery spread eastward, causing the Pikes Peak gold rush of 1859. Thousands of fortune hunters hurried across the plains on foot, on horseback, and in wagons. Most of these failed to find any gold and trudged wearily back home. But they had founded several little clusters of huts, known as Montana City, St. Charles, Auraria, and Denver City (named after General James W. Denver, territorial governor of Kansas); and these gradually grew into the capital city of Colorado.

On May 6, 1859, John H. Gregory discovered the Gregory Lode, a vein of gold-bearing quartz, near present-day Central City. Mines were quickly developed on the branches of Clear Creek, in South Park, and across the Continental Divide on the branches of the Blue River.

In 1859 the land that later became Colorado was within the territories of Kansas, Nebraska, Utah, and New Mexico. But the pioneers felt they should have a government of their own, so they created the Jefferson Territory, containing all of present-day Colorado and liberal strips of what is now Utah and Wyoming. Many of the miners ignored the authority of this territorial government and established local laws of their own, electing officials to enforce them.

On February 28, 1861, a law was signed creating the Colorado Territory. William Gilpin, appointed by President Lincoln, was the first governor. The territory was named for the river that rises in Grand Lake and flows through rugged chasms and fertile valleys to the great depths of the Grand Canyon and finally to the Pacific Ocean. (Other rivers rising in Colorado are the Rio Grande, Gunnison, Yampa, White, San Juan, Dolores, Arkansas, Republican, South Platte, and North Platte).

During the first decade following the Pikes Peak gold rush, Colorado's development was slow. Refractory ore (difficult to extract, process, and transport) was encountered in the mines. The Civil War claimed citizens for soldiers, and Indian resistance threatened the existence of the territory.

After surviving the ordeals of early years, Colorado made rapid progress in her second decade as a territory. Railways were completed to Colorado in 1870, narrow-gauge rail lines in the mountains tapped the mining regions, colony towns were founded, agriculture was extended, new mines were opened in the San Juan region and immigration escalated.

In 1864, Congress passed an Enabling Act to permit Colorado to become a state. However, the people voted against it because they did not want to pay the taxes needed to support a state government. Finally, more than ten years later, Colorado entered the Union as the 38th state on August 1, 1876, and was called the "Centennial State" in honor of the 100th anniversary of the Declaration of Independence.

During the 1880s progress continued on a grand scale. Mineral wealth poured forth from Aspen and other mining centers such as Leadville. Many other towns flourished; colleges and opera houses were built, and brownstone mansions rather than log cabins became representative of the times. Agriculture expanded with the construction of irrigation systems and the introduction of dry farming. The range livestock industry prospered. Wood production soared. Smelters were erected for the reduction of ores. Although the Panic of 1893 (which followed a devaluation of silver) was a severe blow to the mining industry, Colorado rallied. The great gold camp at Cripple Creek aided revival. Farming continued to expand, and new crops such as sugar beets created new wealth. By 1890, Colorado claimed a population exceeding 413,000.

The city of Leadville, mentioned above, was also home to one of the most unusual human-made structures. Built in 1895, Leadville's Ice Palace was constructed by approximately 300 craftsmen in less than 60 days. The main building materials were 8,000 tons of ice and 307,000 board feet of lumber. When completed, this crystal castle housed a skating rink, ballroom, banquet room, riding gallery, lounges, a kitchen and more. It covered over five acres and was electrically lit and heated by coal burning stoves. If you are fond of quirky little pieces of history, get a copy of *Leadville's Ice Palace* published by Ice Castle Productions. Weighing in at 391 pages, this fascinating book is the definitive work on the bizarre project one city used in an attempt to boost its economy.

This brings us up to the beginning of the 20th century. Since the turn of the century, historically significant events have multiplied in geometric proportions. The great depression, World Wars I and II, the Korean War, the civil rights movement, more wars, on and on. To describe Colorado's involvement in all these events would take much more space than can be allotted in this book.

Colorado's Geography/Topography

Colorado is the eighth largest state in the nation, with an area of 104,100 square miles and with over 36% of this area owned by the federal government. The state is rectangular, extending 387 miles east to west and 276 miles north to south.

The main feature of the state's geography is the Continental Divide, extending northeast to southwest and roughly bisecting Colorado into the Eastern and Western Slopes. Waters west of the Divide flow into the Pacific, east of the Divide into the Atlantic. The major rivers are the Arkansas, Platte, Rio Grande and Colorado. The state's largest natural lake is Grand Lake, which human enterprise has outdone with projects like the John Martin Reservoir on the Arkansas River and Blue Mesa Reservoir on the Gunnison River.

Colorado contains 75% of all the area in the United States over 10,000' high. It contains 53 peaks of more than 14,000', with the highest being Mt. Elbert at 14,433', and over one thousand peaks two miles high. In fact, the mountainous area of Colorado is six times that of Switzerland. Three of the nation's highest highways are in Colorado. The roads to the summits of both Pikes Peak and Mt. Evans are over 14,000' above sea level and Trail Ridge Road, which crosses through Rocky Mountain National Park and over the Continental Divide at 12,183', is the nation's highest continuous paved highway. The principal mountain ranges are the eastern Front Range, the central Sawatch Range, the Park Range in the north, the southern Sangre de Cristo Mountains and the San Juan Mountains in the southwest.

Plateaus, mesas, and canyons make up the western 25% of the state with high plains bordering Wyoming, Nebraska, Kansas, Oklahoma and New Mexico. Sloping upward from Kansas, Colorado's central plains gently rise approximately 2,000', from 3,386' to 5,200' above sea level.

Colorado has three national parks, seven national monuments, 12 national forests, 40 state parks, and one national recreation area.

Colorado's 63 counties are divided into five informal substate regions (see map in Appendix B):

Front Range	Adams, Arapahoe, Boulder, Denver, Douglas, El Paso, Jefferson, Larimer, Pueblo, Weld
Western Slope	Archuleta, Delta, Dolores, Eagle, Garfield, Grand, Gunnison, Hinsdale, Jackson, La Plata, Mesa, Moffat, Montezuma, Montrose, Ouray, Pitkin, Rio Blanco, Routt, San Juan, San Miguel, Summit
Eastern Plains	Baca, Bent, Cheyenne, Crowley, Elbert, Kiowa, Kit Carson, Lincoln, Logan, Morgan, Otero, Phillips, Prowers, Sedgwick, Washington, Yuma
San Luis Valley	Alamosa, Conejos, Costilla, Mineral, Rio Grande, Saguache
Eastern Mountains	Chaffee, Clear Creek, Custer, Fremont, Gilpin, Huerfano, Lake, Las Animas, Park, Teller

Colorado's Weather

Unpredictable, unbelievable, unanticipated calm, chaotic, implausible, improbable, beautiful, nasty, wonderful, violent, serene, ominous, threatening, and blissful are a few of the ways I can describe Colorado's weather.

Growing up in Florida, I experienced my share of violent thunderstorms and hurricanes. However, not until I moved to Colorado did I experience a real-life use of the Emergency Broadcast System. I was driving around Denver, listening to one of my favorite songs, when that nasty, high-pitched tone did its job and startled me back into reality. The clouds had been looking ominous but I had not seen any rain, lightening or thunder. The tone was followed by reports of three tornadoes over the area with one touching down and ripping a path along one of Denver's parkways less than a mile from my location. Being a closet thrill-seeker, I stopped my van and climbed on top to watch the show until I realized one mile is not exactly a safe distance from a fast moving, totally unpredictable tornado.

On another occasion, during a morning hike outside of Breckenridge, I experienced bright sunshine, sleet, rain, snow, and more sunshine followed by a heavy misty fog—all before lunch! Fortunately, I had been in Colorado long enough to know to pack the right clothes.

The reason I share these stories is that although I will cover the "for the tourist" descriptions of our weather, such descriptions don't relay the whole story. They consist of basic highs, lows, and averages but don't convey the extreme changes. Every year there are news stories of inexperienced hikers being rescued from snowstorms dressed in shorts and t-shirts. After all, it was 90° in the city when they left for the mountains.

If you look in a guide or tour book or break open an encyclopedia, this is basically what you will find about Colorado's weather:

Colorado enjoys an average of nearly 300 days of sunshine per year, with an average humidity of 33%. Precipitation varies with respect to elevation and location of a given area. This can range from 60" per year on the western slopes to 16" or less on the Great Plains and the Colorado Plateau. Rainfall is concentrated in the spring and summer and the plains are subject to heavy winter snowfalls. The annual average temperature (Fahrenheit) ranges from about 51° on the plains to less than 36° in the mountains. The state's recorded high was 118° in 1888, while in 1985 the lowest recorded temperature was -61°. During cold months, Colorado's front range occasionally experiences Chinooks—fast-moving (up to 100 mph), warm winds—which can cause local temperatures to rise as much as 50° in a matter of hours. First snows may occur as early as September with the last as late as July or August. At lower elevations, winters are fairly mild and snow seldom stays on the ground more than a few days under the warm, bright sun.

Weather/pollution information numbers

Clean Air Hotline 303-758-4848

Wood Burning Hotline 303-692-3280

Smoking Vehicle Hotline 303-777-0517

Public Transit 303-299-6000

Air Quality Information 303-782-0211

Carpools 303-458-7665

For a more rounded, complete picture of Colorado's weather, see the section on high-altitude gardening in chapter 10. The following month-by-month account of interesting weather facts was provided by Mike Nelson of KUSA 9News and Nolan J. Doesken of the Department of Atmospheric Science at Colorado State University.

January	Colorado's coldest New Year's Day occurred in 1979. A morning temperature of -60°F was reported at Maybell.
February	A remarkable "Fog Storm" on February 5-15, 1978, covered much of eastern Colorado. Rime ice several inches thick broke miles of power lines across the region.
March	A massive blizzard over northeast Colorado, March 10-11, 1977. Snow piled into 25' high drifts, killed thousands of cattle, and resulted in the deaths of nine people.
April	A remarkably strong cold front crossed Colorado on Easter Sunday, April 19, 1987. Afternoon temperatures along the Front Range were in the 80s. By evening it was snowing with Denver receiving 3".

May	A late spring snowstorm once dumped 27.8" of snow in Fort Collins within a two-day period. Comparable amounts fell in Boulder with larger totals in the foothills.
June	June is Colorado's severe weather month with an average of 15 tornadoes and 46 damaging hailstorms. On June 6, 1990 a tornado ripped through the town of Limon. Good warnings prevented loss of life although the town itself was almost wiped out.
July	A brutal hailstorm ravaged an area from Estes Park to Colorado Springs on July 11, 1990. In three hours, the storm caused more than $600 million in damages to cars and homes.
August	Denver's all time record high reached 105°F on August 8, 1878. Denver's high temperature on August 10, 1968 reached only 58°F.
September	An early Front Range snowstorm September 16-18, 1971 dropped 1-2' of snow from Fort Collins to Pueblo. Millions of dollars of damage occurred from broken tree branches. In a repeat performance, another early snowstorm hit the Front Range on September 20, 1995. Over 80% of all the trees in Denver were damaged.
October	In 1991, following a very mild autumn, a severe cold wave killed thousands of trees over eastern Colorado. Denver's high temperature on October 30, 1991 was only 21°F.
November	A snowstorm that deposited 20-50" of snow over most of eastern Colorado from November 2-6, 1946 was responsible for at least 13 deaths.
December	The worst and most widespread heavy snow to hit the Colorado Front Range occurred between December 1-5, 1913. In Denver, 46" of snow fell and 86" fell at Georgetown. Many roofs collapsed and locomotives were stranded.

The Powers That Be

2

COLORADO'S
GOVERNMENT

Colorado's Political Process

State Government
Departments and Agencies

As a citizen of Colorado you are guaranteed the right of access to your government. The State's constitution reads "All elections shall be free and open; and no power, civil or military, shall at any time interfere to prevent the right of suffrage." Of course, this is tempered by the old saying "You can't fight city hall." Either way, you have predefined rights and responsibilities as a citizen. This chapter is designed to give you a better understanding of how the state government functions and, more important, who is responsible for what and how to contact them.

Colorado's Political Process

The Voting Process

The qualifications to become a registered voter in Colorado are:

- 18 years of age by Election Day
- United States citizenship

- Address of residence within a given precinct for 30 days by Election Day. A citizen who will reach 18 or become a U.S. citizen during the 30 days prior to the election must register before the 30 days in order to vote

Voter registration is a yearly responsibility of the election commission or county clerk. Both operate during normal business hours and can designate additional sites for registration (shopping malls, grocery stores, etc.) during the weeks preceding an election. If qualified, you can register up to, and including, 30 days before an election. If you have moved or changed your legal address since the last election, you must register the change at any location where voter registrations are completed.

In 1984, Colorado voters passed an initiative known as the Motor Voter, which allows you to register at all offices where driver's licenses are issued. In addition, in 1992, a law was passed that allows a registrar at each high school to register qualified high school students.

Early Voting: You may vote in person at a place designated by the county clerk up to 24 days before any election and no later than the Friday prior to the election. Every county must provide a polling place for early voting.

Mail-in Voting: After January 1 of any election year, you may obtain an application for a mail-in ballot. This option is available the entire year up to the Friday immediately preceding the election.

Election Days: General elections are held on the Tuesday following the first Monday of November in even-numbered years. National and state offices are decided in this election and there may also be ballot issues. Since 1993, initiatives or referenda concerning fiscal matters may be on the ballots of the statewide election held in November in odd-numbered years.

The November general election is held every fourth year and coincides with the presidential election. Colorado's presidential primary is held on the first Tuesday of March during presidential election years. Voters choose their candidates for president and vice-president in the party in which they are affiliated. They also select a slate of delegates to their party's national convention who are committed to support the candidates who win the presidential primary election.

The regular state primary election is on the second Tuesday of August in even-numbered years. Those who have party affiliation decide contested races within the party. This is the final nomination of the candidate who will represent the party. Only those who have declared a choice of party may vote in the primary election. However, any unaffiliated voter may declare a party affiliation at the polling place.

The Voting Process on Election Day

Each precinct has its own polling place, usually located in public places such as schools, fire stations, churches, or other buildings open to the public. To insure each voter has complete information or to offer assistance, election judges staff each polling place.

The polls are open from 7 A.M. to 7 P.M. The polls are not declared closed until all that were in line at 7 P.M. have voted. Precinct results are reported to the county clerk or the election commission and the final report is sent to the Secretary of State.

The League of Women Voters provides nonpartisan information for the public to encourage all that have registered to be informed voters. In addition, a 1994 law requires the nonpartisan research staff of the General Assembly to prepare a ballot information booklet on any initiated or referred constitutional amendment or legislation. This booklet includes the text and title of each measure and a fair and impartial analysis of each measure that includes a summary and the major pros and cons of each issue. The booklet is distributed at no charge to registered voters statewide at least 30 days before the election.

Initiatives and Referendums

In 1910, Colorado adopted the process of direct legislation by Initiative and Referendum to amend either the state constitution or the Colorado Revised Statutes. These types of ballot proposals have two different forms.

In the Initiative process a proposal by citizens who have circulated petitions and gathered the required number of signatures (five percent of the number of votes cast for the secretary of state in the previous election) is placed on the General Election ballot.

A referendum is a proposal passed by two-thirds of the General Assembly, and then placed on the ballot for popular vote. Citizens may initiate a referendum to repeal a law passed by the General Assembly.

There are seven steps that must be complete before an initiative can be placed on the ballot:

- The proponents must prepare a proposal or statement of the issue.

- The Legislative Council and the Office of Legislative Legal Services must review the proposal. A public meeting must follow and the proposal can be resubmitted after any changes.

- Representatives of the Secretary of State, Attorney General and the Office of Legislative Legal Services must conduct a Title Setting Hearing. This hearing is open to the public with testimony by both proponents and opponents allowed. Challenges must be made within seven days.

- The complete text of the proposal must be made available to the media and the public.

- The proponents are provided an approved petition format that they use to have petitions printed and circulated for signatures.

- The circulators of such petitions must be registered voters who may be paid for their work. The number of valid signatures required is covered above and has been approximately 50,000 for the past several years. A six-month window is granted for the circulation and all petitions must be returned to the secretary of state at least three months before the election.

- The Secretary of State has a verification and challenge period of 30 days after the deadline to verify if a sufficient number of the signatures are valid. A fifteen-day cure period is granted the proponents if the number of signatures is ruled insufficient. However, the entire process must be complete no later than three months before the election.

If approved by the Secretary of State, the proposal is given a ballot issue number and appears on the ballot for the November election. The ballot issue must receive a majority of votes in order to be approved.

The Branches of Government

The U.S. Constitution established three branches of Federal Government with a balance of power. Colorado went a step further when they provided for a vote of the people on issues referred by the General Assembly. Although described only briefly herein, a complete understanding of the General Assembly's functions and history can be found in the book *The Colorado General Assembly*. Below is a brief description of the three branches of Colorado's State Government.

The Executive Branch

The Executive Branch encompasses the offices of state elected officials and administrative departments that conduct state business. In 1970 the state constitution was amended to limit the number of executive departments to 20.

The Governor of Colorado

(Bill Owens, Republican, elected in 1998)

The Governor is the head of the Executive Branch. The voters elect the Governor, Lieutenant Governor, Secretary of State, Treasurer, and Attorney General for terms of four years each. Article IV, Section 2 of the state constitution gives the Governor supreme executive power to take care that the laws be faithfully executed.

One of the major powers of this office is the right to appoint approximately 400 judges, heads of departments, board members and commissioners. The Governor also has the power to veto bills passed by the General Assembly and has line item veto of items in the state budget. Also under the control of the Governor's Office are the Office of State Planning and Budgeting, the Office of Energy Conservation, the Office of Business Development, the International Trade Office and the Colorado Office of Space Advocacy.

The Governor's Cabinet consists of the four other elected officials mentioned above and the heads of the state departments. Included by invitation at cabinet meetings are the commissioners of Education and Higher Education.

The Lieutenant Governor
(Joe Rogers, Republican, elected 1998)
The Lieutenant Governor is always elected as a package deal with the Governor and automatically becomes Governor should the office be vacated.

The Commission on Indian Affairs falls under the control of this office and provides services and coordinates relations between the Tribal governments and the State.

The Secretary of State–The Department of State
(Donetta Davidson, Republican, elected 2000)
The Secretary of State administers and enforces the laws and codes concerning elections, registration of licenses and incorporation, and also reports political campaign funding.

Additional offices under the Department of State include the Corporations Division, Licensing Division, Administrative Division, and the Elections Division.

The State Treasurer–The Department of the Treasury
(Mike Coffman, Republican, elected 1998)
This office has three main divisions. The Accounting Division reviews all state bank accounts. The Investment Division is responsible for the safe and profitable investment of state moneys. The Unclaimed Property Program attempts to locate owners of dormant funds. If the owners cannot be found, the moneys go into the state general fund.

The Attorney General–The Department of Law
(Ken Salazar, Democrat, elected 1998)
Charged with protecting the people by enforcing laws concerned with consumer fraud, anti-trust, and consumer credit, the Attorney General acts as the state's lawyer. The Department of Law is the administrative arm of the Attorney General who acts as its executive director. State agencies and the General Assembly receive legal services from assistant attorneys general. They also represent the state in liability cases, review state contracts, and prepare legal opinions. The Attorney General represents the state's interest in state and federal courts.

The Judicial Branch

The Judicial Branch was created to ensure the balance between individual rights and the powers of the state government. Its major function is to protect the rights of individuals as it interprets and applies the laws.

Colorado courts are empowered to resolve conflicts in both criminal and civil matters. Civil cases can include disputes over wills, contracts, personal injuries or family law matters. The Colorado Criminal Code and the Colorado Rules of Procedure govern procedures in a criminal case. A district attorney files criminal charges. A grand jury can hand down an indictment based on probable cause, but this procedure is seldom used in a criminal case.

Small Claims Court

The Small Claims Court is a division of the county court. Civil matters involving no more than $7,500 are argued in this court, without attorneys. Both day and evening sessions are available. *Winning Big in Colorado Small Claims Court* by Charles Brackney is an excellent resource about using the small claims court.

Municipal Courts

Municipal courts handle violations of city laws committed within city limits. This includes offenses of traffic laws, shoplifting (under $300), disturbing the peace, and other petty violations. Any decision of a municipal court can be appealed to a state court. A defendant has the right to a jury trial in this court.

County Courts

These courts handle traffic violations, minor criminal offenses, and civil actions involving no more than $10,000. Denver is somewhat different because it is both a city and a county. The Denver County Court functions as a municipal as well as a county court and is funded entirely by Denver taxes and fines paid by offenders. Denver also has a separate juvenile court and a separate probate court. These types of cases are handled by the district courts in the rest of the state.

District Courts
District courts are organized into 22 judicial districts. There may be more than one district judge who may serve more than one county in their district. A district court decision may be appealed to the Colorado Court of Appeals or the Colorado Supreme Court.

Water Court
This is a division of the District Court. A district judge from within the water district is appointed by the State Supreme Court to preside over cases concerning water rights or the uses of water resources. There are no juries in this court but decisions can be appealed to the Colorado Supreme Court.

The Court of Appeals
The Court of Appeals serves to hear appeals to decisions in civil and criminal cases. There are 16 judges and their decisions are final unless the Colorado Supreme Court agrees to review a case.

The Colorado Supreme Court
A decision by this court is final and case reviews are not guaranteed. This court is headed by the chief justice who is selected by the seven judges of the court from its own membership. The chief justice also serves as the executive head of the judicial branch of the state government.

Duties of the chief justice include the supervision of all other state courts and the attorneys who practice law in Colorado. There are four committees that handle the administrative duties of the Colorado Supreme Court.

The State Board of Law Examiners reviews the educational, professional, ethical, and moral qualifications of people who apply for licenses to practice law in Colorado.

The Attorney Registration System and Advisory Committee (formerly the Grievance Committee), composed of 15 attorneys and four civilians, investigates all complaints about attorneys. The committee has the power to recommend an attorney be censured or suspended, or that his or her license be revoked.

The Public Defender Commission appoints the state public defender, who then appoints assistants in regional offices to serve all the state courts. In mental health cases, a public defender may be appointed as *guardian ad litem* to represent the person in a single lawsuit.

The State Court Administrator is responsible for managing court personnel, finances, data processing, research and other responsibilities under the supervision of the chief justice.

Becoming a Judge

In 1966, the voters of Colorado approved an initiative that allows state judges to be appointed rather than elected. When a vacancy in any state court occurs, a judicial nominating commission interviews applicants and recommends several to the governor for consideration. The governor appoints the judge for a provisional term of two years.

Judges retained by the voters serve the remaining years of the term to which they have been appointed. Upon completion of their term, they may submit their names for retention in the general election. In this manner, voters have the opportunity to decide whether or not the performance of a judge merits continuation on the bench. Terms of judges are different for each jurisdiction. A county judge serves for four years, a district judge for six years, an appeals court judge for eight years, and a supreme court justice for ten years. The exceptions to this are city-counties, such as Denver and Broomfield. In Denver, a vacancy is filled by appointment by the mayor from a list of three candidates recommended by the Denver County Court Nominating Commission. The mayor of Denver also has the authority to dismiss a judge when there is sufficient cause.

Juries
Every citizen of Colorado is subject to summons for jury duty if they meet the following qualifications:
- Citizen of the United States
- At least 18 years of age
- Resident of the county
- Able to read, speak, and understand the English language
- Not currently imprisoned for a felony conviction

Jury summonses are issued at random from a database of the

names of registered voters and those who hold a Colorado driver's license. Jurors in Colorado now serve for only one day or one trial in any calendar year. Employers must pay employed jurors their regular wages for the first three days of a trial and then the state pays $50 per day thereafter. Being summoned to jury duty does not necessarily mean you will serve. However, in the City and County of Denver you can plan on spending the entire day waiting around to find out if you're needed or not.

The Legislative Branch

The General Assembly, with its Senate and House of Representatives, is the heart of the Legislative Branch. The organizational structure, functions, responsibilities, and level of funding for the Executive Branch are determined by the General Assembly. In conjunction with the Executive Branch, the Joint Budget Committee develops the state budget, which, after modifications, is approved by the General Assembly. Laws passed by the General Assembly also define the responsibilities of the judicial system.

The Legislators

The General Assembly has 100 legislators: 35 in the Senate and 65 in the House. Voters in each legislative district elect their representatives to the General Assembly in the general election. Representatives serve two-year terms and senators serve four-year terms with half up for reelection at each general election. Members of the General Assembly are given immunity from arrest except for treason or a felony.

The Legislative Council

The Council is responsible for computerized legislative research and establishes a data bank on state resources, programs, and expenditures. The Council is headed by the majority leader of the Senate and the Speaker of the House who serve *ex officio*, with eight senators and eight representatives serving as the Council. The Council staffs reference, interim, and statutory committees, which include economists who forecast state revenue and costs and prepare fiscal notes estimating the cost of legislation.

The Legislative Committees

Committee on Legal Services: This committee includes the chairs of House and Senate Committees on Judiciary, four members of the House, two from each major political party, and four members from the Senate, two from each party. This committee supervises the operation of the Office of Legislative Legal Services, which consists of lawyers, technical experts, and clerical personnel who are responsible for drafting all bills, resolutions, and memorials introduced in the General Assembly.

Legislative Audit Committee: Members of the General Assembly vote on the selection of a state auditor, who must be a certified public accountant. This official is appointed for a five-year term. The eight-member committee oversees the review of audits of financial transactions and accounts, performance audits, and management studies of all state agencies. The committee consists of two senators from each party and two representatives from each party.

Capital Development Committee: This committee was created in 1985 to deal with long-range planning to meet the capital requirements of the state government. It studies capital construction needs and the maintenance requests of state agencies. It also holds public hearings, determines priorities for proposals, and makes recommendations to the General Assembly.

Sunrise and Sunset Review Committee: The House and Senate Majority leadership appoints six or more legislators to serve on the Sunrise and Sunset Review Committee, which conducts studies of state boards and commissions and may recommend their termination.

The Sunset Law provides that agencies that no longer serve a purpose shall be terminated. When an occupational group requests state regulation, such as licensing, the committee may recommend it be provided—a Sunrise.

The Joint Budget Committee: This committee reviews the fiscal needs and management of all state agencies and institutions, holds hearings on budget requests, estimates tax revenues, reviews the state's fiscal structure, and prepares the annual budget.

Committees of Reference. These committees have been formed to review proposed legislation and make recommendations to the entire legislative body. A Legislative Council member who prepares a report of the discussions and decisions is on the staff of each committee. These reports are available to the public. The Senate and House have ten separate committees of reference.

As bills are introduced, they are given a number. Bills introduced to the Senate begin each session with the number SB1. In the House they begin with HB 1001. A prefix is added to identify the year of introduction, such as HB 97-1001. These committees also handle concurrent resolutions, joint resolutions, memorials and tributes.

State Departments and Agencies

This section provides information about the responsibilities and points of contact for every department and agency of the state government.

Colorado State Government
www.state.co.us
General Information: 303-866-5000

Governor's Office
www.state.co.us/gov_dir/governor_office.html
136 State Capitol
Denver, CO 80203-1792
Advocate Contact: 303-866-2885   Fax: 303-866-4824
Main Office: 303-866-2471   Fax: 303-866-2003

Department of Agriculture
www.ag.state.co.us
700 Kipling St., #4000
Lakewood, CO 80215-5894
Main Office: 303-239-4100   Fax: 303-239-4125

Responsibilities:
- Pesticide use (agricultural and residential)

- Livestock brand inspection
- Weights and measures certification
- Animal welfare (neglect and cruelty), rodent and predator control

Department of Corrections
www.doc.state.co.us/index.html
2862 S. Circle Drive, #400
Colorado Springs, CO 80906
Main Office: 719-579-9580

Responsibilities:
- Prisons and parole supervision
- Transitional community correction
- Victim notification program

Other numbers:
    Parole Board: 719-546-0141   Fax: 719-540-0363

Department of Education
www.cde.state.co.us
201 E. Colfax Avenue
Denver, CO 80203-1799
Main Office: 303-866-6806   Fax: 303-866-6938

Responsibilities:
- K-12 standards and assessments
- State Board of Education
- Teacher and administrator licensing
- School for the Deaf and the Blind
- State library services and Charter schools

Other numbers:
Educator Licensing: 303-866-6628
Special Education Services Office: 303-866-6694
Colorado School for the Deaf and Blind: 719-578-2100
Colorado State Library: 303-866-6900

Department of Health Care Policy and Financing
www.chcpf.state.co.us
State Human Services Building
1575 Sherman St., 10th floor
Denver, CO 80203
Main Office: 303-866-2993   Fax: 303-866-4411

Responsibilities:
- Health Care Reform and Medicaid
- Health Data Commission

Department of Higher Education
www.state.co.us/cche_dir/hecche.html
First contact the individual college or university.
If the problem is not resolved, contact Department
of Higher Education
1380 Lawrence St., Suite 1200
Denver, CO 80204-2059
Main Office: 303-866-2723   Fax: 303-866-4266

Department of Human Services
(formerly Departments of Social Services and Institutions)
www.cdhs.state.co.us/
State Social Services Building
1575 Sherman St., 8th Floor
Denver, CO 80203-1714
Main Office: 303-866-5700   Fax: 303-866-4740

Responsibilities:
- Public assistance (AFDC, Food Stamps, and OAP, LEAP)
- Medicaid eligibility and services for the elderly
- Protection of dependent adults
- Vocational rehabilitation services
- Child protection, social services to families, and foster care
- Child care assistance
- Child support enforcement

- State mental institutions/mental health
- Developmentally disabled services
- Juvenile delinquency
- Alcohol and drug abuse services

Other numbers:

Low-Income Energy Assistance (LEAP): 303-866-5968

Colorado Coordinating Council on
  Housing and the Homeless: 303-762-4457

Division of Youth Corrections: 303-866-7345

Child Support Enforcement: 720-947-5000

Division of Child Care: 303-866-5958

Mental Health Services: 303-866-7400

Alcohol and Drug Abuse: 303-866-7480

Department of Labor and Employment

www.cdle.state.co.us/default.asp
1515 Arapahoe Street
Tower 2, Suite 400
Denver, CO 80202
Main Office: 303-620-4718   Fax: 303-620-4714

Responsibilities:

- Labor standards
- Unemployment insurance
- Workers' compensation
- Job services

Department of Local Affairs

www.dola.state.co.us
Centennial Building
1313 Sherman St., Suite 323
Denver, CO 80203
Main Office: 303-866-2771   Fax: 303-866-2251

Responsibilities:
- Property tax administration/appeals
- Financial and technical assistance to local governments
- Rural job training
- Disaster response
- State housing development programs

Other numbers:

Division of Property Taxation: 303-866-2371

Motion Picture & TV Advisory Commission: 303-620-4500

Department of Military Affairs
www.coloradoguard.com
6848 S. Revere Parkway
Englewood, CO 80112
Main Office: 303-397-3000   Fax: 303-397-3003

Responsibilities:
- Army and Air National Guard, Civil Air Patrol

Department of Natural Resources
www.dnr.state.co.us/index.asp
Centennial Building
1313 Sherman St., Suite 718
Denver, CO 80203
Main Office: 303-866-3311   Fax: 303-866-2115

Responsibilities:
- Mining, energy development, and geology
- Parks and recreation, wildlife management
- Water supply, storage, and management
- Soil and water conservation, state land management

Other numbers:

Division of Wildlife: 303-297-1192   Fax: 303-866-5417

Department of Personnel
www.state.co.us/gov_dir/gss/index.html
Colorado State Bank
1600 Broadway, Suite 1030
Denver, CO 80202
Main Office: 303-866-6566

Responsibilities:
- State employment, testing and recruitment
- Classification and pay, including Fair Labor
- Standards Act for state employment
- Equal Employment Opportunity/Affirmative
- Action for state employment
- State employee benefits

Department of Public Health and Environment
(formerly Department of Health)
www.cdphe.state.co.us/cdphehom.asp
4300 Cherry Creek Drive S., Bldg. A, 1st floor
Denver, CO 80246-1530
Advocate Contact: 303-692-2035
Main Office: 303-692-2000   Fax: 303-782-0095

Responsibilities:
- Environmental permits and regulations
- Water supply safety
- Air quality and landfill monitoring
- Food sanitation and product safety
- Disease monitoring
- Women, infant and children (WIC) nutrition program
- Family planning and prenatal care
- Immunizations and home health care
- Programs for children with special needs
- Emergency medical services/trauma

Other numbers:

Vital Records: 303-756-4464

Air Pollution Control Division: 303-692-3100

Consumer Protection Division: 303-692-3620

Disease Control & Environmental Epidemiology: 303-692-2700

Emergency Medical Services & Prevention: 303-692-2500

Hazardous Materials/Waste Management: 303-692-3300

Department of Public Safety
www.state.co.us/gov_dir./cops/cosp.htm
700 Kipling St., Suite 3000
Lakewood, CO 80215
Main Office: 303-239-4400   Fax: 303-231-9708

Other numbers:

State Patrol: 303-239-4500

Division of Criminal Justice: 303-239-4442

Division of Fire Safety: 303-239-4463 or 800-317-3473

Department of Regulatory Agencies (DORA)
www.dora.state.co.us
Civic Center Plaza
1560 Broadway, Suite 1550
Denver, CO 80202
Main Office: 303-894-7855   Fax: 303-894-7885

Responsibilities:

- Licensed occupations (doctors, dentists, plumbers, etc.)
- Insurance issues
- Real estate and investment issues
- Discrimination issues

For a complete breakdown of this department and all regulatory agencies and responsibilities, see the DORA section that follows.

Department of Revenue
www.revenue.state.co.us
State Capitol Annex
1375 Sherman St., Suite 404
Denver, CO 80261
Main Office: 303-866-3091   Fax: 303-866-2400

Responsibilities:
- State sales tax and income tax
- Driver's licensing
- Colorado Lottery
- Limited stakes gaming and regulation
- Horse and dog racing regulation
- Liquor license enforcement

Other numbers:
Income Tax Information: 303-232-2446
Income Tax Forms: 303-232-2414
Trade Name Registration Information: 303-232-2434
Income Tax Refund Inquiries: 303-232-2438
Liquor Enforcement Division: 303-205-2300
Motor Vehicle Division: 303-205-5600
Driver License: 303-205-5646
Emissions: 303-205-5603
Gaming Division: 303-205-1355
Sales Tax and Estate Tax Information: 303-232-2416

Department of Transportation
www.dot.state.co.us
4201 E. Arkansas Ave., Suite 277
Denver, CO 80222
Main Office: 303-757-9011   Public Information: 303-757-9228

Responsibilities:
- Construction and maintenance of state highways

- Long and short range planning for state transportation
- Coordination and implementation of transportation safety programs, including combating drunken driving
- Support aviation interests, safety, and maintenance needs of airports
- Assisting with alternate modes of transportation, such as public transit in rural areas, bicycle and pedestrian safety programs

Other numbers:

Statewide highway conditions: 303-639-1111

Metro highway conditions (within two driving hours of Denver): 303-639-1111

Metro Denver Road and Highway Construction Information: 303-573-7623

DORA

www.dora.state.co.us

The Colorado Department of Regulatory Agencies (DORA) consists of nine different divisions and several support offices. The major purpose of DORA is to regulate businesses and individuals when the state legislature believes such regulation is necessary for the protection of Colorado citizens. Below is a brief description of the support offices, divisions and the boards that regulate professions and occupations that require licensing.

Office of the Executive Director

1560 Broadway, Suite 1550
Denver, CO 80202
303-894-7850

The Executive Director is responsible for the overall management of the Department and its divisions. The Executive Director appoints Division Directors (with the exception of Insurance and Public Utilities Commissioners who are appointed by the Governor). The Governor makes appointments to boards and commissions and the Executive Director plays a significant role in recommending the names of people for those appointments. The

Executive Director presents the Department budget to the Joint Budget Committee, and initiates and recommends legislation affecting the Department.

The Executive Director gives advice to the general assembly and the general public on questions relating to the role of the state in regulating professions and occupations.

Division of Administrative Services

www.dora.state.co.us/administration
1560 Broadway, Suite 1550
Denver, CO 80202
303-894-7856

The Division of Administrative Services provides services to the department in the areas of planning, budget and fiscal management, payroll and data processing and personnel. The Division provides centralized support in the above areas to all divisions in the Department and also coordinates record management and space planning for the Department. The Division also completes special projects as assigned by the Executive Director, and is responsible for implementation of the Americans with Disabilities Act.

The personnel section serves as a liaison between employees in the Department and the State Department of Personnel. The staff addresses employee questions and concerns about personnel policies and procedures, and advises employees about job advancement and job enhancement opportunities in state government.

The Division serves as the liaison between the Department and the State Controller, State Archives, State Treasurer, State Department of Personnel, the Office of State Planning and Budgeting, and the Joint Budget Committee staff.

Office of Consumer Counsel

www.dora.state.co.us/occ
1580 Logan Street, 6th Floor
Denver, CO 80203
303-894-2121

The Office of Consumer Counsel (OCC) represents the interests of residential, small business and agricultural consumers before the

Public Utilities Commission, certain federal agencies (such as the FCC), and in the courts on appeal. The OCC is Colorado's consumer advocate in electric, gas, and telecommunications utility rate- and rule-making matters. The office represents consumers by participating in complex utility cases. The OCC examines the technical evidence filed by the utility, provides expert testimony on consumers' behalf, cross-examines other witnesses, makes legal arguments, and represents consumers in settlement negotiations. Approximately 40 other states have utility consumer advocate offices similar to the OCC.

The OCC has a staff of technical and administrative personnel as well as legal representation through the Department of Law. In addition, a statutorily-authorized board appointed by the governor gives policy guidance to the OCC. The eleven-member board is appointed to represent the public interest and, specifically, the interests of residential, small business, and agricultural utility consumers. Board members come from all geographic areas of the state.

The office is funded by an assessment on the state's regulated utilities. Since utility companies pass this cost on to their customers, ratepayers fund the office. Each Colorado consumer pays about five cents per month in combined utility bills to fund the OCC. The Office of Consumer Counsel helps consumers by lowering or eliminating utility rate increases and by ensuring that utility rates, regulations and policies are more equitable for residential, small business and agricultural consumers. The OCC is charged with representing the small consumer before the PUC, but is prohibited by statute from representing individuals in complaints with utilities. Instead, the PUC is staffed to resolve individual complaints. The OCC is interested in individual complaints when they show a pattern of rate or service problems the office believes should be addressed.

Office of Policy and Research
www.dora.state.co.us/OPR
1560 Broadway, Suite 1550
Denver, CO 80202
303-894-7848
OPR is the research arm of the Executive Director of DORA. It

prepares "sunrise" and "sunset" reports. DORA is required to evaluate both the need for regulation of different occupational groups seeking state regulation and the need for and effectiveness of existing regulatory agencies and functions that are scheduled for termination. The director of OPR coordinates the research and evaluation effort and the executive director submits DORA's findings and recommendations to the Legislature. Final reports are on file in the Executive Director's office and are available to the public. Interested members of the public who wish to provide input on agencies subject to sunset or sunrise evaluations should contact the director.

Office of Certification
www.dora.state.co.us/Certification

Disadvantaged Business Certification (DBE): The Office of Certification offers the Disadvantaged Business Enterprise certification program. The Office conducts certifications for the Colorado Department of Transportation, Regional Transportation District, and the Denver Board of Water Commissions. A business must be owned and controlled by women or minorities to be certified.

Division of Banking
www.dora.state.co.us/Banking
1560 Broadway, Suite 1175
Denver, CO 80202
303-894-7575

The Division of Banking is responsible for the regulation of state-chartered commercial banks, trust companies, and industrial banks and of money order companies and debt management companies. The Division holds charter and license application hearings and issues rules and regulations affecting institutions and licenses. The Division works closely with the Federal Reserve Bank and the FDIC in the regulation of commercial banks and industrial banks and certain federally insured trust companies.

Activities include chartering and licensing financial institutions, performing examinations, supervising operations, and closing state chartered banks, industrial banks, and trust companies when necessary. Also, the Division is responsible for the enforcement of the Public Deposit Protection Act, to protect public entity deposits held by state and national banks.

There is an eight-member banking board that is the policy- and rule-making authority for the Division. The board conducts monthly meetings and the public is encouraged to attend these meetings. Board members are appointed for four-year terms.

Colorado Civil Rights Division

www.dora.state.co.us/Civil-Rights/
1560 Broadway, Suite 1050
Denver, CO 80202
303-894-2997

The Civil Rights Division is a state agency established in 1957 to administer and enforce Colorado civil rights laws in employment, housing, and public accommodations. The Division works with federal agencies, such as the Equal Employment Opportunity Commission (EEOC) and the Department of Housing and Urban Development (HUD), and with local human rights agencies. Colorado civil rights laws prohibit discrimination in employment, housing, and public accommodations on the basis of race, sex, national origin, ancestry, physical or mental handicap, creed, color, or marital status (housing and public accommodations only). Discrimination based on age and marriage to a coworker in employment is also prohibited.

The Colorado Civil Rights Commission is a seven member bi-partisan panel appointed by the Governor. The Commission members are selected from across the State to serve four-year terms. Two members represent the business community, two represent state or local government entities, and three are from the community at large. At least four commissioners must be from groups who have been or might be discriminated against because of handicap, race, creed, color, sex, national origin or ancestry, marital status, religion, or age. The Commission meets monthly to formulate policy and to hear appeals in discrimination cases. The public may attend such meetings.

Division of Financial Services

www.dora.state.co.us/Financial-Services
1560 Broadway, Suite 1520
Denver, CO 80202
303-894-2336

The Division of Financial Services regulates state-chartered savings and loan associations, credit unions, life care institutions, and small business development credit corporations. It also administers the public deposit protection program that covers all uninsured governmental unit deposits in state and federal savings and loan associations.

The Division operates under the policy-making and rule-making authority of the Financial Services Board. The Financial Services Board issues rules and regulations governing the industries regulated by the Division, may delegate many of its authorities to the Commissioner, and hears appeals of actions taken by the Commissioner under delegated authority.

The Division is empowered to approve applications to incorporate new state-chartered savings and loan associations, approve branch office applications for existing associations, approve mergers between associations, and approve changes of ownership.

State-chartered credit unions operate under the supervision of the Division. The Division is empowered to approve applications to incorporate new state credit unions and to approve mergers between credit unions. State credit unions are subject to periodic examination by the Division staff.

The Division regulates certain financial activities of life care institutions, which provide long-term residence and care for the elderly. The Division may initiate enforcement action against violations of the law by life care providers.

The Division is empowered to consider applications for licensure of, grant licenses to, and periodically examine small business development credit corporations, which are designed to provide a variety of financing options to small businesses.

The Division also handles consumer complaints and information requests regarding the industries it regulates and has available, at a nominal cost, the annual *Financial Report on Colorado State Chartered Savings and Loan Associations and Credit Unions* as well as copies of the statute and regulations for the industries it regulates.

Division of Insurance

www.dora.state.co.us/insurance
1560 Broadway, Suite 850
Denver, CO 80202
303-894-7499

The Division of Insurance has responsibility for the regulation of approximately 1800 insurance companies doing business in Colorado. Entities regulated by the Division include traditional insurance companies such as auto, health and workers' compensation carriers, as well as pre-need funeral companies, bail bond companies, fraternal benefit societies, captive organizations and self-insurance pools.

The Division's consumer protection mission includes:

- Resolving consumer complaints against insurers
- Monitoring companies for financial solvency and law compliance
- Licensing agents and brokers
- Investigating illegal activities

Public Utilities Commission

www.dora.state.co.us/puc
1580 Logan Street, 2nd Floor
Denver, CO 80203
303-894-2000

The Public Utilities Commission achieves a regulatory environment that provides safe and reliable utility services to all on just and acceptable terms. The Commission strives to assure that the public receives utility services at affordable prices. It also assures that utilities have the opportunity to receive a reasonable return on their investments. This return on investments allows Colorado utilities to obtain the necessary funds to build new facilities or to upgrade existing ones.

The Commission regulates investor-owned electric, gas, telephone, and water utilities, transportation companies, and some electric cooperatives. Municipal utilities are not regulated except for wholesale activities. Over the past few years, some types of telecommunications services and products and some types of transportation carriers have been deregulated.

The Commission holds public hearings to consider rate change requests by large public utilities such as Public Service Company/ Xcel Energy and Qwest Communications, as well as rate change requests by smaller utility companies.

The Commission has established safety regulations and permit requirements for common and contract carriers, and has established safety regulations for the transportation of hazardous materials.

Commission consumer affairs specialists work to resolve complaints against regulated utilities and provide general information about utilities and the Commission. The Commission publishes many consumer brochures that are available to the public free of charge.

Division of Real Estate

www.dora.state.co.us/Real-Estate
1900 Grant Street, Room 600
Denver, CO 80203
303-894-2166

The Division of Real Estate regulates real estate salespersons and brokers through licensure and discipline. Licensees must comply with established educational and experience requirements, and pass a test prior to licensure. The Division regulates earnest money deposits and escrow and trust funds.

The Division administers the real estate recovery fund, which can be used by persons to recover sums lost because of the actions of a licensee. Persons who obtain a final judgment against a broker or salespersons can regain their actual loss suffered in a transaction up to $15,000 per claimant and up to $50,000 in the aggregate against any one licensee.

The Division regulates all time-share projects sold in Colorado, and regulates developers of subdivisions consisting of 10 or more residential sites, tracts or lots.

A five-member Commission meets monthly to conduct rule making hearings, make policy decisions, consider licensing matters, review complaints and take disciplinary action against licensees. Commission members serve three-year terms, and members are appointed as follows: three real estate brokers, one person with expertise in subdivision development, and one public member.

The Division also regulates real estate appraisers pursuant to the requirements of the federal Real Estate Appraisal Reform Amendments of the Financial Institutions Reform, Recovery, and Enforcement Act of 1989. The Board of Real Estate appraisers consists of seven members appointed by the governor: four licensed or certified appraisers, one of whom must have expertise in eminent domain, a county assessor, an officer or employee of a commercial bank experienced in real estate lending, and one public member.

Division of Registrations
www.dora.state.co.us/Registrations
1560 Broadway, Suite 1300
Denver, CO 80202
303-894-7690

The Division of Registrations includes most of the professional and occupational licensing boards in Colorado. These boards have been created by the Colorado legislature to protect the public from unqualified and incompetent practitioners. Boards typically are empowered to determine the qualifications necessary to obtain a license, regulate the standards of conduct for the profession, review complaints against licensees, and take disciplinary action as they determine necessary. Boards can suspend or revoke licenses, but they cannot order a licensed individual to refund money or perform repairs.

Most of the boards in the Division meet on a monthly basis, and the public is invited to attend board meetings. For information on the time and location of a particular board meeting, contact the administrator for that board at the telephone number listed.

Although each board handles the disciplinary proceedings against its licensees, the Division has established a centralized complaint process for all the boards. When complaints are received, they are ordinarily assigned to an investigator who notifies the licensee that a complaint has been filed against him or her and asks the licensee to respond by letter, stating his or her side of the story. An investigation is then initiated to try to determine the facts of the situation. Staff of the Complaints and Investigations Section (303-894-7690) can answer general questions about the investigative process or specific questions about the status of the case.

The Division has available a brochure entitled *A Guide for Filing Consumer Complaints Against Licensed Professions and Occupations*. It also publishes a brochure for licensees entitled *Questions and Answers Concerning the Complaint Against Your License*.

Board of Accountancy
303-894-7800

The Board regulates the profession of Certified Public Accountants, both individuals and public accounting firms. The practice of public accounting includes issuance of reports on financial statements, management advisory or consulting services, preparation of tax returns, and furnishing advice on tax matters.

Acupuncturists Registration
303-894-2440

The Division registers individuals providing acupuncture services, described as the insertion of needles into the human body by piercing the skin of the body at specific locations based on traditional Oriental concepts of evaluation and treatment. The Division also registers individuals in training who are under the direct supervision of a registered acupuncturist.

State Board of Architects
303-894-7800

The Board licenses persons to practice architecture, which means the planning and design of buildings, preparation of construction contract documents, observation of construction as agreed upon, and administration of construction contracts for the construction, but not the performance, of buildings.

Board of Barbers and Cosmetologists
303-894-7772

The Board licenses barbers, cosmetologists, cosmeticians, and manicurists. The Board also registers locations at which any of the above professional services are provided. The Board investigates, upon written consumer complaint, all suspected or alleged violations relating to its area of responsibility.

Board of Chiropractic Examiners
303-894-7759 x301

The Board licenses chiropractors. Chiropractors who wish to practice electrotherapy or acupuncture must provide the Board with proof of additional education in that area. The Board sets standards for unlicensed personnel who operate an X-ray machine or administer radiation for diagnostic purposes.

Board of Dental Examiners
303-894-7759 x307

The Board licenses dentists and dental hygienists, and specifies the tasks that unlicensed dental auxiliaries may perform. Additionally, the Board administers a dentist peer assistance program.

State Electrical Board
303-894-2300

The Board licenses journeyman electricians, master electricians, electrical contractors and residential wiremen. Electrical apprentices are required to register with the Board. The Board also performs electrical inspections on new and remodeled facilities throughout the state in its areas of jurisdiction. The standard used by the Board is the National Electrical Code.

Board of Registration for Professional Engineers and Professional Land Surveyors
303-894-7788

The Board licenses engineers and land surveyors, and certifies engineers-in-training and surveyors-in-training. The Board enforces minimum survey standards as set by law. Land surveyors are required to file monument records with the Board.

State Grievance Board
303-894-7766

The Board hears disciplinary matters and can bring injunctive actions relating to licensed psychologists, clinical social workers, marriage and family therapists, and licensed professional counselors, and also relating to certified school psychologists and unlicensed psychotherapists. The Board maintains a database for licensed and unlicensed psychotherapists, which includes information about their methods of practice and years of experience. For this information call 303-894-7771.

State Board of Marriage and Family Therapists Examiners
303-894-7766

The Board licenses persons who practice psychotherapy and who are marriage and family therapists. Disciplinary matters are referred to the State Grievance Board.

Colorado State Board of Medical Examiners
303-894-7690

The Board licenses qualified physicians and physician assistants. In addition, the Board reviews complaints in order to determine whether action is necessary to protect patients. The Board administers a physician's peer health assistance program.

Midwives Registration
303-894-2440

Effective July 1, 1993, the Division implemented a program to register direct-entry midwives, also known as "lay" midwives. Direct-entry midwifery means the advising, attending, or assisting of a woman during pregnancy, labor, and natural childbirth at home and during the postpartum period. This program administers examinations to graduates of educational programs that meet the standards established by the Division. The Division also establishes standards of practice and has authority to investigate complaints and take disciplinary action if necessary.

State Board of Nursing
303-894-2430

The Board licenses Registered Nurses, Licensed Practical Nurses,

Psychiatric Technicians, and Certified Nurse Aides. The Board approves educational programs for all types of licenses. The Nurse Aide Advisory Committee assists the Board in their duties. Additionally, the Board administers a nursing peer health assistance diversion program to assist licensees experiencing impaired practice.

Board of Examiners of Nursing Home Administrators
303-894-7759 x302

The Board licenses nursing home administrators in an effort to ensure quality administration and sound management of nursing homes. Nursing home administrators are individuals who are responsible for planning, organizing, directing, and controlling the operations of a nursing home. The Board administers a nursing home administrator-in-training program.

Board of Optometric Examiners
303-894-7750

The Board licenses optometrists and authorizes them to prescribe and administer certain pharmaceutical agents upon meeting minimum educational and practical requirements.

Office of Outfitters Registration
303-894-7778

The Office regulates outfitters who provide services for the purpose of hunting or fishing by requiring insurance, bonding and proficiency in first aid, and setting standards for operation. The Office works cooperatively with the Division of Wildlife, the Bureau of Land Management, the U.S. Forest Service, various District Attorneys throughout the state, and other state and federal game and land management agencies.

Passenger Tramway Safety Board
303-894-7785

The Board regulates aerial tramways, surface lifts, and tows used for recreational purposes in Colorado. While the focus is ski-related equipment, the Board also licenses other types of tramways. The

Board promulgates design, operation, and maintenance standards, reviews requests for variance from the rules, and investigates accidents related to the operation of tramways. Each licensed tramway is inspected at least twice annually.

State Board of Pharmacy
303-894-7750

The Board licenses pharmacists and pharmacy interns. Prescription and other drug outlets must be registered with the Board. The Board is responsible for the control and regulation of drugs, and administers the Controlled Substances Act with the Department of Health. It cooperates extensively with other state and federal agencies. Additionally, the Board's inspectors perform routine inspections of pharmacies and conduct special investigations.

State Board of Physical Therapy
303-894-2440

All persons practicing physical therapy or physiotherapy must register with the Division. An advisory committee appointed by the Director assists in registration. The rules also specify supervisory requirements for physical therapist assistants.

Examining Board of Plumbers
303-894-2319

The Board is responsible for the licensing of residential plumbers, journeyman plumbers, and master plumbers. Plumbing apprentices who work for a plumbing contractor must register with the Board. The Board employs inspectors responsible for performing inspections in designated areas of the state. The Board establishes and administers the Colorado plumbing code, which represents the minimum standards for installation, alteration, and repair of plumbing equipment and systems.

Colorado Podiatry Board
303-894-2440

The Board licenses qualified podiatrists and reviews complaints in order to determine whether action is necessary to protect patients.

State Board of Professional Counselors
303-894-7766

The Board licenses persons who practice psychotherapy and who are professional counselors. Disciplinary matters are referred to the State Grievance Board.

Colorado State Board of Psychologist Examiners
303-894-7766

The Board licenses persons who practice psychotherapy and who are psychologists. Disciplinary matters are referred to the State Grievance Board.

State Board of Social Work Examiners
303-894-7766

The Board licenses persons who practice psychotherapy and who are clinical social workers. Disciplinary matters are referred to the State Grievance Board.

State Board of Veterinary Medicine
303-894-7750

The Board licenses veterinarians and specifies what tasks veterinary students may perform under the direct supervision of a licensed veterinarian. Veterinary medicine includes surgery, obstetrics, dentistry, and all other branches or specialties of animal medicine.

Division of Securities
1580 Lincoln, Suite 420
Denver, CO 80203
303-894-2320

The Division registers securities and licenses people who distribute securities. The Division investigates complaints and monitors broker-dealer activities and sales promotions. The thrust of the Colorado regulation is to bring actions against fraudulent conduct; the Division enforcement staff works with local, state and federal law enforcement authorities. The Division performs broker-dealer field examinations of intrastate and NASD member firms.

The Division also administers and enforces the Colorado Commodity Code, enacted in 1989 to protect investors and to prevent and prosecute illegal and fraudulent schemes involving precious metals and other off-exchange commodities.

In addition, the Division regulates and monitors the issuance of certain kinds of municipal bonds in Colorado, and local government investment pool trust funds.

The Division has a publication available that lists the most common areas of investment schemes and the types of solicitation techniques used by promoters. Entitled *How to Protect Your Savings Against Con Artist Hypnosis*, the brochure is free of charge. The Division also has available a videotape cassette entitled *Calling for Your Dollars*, a consumer protection program about boiler rooms and a series of publications called *Investor Alert*, quarterly warnings to investors produced in cooperation with the Council of Better Business Bureaus.

Business Assistance Center

Part of the Office of Economic Development, the Business Assistance Center helps new and existing businesses with pertinent issues. The Center offers information on permits, licenses and regulatory requirements for starting a new business or expanding an existing business. It helps small businesses with their concerns in the formation of rules and regulations, and investigating and facilitating resolution of complaints and disputes. The *Colorado Business Resource Guide* is available free from the Center. The topics covered in the guide include Business Entry Options, Trademarks, Copyrights and Patents, Income and Property Tax, and a checklist for starting a business. Call 303-592-5920 or 800-333-7798.

School's Out Forever

STATE
SCHOOL
SYSTEMS

Public

Private

Higher Education

Libraries

An Overview of Public Schools

School Districts: In 1957, there were 239 non-operating districts in the state and 203 one-room school districts. Through the voluntary process of the School District Reorganization Act, the number of school districts was reduced to 176. Today 20 counties have only one school district, 17 counties have two school districts, and 12 counties have no more than three districts. County superintendents have been abolished.

The 176 school districts are not necessarily coterminous with any other political boundaries. Most districts maintain elementary, middle/junior high schools, and senior high schools.

Many elementary schools include kindergarten classes. A local board may establish and maintain a kindergarten; law does not mandate it. Kindergartens may be paid for from the general school fund.

Entrance Age to school is determined by local board policy. The School Attendance Law entitles state residents between the ages of six and 21 to a free education, and requires persons between the ages of seven and 16 to attend school. The Constitution entitles the legislature to require by law that children of sufficient physical and mental ability attend school during at least a three-year period between the ages of six and 18 years unless educated by other means.

The Exceptional Children's Educational Act defines a handicapped child as one between the ages of five and 21, and requires that administrative units serve every handicapped child. Thus, a handicapped child may enter school at age five. There are some programs for younger children. Over half of Colorado's school districts offer programs for three-to-five-year-olds that are handicapped or "at risk."

Enrollment Requirements (including entrance age for school) vary from district to district, but usually include legal proof of age (preferably a birth certificate) and various immunizations. Transfer students register in the district of prospective residence. Registration requirements and grade placement vary among school districts, but transcripts of the student's records from the school previously attended are usually required. In general, school authorities will send for transcripts.

Local Control of Instruction: The Constitution of the State of Colorado, Article IX, Section 15, states: "School districts—boards of education. The general assembly shall, by law, provide for organization of school districts of convenient size, in each of which shall be established a board of education ... Said directors shall have control of instruction in the public schools of their respective districts." In 1993, the Colorado General Assembly enacted legislation aimed at bringing about coordinated improvement in the performance and accountability of the state's K-12 education system. House Bill 93-1313 requires local school districts to redesign curriculum, instruction, testing and teacher development around academic standards that spell out what students should know and be able to do, at various stages in their schooling, in 11 areas: math, science, reading, writing, history, geography, civics, art, music, physical education, and foreign language.

Colorado's education reform effort has been further enhanced by the passage of SB 00-186. This bill mandated a number of items as a part of an education reform strategy. Among a long list of items the bill provided for:

- Expansion of the Colorado Student Assessment Program (CSAP) by moving to annual testing of grades 3 through 10.
- Mandating the development of a Colorado State reporting program which includes, among other things, the production of a report card for each public school in the state.
- Development of a web site at *http://reportcard.cde.state.co.us/reportcard/CommandHandler.jsp* to provide public access to the report cards as well as access to output and reporting formats that will provide school districts and the public with information for making informed decisions.

The law requires that history and civil government of Colorado, as well as the history and civil government of the United States (incorporating history, culture, and contributions of minorities, including but not limited to Spanish-Americans and African-Americans) be taught in the public schools of the state. The U.S. Constitution is also to be taught, as well as the honor and use of the flag. In addition, students must be given information on the effect of use of alcohol and controlled substances.

Textbooks: In addition to curriculum, our Constitution states: "Textbooks in public schools: Neither the general assembly nor the state board of education shall have power to prescribe textbooks to be used in the public schools." We do not have statewide approved/mandated/adopted textbooks.

Local Boards of Education: Colorado Revised Statutes, 22-32-109 and 110 enumerate local boards' powers and duties. Their curricula normally include general, college preparatory, business, and vocational-technical courses. Their high school graduation requirements usually include one or more units of English, math, social studies, science, and physical education.

Meetings of local boards of education are open to the public; however, they may go into executive session.

Discipline: Local boards of education are required by law to adopt discipline codes as well as written policies, rules, and regulations which relate to the study, discipline, conduct, safety, and welfare of all pupils.

Accreditation: The Colorado Department of Education accredits school districts; additionally, the North Central Association accredits some schools. Districts are not ranked or rated as to which is best.

Home Study and Nonpublic Schools: The School Attendance Law distinguishes between nonpublic schools and home study. Home study is permitted in Colorado under this law. Nonpublic schools are required to provide a basic academic education, but are protected from untoward interference by any board of education, state or local.

School Choices in Colorado*

We know when it comes to education, one size does not fit all. Children learn in different ways and have different learning strengths and interests. Students are more excited about learning and learn more when they are in educational programs that suit their learning styles and special strengths, needs, and interests. To take the best advantage of public school opportunities now available, you need to know about the choices available to you.

Open Enrollment: Legislation enacted in 1994 created open enrollment throughout Colorado. This means you may enroll your children in any public school in the state, assuming there is space available, without paying extra money.

Charter Schools: Colorado has 69 charter schools and more are under development. Charter schools are public schools created by groups of parents, teachers, or community members to reflect different educational approaches or philosophies. These schools are self-governing, enjoy some independence from the local school district, and have a clear plan for how and what students should learn. They are open to all interested students on a space-available basis.

Magnet Schools: Many districts offer magnet schools—also called "focus" or "alternative" schools—that have specific educational approaches or philosophies. Examples include special emphasis schools in science or performing arts, as well as Montessori or

Waldorf schools that reflect a particular educational philosophy. They range from highly structured schools to open schools. These schools are open to all interested students on a space-available basis. Admission is usually done by lottery.

College Classes: High school students have the opportunity to take college courses or to earn college credit for certain high school classes. These opportunities serve two important purposes: they provide challenging academic experiences for students and they can help reduce the length and expense of college.

Finally, it's important to note you don't necessarily need to look outside your neighborhood school to have an impact on your children's educational program. You can discuss your child's learning style and special interests with his or her teacher. You can help set the direction for the educational approach in your child's school by getting involved in school committees that help make educational decisions. You also can have an impact on the educational philosophy of the district by voting in school board elections. You can attend and participate in school board meetings and share your ideas and concerns with teachers, principals, and school board members. There are many ways to make your neighborhood school your school of choice.

* Excerpted from *A Parent's Guide to Colorado Public Schools*, published 1994 by Governor Romer's Office.

Selecting the Right School

When it comes time to select a school for your children, the responsibility for doing so falls squarely on your shoulders! Don't assume anything! Don't accept as fact any reputation a school may or may not have. Don't expect your realtor or local school administrator to "fill you in" on the downside to any given school. Visit all prospective schools and check them out for yourself.

This chapter contains the basic information for you to do the necessary research. First and foremost, you must determine what is important to your child's education. Use the Parent Inventory of Educational Preferences below to clarify exactly what you are looking for in a school. Keeping in mind the various options available to Colorado residents, find the appropriate point of contact for your school district and start with some phone calls. After you get a feel for what's offered by the schools in your area, plan on spending an entire day making personal visits to your top choices. If you live in the greater Denver Metro area, I highly suggest you obtain a copy of *The Guide to Metro Denver Public Schools* published by Magnolia Street Press. If you are considering a private school anywhere in Colorado, the book you need is *Colorado Private Elementary and Secondary Schools*, also available from Magnolia Street Press. Both these books contain complete, accurate and up-to-date information on a school-by-school basis. See the publishers listing in Appendix A for details.

While visiting the schools, make sure all your questions are answered by the administrators and if school is in session, stroll around and note the teacher/student ratio, the general atmosphere of the classrooms and things of special interest to you or your child. Many school systems have cut back or eliminated special classes like fine arts, music, etc., due to budget cuts. If you see temporary classrooms on the grounds, you can assume this means overcrowding. Many counties in Colorado are growing at such an explosive rate an adequate number of new school facilities may be years in the making. Check with the school district about future plans and budgets.

Finally, for the best possible inside information, visit with the parents of other children currently enrolled in the schools. The easiest way to do this is in front of the schools during normal drop-off/pick-up times or at designated bus stops.

Time spent doing this properly now can save you a lot of regrets years later.

The form below was taken from *The Guide to Metro Denver Public Schools*, published by Magnolia Street Press.

Parent Inventory of Educational Preferences
What is important to you in a school for your children? Rank the following list of criteria or pick a few of greatest importance.

_____ Specific philosophy, curriculum or educational strategy _____

_____

_____ Structured/unstructured environment *(circle one)*

_____ Small teacher/student ratio *(state ideal number)* _____

____ College-preparatory/vocational emphasis of curriculum *(circle one)*

____ School's capability to meet special needs _____

____ Enrichment for gifted/talented children

____ Enrichment for all children

____ Handicap access

____ High level of teacher experience and training

____ Neighborhood school, close to home, walking distance

____ On-site before- and after-school day care

____ Other services such as transportation, lunch program, or boarding

____ New building, modern facilities

____ Older building, historical awareness

____ Non-traditional school building and/or environment

____ State-of-the-art technology and emphasis in curriculum

____ High standardized test scores of other students

____ No tuition or low tuition

____ Religious instruction and environment

____ Cultural, racial, ethnic, and/or economic diversity of students

____ Small school enrollment (state ideal number) _____

____ High level of involvement and input by parents or community

____ Specific athletic offerings _____

____ Specific extracurricular offerings _____

What educational goals do you have for your children? _____

_____

_____

What special needs do your children have which may require services
beyond the "regular" classroom?_____

_____

_____

_____

What expectations or desires do your children have for school programs
in addition to or differing from yours?_____

_____

_____

_____

Index of Cities and School Districts

www.cde.state.co.us
http://reportcard.cde.state.co.us/reportcard/CommandHandler.jsp

City	District	Phone
Agate	Agate 300	719-764-2741
Aguilar	Aguilar Reorganized 6	719-941-4614
Akron	Akron R-1	970-345-2268
Alamosa	Alamosa RE-11J	719-587-1600
Anton	Arickaree R-2	970-383-2202
Antonito	South Conejos RE-10	719-376-5512
Arvada	Jefferson County R-1	303-982-6500
Arvada	Westminster 50	303-428-3511
Aspen	Aspen 1	970-925-3460
Ault	Ault-Highland RE-9	970-834-1345
Aurora	Aurora 28J (Adams-Arapahoe 28J)	303-344-8060
Aurora	Cherry Creek 5	303-773-1184
Avon	Eagle County RE 50	970-328-6321
Avondale	Pueblo County Rural 70	719-947-3484
Bailey	Jefferson County R-1	303-982-6500
Bailey	Platte Canyon 1	303-838-7666
Basalt	Roaring Fork RE-1	970-945-6558
Bayfield	Bayfield 10 JT-R	970-884-2496
Bellvue	Poudre R-1	970-482-7420
Bennett	Bennett 29J	303-644-3234
Berthoud	Thompson R-2J	970-613-5000
Bethune	Bethune R-5	719-346-7513
Beulah	Pueblo County Rural 70	719-485-3127
Black Hawk	Gilpin County RE-1	303-582-0625
Blanca	Sierra Grande R-30	719-379-3259
Boulder	Boulder Valley RE-2	303-447-1010
Branson	Branson Reorganized 82	719-946-5531
Breckenridge	Summit RE-1	970-668-3011
Briggsdale	Briggsdale RE-10	970-656-3417
Brighton	Brighton 27J	303-655-2900
Brighton	Northglenn-Thornton 12	303-872-4000
Broomfield	Boulder Valley RE-2	303-447-1010
Broomfield	Jefferson County R-1	303-982-6500

Broomfield	Northglenn-Thornton 12	303-872-4000
Brush	Brush RE-2(J)	970-842-5176
Buena Vista	Buena Vista R-31	719-395-7000
Burlington	Burlington RE-6J	719-346-8737
Byers	Byers 32J	303-822-5292
Calhan	Calhan RJ-1	719-347-2541
Calhan	Ellicott 22	719-683-2700
Campo	Campo RE-6	719-787-2226
Canon City	Canon City RE-1	719-269-5700
Carbondale	Roaring Fork RE-1	970-945-6558
Castle Rock	Douglas County RE 1	303-688-3195
Cedaredge	Delta County 50(J)	970-874-4438
Center	Center 26 JT	719-754-3442
Cheraw	Cheraw 31	719-853-6655
Cheyenne Wells	Cheyenne County RE-5	719-767-5656
Chipita Park	Manitou Springs 14	719-685-2024
Clifton	Mesa County 51	970-245-2422
Collbran	Plateau Valley 50	970-487-3547
Colorado City	Pueblo County Rural 70	719-542-0220
Colorado Springs	Academy 20	719-598-2566
Colorado Springs	Cheyenne Mountain 12	719-475-6100
Colorado Springs	Colorado Springs 11	719-520-2000
Colorado Springs	Falcon 49	719-495-3601
Colorado Springs	Hanover 28	719-579-2000
Colorado Springs	Harrison 2	719-576-8360
Colorado Springs	Lewis-Palmer 38	719-488-4700
Colorado Springs	Widefield 3	719-391-3000
Commerce City	Adams County 14	303-853-3333
Conifer	Jefferson County R-1	303-982-6500
Cortez	Montezuma-Cortez RE-1	970-565-7282
Cotopaxi	Cotopaxi RE-3	719-942-4131
Craig	Moffat County RE: No. 1	970-824-3268
Crawford	Delta County 50(J)	970-874-4438
Creede	Creed Consolidated 1	719-658-2220
Crested Butte	Gunnison Watershed RE1J	970-641-7760
Cripple Creek	Cripple Creek-Victor RE-1	719-689-2685
De Beque	De Beque 49JT	970-283-5597
Deer Trail	Deer Trail 26J	303-769-4421

Index of Cities and School Districts

Del Norte	Del Norte C-7	719-657-4040
Delta	Delta County 50(J)	970-874-4438
Denver	Cherry Creek 5	303-773-1184
Denver	Denver County 1	303-764-3200
Denver	Mapleton 1	303-853-1000
Denver	Northglenn-Thornton 12	303-872-4000
Denver	Westminster 50	303-428-3511
Dillon	Summit RE-1	970-668-3011
Dinosaur	Moffat County RE: No. 1	970-824-3268
Divide	Woodland Park RE 2	719-687-6048
Dolores	Dolores RE-4A	970-882-7255
Dove Creek	Dolores County RE No.2	970-677-2522
Durango	Durango 9-R	970-247-5411
Eads	Eads RE-1	719-438-2218
Eagle	Eagle County RE 50	970-328-6321
Eastlake	Northglenn-Thornton 12	303-872-4000
Eaton	Eaton RE-2	970-454-5193
Edgewater	Jefferson County R-1	303-982-6500
Edwards	Eagle County RE 50	970-328-6321
Egnar	Dolores County RE No.2	970-677-2522
Elbert	Elbert 200	303-648-3030
Elizabeth	Elizabeth C-1	303-646-4441
Empire	Clear Creek RE-1	303-567-4467
Englewood	Cherry Creek 5	303-773-1184
Englewood	Englewood 1	303-761-7050
Englewood	Sheridan 2	303-761-8640
Erie	St. Vrain Valley RE 1J	303-776-6200
Estes Park	Park (Estes Park) R-3	970-586-2361
Evans	Greeley 6	970-352-1543
Evergreen	Clear Creek RE-1	303-567-4467
Evergreen	Jefferson County R-1	303-982-6500
Fairplay	Park County RE-2	719-836-3114
Falcon	Falcon 49	719-495-3601
Flagler	Arriba-Flagler C-20	719-765-4684
Fleming	Frenchman RE-3	970-265-2111
Florence	Florence RE-2	719-784-6312
Fort Carson	Fountain 8	719-382-1300

Fort Collins	Poudre R-1	970-482-7420
Fort Collins	Thompson R-2J	970-613-5000
Fort Lupton	Weld County RE-8	303-857-6291
Fort Morgan	Fort Morgan RE-3	970-867-5633
Fountain	Fountain 8	719-382-1300
Fountain	Widefield 3	719-391-3000
Fowler	Fowler R-4J	719-263-4224
Franktown	Douglas County RE 1	303-688-3195
Fraser	East Grand 2	970-887-2581
Frederick	St. Vrain Valley RE 1J	303-776-6200
Frisco	Summit RE-1	970-668-3011
Fruita	Mesa County 51	970-245-2422
Galeton	Eaton RE-2	970-454-5193
Gardner	Huerfano RE-1	719-738-1520
Gateway	Mesa County 51	970-245-2422
Georgetown	Clear Creek RE-1	303-567-4467
Gilcrest	Gilcrest RE-1	970-737-2403
Glenwood Springs	Roaring Fork RE-1	970-945-6558
Gold Hill	Boulder Valley RE-2	303-447-1010
Golden	Jefferson County R-1	303-982-6500
Granada	Granada RE-1	719-734-5492
Granby	East Grand 2	970-887-2581
Grand Junction	Mesa County 51	970-245-2422
Grand Lake	East Grand 2	970-887-2581
Greeley	Greeley 6	970-352-1543
Grover	Pawnee RE-12	970-895-2222
Guffey	Park County RE-2	719-836-3114
Gunnison	Gunnison Watershed RE1J	970-641-7760
Gypsum	Eagle County RE 50	970-328-6321
Haxtun	Haxtun RE-2J	970-774-6111
Hayden	Hayden RE-1	970-276-3864
Henderson	Brighton 27J	303-659-4820
Highlands Rangh	Douglas County RE 1	303-688-3195
Hoehne	Hoehne Reorganized 3	719-846-4457
Holly	Holly RE-3	719-537-6616
Holyoke	Holyoke RE-1J	970-854-3634
Hooper	Sangre De Cristo RE 22J	719-378-2321

Index of Cities and School Districts

Hotchkiss	Delta County 50(J)	970-874-4438
Hudson	Keenesburg RE-3(J)	303-732-0248
Hugo	Genoa-Hugo C113	719-743-2428
Hygiene	St. Vrain Valley RE 1J	303-776-6200
Idaho Springs	Clear Creek RE-1	303-567-4467
Idalia	East Yuma County RJ-2	970-332-5764
Ignacio	Ignacio 11 JT	970-563-4521
Iliff	Valley RE-1	970-522-0792
Indian Hills	Jefferson County R-1	303-982-6500
Jamestown	Boulder Valley RE-2	303-447-1010
Joes	West Yuma County RJ-1	970-848-5831
Johnstown	Johnstown-Milliken RE-5J	970-587-2336
Julesburg	Julesburg RE-1	970-474-3365
Karval	Karval RE-23	719-446-5311
Keenesburg	Keenesburg RE-3(J)	303-732-0248
Kersey	Platte Valley RE-7	970-352-6177
Kim	Kim Reorganized 88	719-643-5295
Kiowa	Kiowa C-2	303-621-2220
Kit Carson	Kit Carson R-1	719-962-3219
Kremmling	West Grand 1-JT	970-724-3217
La Jara	North Conejos RE-1J	719-274-5174
La Junta	East Otero R-1	719-384-6900
La Porte	Poudre R-1	970-482-7420
La Salle	Gilcrest RE-1	970-737-2403
La Veta	La Veta RE-2	719-742-3562
Lafayette	Boulder Valley RE-2	303-447-1010
Lake City	Hinsdale County RE-1	970-944-2314
Lake George	Park County RE-2	719-836-3114
Lakewood	Jefferson County R-1	303-982-6500
Lamar	Lamar RE-2	719-336-3251
Larkspur	Douglas County RE-1	303-688-3195
Las Animas	Las Animas RE-1	719-456-0161
Leadville	Lake County R-1	719-486-6800
Limon	Limon RE-4J	719-775-2350
Littleton	Cherry Creek 5	303-773-1184
Littleton	Douglas County RE-1	303-688-3195
Littleton	Jefferson County R-1	303-982-6500

Littleton	Littleton 6	303-347-3300
Livermore	Poudre R-1	970-482-7420
Loma	Mesa County 51	970-245-2422
Longmont	St. Vrain Valley RE-1J	303-776-6200
Louisville	Boulder Valley RE-2	303-447-1010
Loveland	Thompson R-2J	970-613-5000
Lyons	St. Vrain Valley RE-1J	303-776-6200
Manassa	North Conejos RE-1J	719-274-5174
Mancos	Mancos RE-6	970-533-7748
Manitou Springs	Manitou Springs 14	719-685-2024
Manzanola	Manzanola 3J	719-462-5527
Maybell	Moffat County RE: No. 1	970-824-3268
Mc Clave	Mc Clave RE-2	719-829-4517
Mead	St. Vrain Valley RE-1J	303-776-6200
Meeker	Meeker RE-1	970-878-3701
Merino	Buffalo RE-4	970-522-7424
Milliken	Johnstown-Milliken RE-5J	970-587-2336
Minturn	Eagle County RE 50	970-328-6321
Moffat	Moffat 2	719-256-4710
Monte Vista	Monte Vista C-8	719-852-5996
Monte Vista	Sargent RE-33J	719-852-4023
Montrose	Montrose County RE-1J	970-249-7726
Monument	Lewis-Palmer 38	719-488-4700
Morrison	Jefferson County R-1	303-982-6500
Mosca	Sangre De Cristo RE-22J	719-378-2321
Naturita	West End RE-2	970-864-2290
Nederland	Boulder Valley RE-2	303-447-1010
New Castle	Garfield RE-2	970-625-7600
New Raymer	Prairie RE-11	970-437-5386
Northglenn	Northglenn-Thornton 12	303-872-4000
Norwood	Norwood R-2J	970-327-4336
Nucla	West End RE-2	970-864-2290
Oak Creek	South Routt RE 3	970-736-2313
Olathe	Montrose County RE-1J	970-249-7726
Ordway	Crowley County RE-1-J	719-267-3117
Otis	Lone Star 101	970-848-2778
Otis	Otis R-3	970-246-3413

Index of Cities and School Districts

Ouray	Ouray R-1	970-325-4218
Ovid	Platte Valley RE-3	970-463-5414
Pagosa Springs	Archuleta County 50 JT	970-264-2228
Palisade	Mesa County 51	970-245-2422
Palmer Lake	Lewis-Palmer 38	719-488-4700
Paonia	Delta County 50(J)	970-874-4438
Parachute	Garfield 16	970-285-7759
Paradox	West End RE-2	970-864-2290
Parker	Douglas County RE-1	303-688-3195
Peetz	Plateau RE-5	970-334-2361
Penrose	Florence RE-2	719-784-6312
Peyton	Peyton 23 JT	719-749-2330
Pierce	Ault-Highland RE-9	970-834-1345
Pine	Jefferson County R-1	303-982-6500
Platteville	Gilcrest RE-1	970-737-2403
Pritchett	Pritchett RE-3	719-523-4045
Pueblo	Pueblo City 60	719-549-7100
Pueblo	Pueblo County Rural 70	719-542-0220
Pueblo West	Pueblo County Rural 70	719-547-2191
Rangely	Rangely RE-4	970-675-2207
Red Feather Lakes	Poudre R-1	970-482-7420
Ridgway	Ridgway R-2	970-626-4230
Rifle	Garfield RE-2	970-625-7600
Rocky Ford	Rocky Ford R-2	719-254-7423
Rush	Miami/Yoder 60 JT	719-478-2186
Rye	Pueblo County Rural 70	719-489-2272
Saguache	Mountain Valley RE-1	719-655-0268
Salida	Salida R-32	719-530-5300
San Luis	Centennial R-1	719-672-3691
Sanford	Sanford 6J	719-274-5167
Security	Widefield 3	719-391-3000
Sedalia	Douglas County RE-1	303-688-3195
Sedgwick	Platte Valley RE-3	970-463-5414
Seibert	Hi-Plains R-23	970-664-2636
Sheridan Lake	Plainview RE-2	719-727-4361
Silt	Garfield RE-2	970-625-7600
Silverthorne	Summit RE-1	970-668-3011

Index of Cities and School Districts

Silverton	Silverton 1	970-387-5543
Simla	Big Sandy 100J	719-541-2292
Springfield	Springfield RE-4	719-523-6654
Steamboat Springs	Steamboat Springs RE-2	970-879-1530
Sterling	Valley RE-1	970-522-0792
Strasburg	Strasburg 31J	303-622-9211
Stratton	Stratton R-4	719-348-5369
Swink	Swink 33	719-384-8103
Telluride	Telluride R-1	970-728-4377
Thornton	Mapleton 1	303-853-1000
Thornton	Northglenn-Thornton 12	303-872-4000
Timnath	Poudre R-1	970-482-7420
Trinidad	Trinidad 1	719-846-3324
USAF Academy	Academy 20	719-598-2566
Vail	Eagle County RE 50	970-328-6321
Vilas	Vilas RE-5	719-523-6738
Vona	Hi-Plains R-23	970-664-2636
Walden	North Park R-1	970-723-3300
Walsenburg	Huerfano RE-1	719-738-1520
Walsh	Walsh RE-1	719-324-5632
Weldona	Weldon Valley RE-20(J)	970-645-2411
Wellington	Poudre R-1	970-482-7420
Westcliffe	Consolidated C-1	719-783-2357
Westminster	Jefferson County R-1	303-982-6500
Westminster	Northglenn-Thornton 12	303-872-4000
Westminster	Westminster 50	303-428-3511
Weston	Primero Reorganized 2	719-868-2715
Wheat Ridge	Jefferson County R-1	303-982-6500
Wiggins	Wiggins RE-50(J)	970-483-7762
Wiley	Wiley RE-13 JT	719-829-4806
Windsor	Windsor RE-4	970-686-7411
Woodland Park	Woodland Park RE-2	719-687-6048
Woodrow	Woodlin R-104	970-386-2223
Wray	East Yuma County RJ-2	970-332-5764
Yampa	South Routt RE 3	970-736-2313
Yoder	Edison 54 JT	719-478-2125
Yuma	West Yuma County RJ-1	970-848-5831

Index of Cities and School Districts

Private Schools

- Colorado has more than 350 private elementary and secondary schools
- 73% of those schools have a religious affiliation
- None are military schools
- A number of those schools focus on the special needs of children
- 43% of the schools offer foreign languages in the curriculum
- At least two schools provide support to home schoolers
- Many schools feature specialized curricula such as Montessori, Waldorf, British Primary, and Core Knowledge
- The Denver Metro area has 180 private schools; Boulder has 21 private schools; Colorado Springs has 37 private schools. There are an additional 135 private schools scattered around Colorado.

The information available about private schools in Colorado is vast. If you are considering enrolling your children in a private school it is highly recommended you obtain a copy of *Colorado Private Elementary and Secondary Schools* published by Magnolia Street Press.

Higher Education

www.state.co.us/cche_dir/hecche.html

The Colorado Commission on Higher Education

The Colorado Commission on Higher Education (303-866-2723) is a nine-member lay board, appointed by the Governor and confirmed by the Senate, that acts as a central policy and coordinating board for Colorado public higher education. The Commission meets monthly on campuses throughout the state, to discuss and act on statewide higher education policy. The Commission works in consultation with governing boards of higher education institutions in the development and implementation of legislative directives and statewide higher education policy. In addition, the Commission receives assistance from an advisory committee that includes legislative, faculty, student, and citizen representation. The responsibilities of the Commission are to:

- Develop long-range plans for an evolving state system of higher education
- Review and approve degree programs
- Establish the distribution formula for higher education funding; recommend statewide funding levels to the legislature
- Approve institutional capital construction requests; recommend capital construction priorities to the legislature
- Develop policies for institutional and facility master plans
- Administer statewide student financial assistance programs through policy development, program valuation, and allocation of funds
- Develop and administer a statewide off-campus (extended studies), community service, and continuing education program
- Determine institutional roles and missions
- Establish statewide enrollment policies and admission standards
- Conduct special studies as appropriate or directed, regarding statewide education policy, finance, or effective coordination.
- Provide the public with various publications concerning all aspects of higher education

Student Financial Assistance Programs
Colorado student aid is appropriated by the state legislature and allocated by the Colorado Commission on Higher Education to eligible Colorado colleges and universities. Colorado student aid awards are made by institutions to students based upon state guidelines and according to institutional policies and procedures. Any aid received must be used for tuition, fees, room, board, books, and supplies or other expenses related to attendance at Colorado institutions.

General Student Eligibility Requirements:

1. Colorado residency for tuition purposes (A small percentage of Undergraduate Merit and Graduate Fellowship awards may be made by some institutions to non-residents of Colorado.)

2. Enrollment in an eligible program at an eligible Colorado postsecondary institution

3. Satisfactory progress toward completion of a course of study

4. No defaulted educational loans or grants

Types of State Aid Available:

Colorado Diversity Grant: Available as part of a statewide effort to increase participation of under-represented groups in the Colorado public higher education system.

Colorado Nursing Scholarships: Designed to provide assistance to individuals seeking nursing education that agree to practice in Colorado. Applications are available from the Colorado Commission on Higher Education annually.

Colorado Part-time Grants: Need-based grants for less than full-time students attending eligible Colorado institutions.

Colorado Student Grants (CSG): Available to qualified undergraduates with documented financial need.

Colorado Student Incentive Grants (CSIG): Available to qualified undergraduates with substantial financial need. (Student grants under this program are comprised of both federal and state funds).

Colorado Work-Study: Part-time employment program designed to assist students with financial need or work experience.

Undergraduate Merit: Available to students who demonstrate superior scholarship or talent as defined by the college or university they attend.

Colorado Graduate Grants: Available to graduate students with financial need.

Colorado Graduate Fellowships: Provide merit-based awards to graduate students.

Dependents Tuition Assistance Program: Pays tuition for dependents of Colorado law enforcement officers, fire, or National Guard personnel killed or disabled in the line of duty, and for dependents of prisoners of war or service personnel listed as missing in action. Dependents of disabled personnel must have demonstrated financial need for the assistance. Applications are available at the Colorado Commission on Higher Education.

Paul Douglas Teacher Scholarships: Federal program designed to encourage outstanding individuals to enter the teaching profession. Federal law stipulates that recipients must be (or have been) in the top 10% of their high school graduating class, or have comparable GED scores.

Contact individual institutions for complete information and details about application procedures and deadlines. Information about other sources of financial aid may be obtained at many local libraries.

Definition of Degrees

Certificates: Requires the completion of a program that would be completed in 30 to 120 credit hours. Includes one, two, and four-year certificate programs as well as post-bachelor's and post-master's certificates.

Academic Associate: Normally requires at least two, but fewer than four years of full-time equivalent college work in an academic field of study.

Vocational Associate: Normally requires at least two, but fewer than four years of full-time equivalent college work whose expressed intent is to impart work-related knowledge and skills.

Bachelor: Normally requires at least four but not more than five years of full-time equivalent college-level work. Includes all bachelor's degrees conferred in a cooperative or work-study plan or program. Also includes bachelor's degrees in which the normal four years of work is completed in three years.

Master's: Requires the successful completion of a program of study of at least the full-time equivalent of one, but not more than two academic years of work beyond the bachelor's degree.

First Professional: Requires completion of a program that meets all three of the following:

1. Completion of the academic requirements to begin practice in the profession
2. At least two years of college work prior to entrance to the program
3. A total of at least six academic years of college work to complete the degree program, including prior required college work plus the length of the professional program itself.

Colorado Institutions of Higher Education
2-Year Colleges and Vocational Schools

Aims Community College	Greeley	970-330-8008
Arapahoe Community College	Littleton	303-794-1550
Colorado Mountain College-Alpine Campus	Steamboat Springs	970-879-3288
Colorado Mountain College-Roaring Fork	Glenwood Springs	970-945-7481
Colorado Mountain College-Timberline Campus	Leadville	719-486-2015
Colorado N.W. Community College	Rangely	970-675-2261
Community College of Aurora	Aurora	303-360-4700
Community College of Denver	Denver	303-556-2600
Delta-Montrose Vo-Tech	Delta	970-874-7671
Emily Griffith Opportunity Center	Denver	303-575-4700
Front Range Community College	Westminster	303-404-5550
Front Range Community College	Aurora	303-340-7001
Front Range Community College	Boulder	303-516-8000
Front Range Community College	Brighton	303-404-5098
Front Range Community College	Fort Collins	970-226-2500
Front Range Community College	Fort Collins	303-204-8135
Front Range Community College	Longmont	303-516-8999
Lamar Community College	Lamar	719-336-2248
Morgan Community College	Fort Morgan	970-542-3100
Northeastern Junior College	Sterling	970-522-6600
Otero Junior College	La Junta	719-384-6831
Pikes Peak Community College	Colorado Springs	719-576-7711
Pueblo Community College	Pueblo	719-549-3200
Red Rocks Community College	Lakewood	303-988-6100
San Juan Basin Vo-Tech	Cortez	970-565-8457

San Luis Valley Educational Center	Alamosa	719-589-5871
Pickens Technical Center	Aurora	303-344-4910
Trinidad State Junior College	Trinidad	719-846-5011

4-Year Colleges and Universities

Adams State College	Alamosa	719-587-7011
Colorado School of Mines	Golden	303-273-3220
Colorado State University	Fort Collins	970-491-1101
Fort Lewis College	Durango	970-247-7010
Mesa State College	Grand Junction	970-248-1020
Metropolitan State College of Denver	Denver	303-556-3058
University of Colorado	Boulder	303-492-1411
University of Colorado	Colorado Springs	719-262-3000
University of Colorado	Denver	303-556-2400
University of Colorado Health Sciences Center	Denver	303-399-1211
University of Northern Colorado	Greeley	970-351-1890
University of Southern Colorado	Pueblo	719-549-2100
Western State College	Gunnison	970-943-2119

Private Colleges And Universities

Colorado Christian University	Lakewood	303-202-0100
Colorado College	Colorado Springs	719-389-6651
Regis University	Denver	303-458-4066
Denver University	Denver	303-871-2000
University of Phoenix, Denver Campus	Englewood, CO	303-755-9090

Private Vocational Schools

Academy of Beauty Culture *www.cosmetologyschool.com*	Grand Junction	970-245-5570
The Art Institute of Colorado *www.artinstitutes.edu*	Denver	303-837-0825
Bartending College *www.bartendingcollege.com*	Denver	303-758-5000
Colorado Cranial Institute	Boulder	303-449-0322
Colorado Floral Education Center	Westminster	303-426-6123
Colorado Insurance Education	Denver	303-757-3404
Colorado School of Healing Art *www.cstia.net*	Lakewood	303-986-2320

Private Vocational Schools *(continued)*

Colorado Technical Institute	Colorado Springs	719-598-0200
Concorde Career Institute	Denver	303-861-1151
www.concordecareercolleges.com		
Denver Paralegal Institute	Colorado Springs	719-444-0190
www.paralegal-education.com/campuses/denver		
Denver Paralegal Institute	Denver	303-295-0550
www.paralegal-education.com/campuses/cosprings		
Hair Dynamics Education Center	Fort Collins	970-223-9943
Healing Arts Institute	Fort Collins	970-223-9741
www.HAI-Colo.com		
ITT Technical Institute	Thornton	303-288-4488
www.itt-tech.edu/campus		
Mr. K's Floral Design School	Denver	303-936-4141
Naomi's Mile High Beauty College	Denver	303-455-3687
Noble School of Cosmetology	Colorado Springs	719-528-8532
Parks College	Denver	303-457-2757
www.parkscollege.com		
Platt College	Aurora	303-369-5151
www.plattcolorado.edu		
Real Estate Training Center	Lakewood	303-421-9078
www.coloradorealestate.net		
Real Estate Training Center	Breckenridge	970-453-2160
Rocky Mt. College of Art & Design	Denver	303-753-6046
www.RMDCAD.edu		
United States Truck Driving School	Wheat Ridge	303-431-7600
www.ustruck.com		
Westwood College of Technology	Denver	303-650-5050
www.westwood.edu		

Libraries

Books are vehicles of ideas, instruments of education, vessels of literature and sources of entertainment.[1] The world of books is the most remarkable creation of man. Nothing else he builds ever lasts. Monuments fall, nations perish and civilizations die out. Yet books live on, still as fresh at the day they were written.[2] In the five-and-a-half centuries since the invention of movable type, one thing hasn't

[1]Based on remarks in *Book Printing: A Basic Introduction* by John P. Dessauer, The Continuum Publishing Co., New York, 1989.
[2]From *To Advance Knowledge: A Handbook on American University Press Publishing* by Gene R. Hawes, American University Press Service, Inc., New York, 1967.

changed—the ability of books to move mankind. The book is imagination. It is comfort and companionship. It is solace and inspiration. It is frivolity and formality. It is recipes and revelations. It is a tour down the Danube, a guide to the Louvre, an armchair adventure to the streams of the Rockies.

To learn a craft, professionals must devour huge amounts of information. To excel, they must continue to read. There is virtually nothing, from gardening to home repairs to constructing an atomic bomb, that cannot be learned from books. Anyone with average reading ability has the opportunity to learn, to improve and expand her or his base of knowledge, to find the answer to almost any question.

Today's modern libraries are a cross between repositories of books and the latest high-tech computer centers. The "information highway" is here and growing at a phenomenal rate. With the advent of the CD-ROM and online services, there exists no information that cannot be located and studied.

One of the intentions for this chapter was to list every public library in Colorado. However, when I discovered there are over 300 such facilities, and because space in this book is limited, I decided to reduce the text presented to information not easily obtained through Directory Assistance or local phone books. Below you will find interesting facts about the newest and best-equipped library in Denver and a list of unique corporate and private libraries which house proprietary, technical and research related material which may be difficult to find elsewhere.

Denver Public Library: Central Branch
www.denver.lib.co.us

In the spring of 1995, Denver unveiled its renovated and expanded central library (phone: 720-865-1111). The new structure has seven floors above ground and three below for a total of 540,000 square feet. In 2001, the DPL was ranked number one in the U.S. among libraries serving more than 500,000 people. A few facts:

- In 1999 the DPL loaned 10,798,758 books and other materials.
- The staff (505 employees) answered 1,344,164 reference questions.
- Collections included 2,092,199 books, CDs, videos and periodicals, as well as 2,234,732 government documents.

This library has many special features that include:

Western History and Genealogy Department: Map room with 5,000 maps for browsing and study, computer access to extensive, world-famous photo collection, two-story seminar room, manuscript reading room, and separate genealogy collection.

Children's Library and Story Pavilion: Study rooms with word processors, audiovisual study areas, children's story pavilion for special programs, enclosed patio and play area, multicultural and foreign language book collections.

Technology: Offers a touch-screen building directory, CD-ROM high-storage jukebox, CARL computerized public access catalog, access to the information highways of the world, online periodical delivery service, digitized photographic imaging, self-checkout systems, 24-hour dial-up access via modem, to databases, statewide network linking 120 academic and public library catalogs, equipment for people with disabilities.

General: Orientation theater, bookstore and gift shop, centralized reference service, young adult reading room, popular browsing collection, two multipurpose rooms seating 90 and 100 each, ten study rooms, seven public meeting rooms each seating up to 30, full accessibility to people with disabilities, security systems and personnel, four passenger elevators, plus escalators on first through fourth floors.

Corporate, Special, and Private Libraries

Many large corporations, hospitals, government agencies, and private foundations maintain their own libraries. These special libraries can be an unbelievable source of information not found in public libraries. Although not "public" in nature, most special libraries allow access to material by individuals for specific projects or purposes. This alphabetical list is presented because most special libraries are not listed in any phone book.

American Humane Association Children's Div. Resource Lib. *www.virtualref.com/scic/76.htm*	Englewood	303-792-9900
American Numismatic Association Library *www.money.org/resourcecenter.html*	Colorado Springs	719-632-2646

American Water Works Association *www.awwa.org*	Denver	303-794-7711
Arthur Andersen & Company Library	Denver	303-291-9444
Aspen Historical Society *www.aspenhistory.org*	Aspen	970-925-3721
Assn. of Operating Room Nurses Library *www.aorn.org/library*	Denver	303-755-6304
Augustana Lutheran Church Library	Denver	303-388-4678
Ball Aerospace Library Service *www.ball.com.aerospace/index.html*	Boulder	303-939-5755
Beet Sugar Development Foundation *www.bsofassbt.org/assbt/assbtljb.org*	Denver	303-832-4460
Boulder Community Hospital Medical Library	Boulder	303-440-2091
Boulder County Corrections Library	Boulder	303-441-4686
Brega & Winters PC Law Library	Denver	303-866-9400
Central Colorado Library System *www.cclsweb.org*	Wheat Ridge	303-422-1150
Centura St. Anthony Hospital Medical Reference Library *www.centura.org*	Denver	303-629-3790
Cherry Creek Schools Professional Library *www.ccsd.k12.co.us/dept_prolib.*	Englewood	303-486-4081
Children's Hospital Medical Library *www.tchden.org*	Denver	303-861-6400
Colorado Agency for Jewish Education Library *www.caje-co.org*	Denver	303-321-3191
CO Department of Local Affairs State Planning Library	Denver	303-866-4189
CO Department of Public Health & Env. Rocky Flats Reading Room	Denver	303-692-2037
CO Department of Revenue Office of Tax Analysis	Denver	303-866-3089
CO Department of Transportation Library *www.dst.state.colo/communications/ publications/library*	Denver	303-757-9972
CO Developmental Disabilities Planning Council	Denver	720-941-0176

Corporate, Special and Private Libraries

CO Division of Wildlife Library *www.dnr.state.co.us/edo/wildlife*	Denver	303-297-1192 x7319
CO Division of Wildlife Research Center Library	Fort Collins	970-472-4353
Colorado Historical Society Stephen H. Hart Library *www.coloradohistory.org*	Denver	303-866-2305
Colorado Legislative Council	Denver	303-866-3521
Colorado Mental Health Institute at Pueblo *www.cdhs.state.co.us*	Pueblo	719-546-4677
Colorado Springs Fine Arts Center Library	Colorado Springs	719-634-5581
Colorado Springs Pioneer Museum Center for Local History *www.colorado_springs.com/fmp/cspm/archives*	Colorado Springs	719-385-5990
Colorado State Bank Building Law Library	Denver	303-837-0287
Colorado State Library *www.cde.state.co.us/index_library.htm*	Denver	303-866-6900
Colorado Supreme Court Library *www.state.co.us/courts/sctlib*	Denver	303-837-3720
Colorado Talking Book Library *www.cde.state.co.us/ctbl*	Denver	303-727-9277
Coors Brewing Company Technical Library	Golden	303-277-3506
Denver Art Museum Library *www.denverartmuseum.org*	Denver	720-913-0100
Denver Botanic Gardens Helen K. Fowler Library *www.botanicgardens.org/library*	Denver	303-370-8014
Denver Health Medical Center Medical Library *www.library.uchsc.eov*	Denver	303-436-6360
Denver Medical Library *www.denvermedlib.org*	Denver	303-839-6670
Denver Museum of Nature & Science Library *www.dmns.org*	Denver	303-370-6362
Denver Public Schools Education Resource Services	Denver	303-405-8105
El Paso County Department of Health and Environment *www.co.el-paso.co.us/health*	Colorado Springs	719-578-3109
El Paso County Law Library	Colorado Springs	719-448-7780

Exempla St. Joseph Hospital Medical Library *www/saintjosephdenver.org/medlib*	Denver	303-837-7848
First Presbyterian Church Gardner Memorial Library	Colorado Springs	719-471-3763
Ft. Carson Post Grant Library	Ft. Carson	719-526-2350
Gates Rubber Company Information Center *www.gates.com*	Denver	303-744-4150
Great Sand Dunes National Monument Library	Mosca	719-378-2312
Hewlett Packard Company Fort Collins Site Library	Fort Collins	970-898-3830
Hewlett Packard Company Library	Loveland	970-679-2460
Hewlett Packard S. Colorado Regional Library	Colorado Springs	719-590-2708
Holland and Hart Law Library *www.hollandhart.com*	Denver	303-295-8096
Holman Inc. Technical Services Development Lab	Laporte	303-482-5600&
Int'l. Federation of Petroleum & Chemical Works Library	Denver	303-333-1543
Jefferson Center for Mental Health Library *www.jeffersonmentalhealth.org*	Lakewood	303-234-9557
Johns Manville Corp. Library *www.jm.com*	Littleton	303-978-5373
KRMA-TV Channel 6 Educational Services *www.rmpbs.org/aboutus/krma*	Denver	303-892-6666
City of Lakewood Library Resources	Lakewood	303-987-7704
Lutheran Church of the Master Library	Lakewood	303-988-6400
Lutheran Medical Center Exempla Medical Library	Wheat Ridge	303-425-8662
Marathon Oil Co. Production Technology Library *www.marathon.com*	Littleton	303-347-5530
Medical Centers of Aurora Library	Aurora	303-873-5766
Medical Group Management Assn. Library Research Center	Englewood	303-397-7887

Corporate, Special and Private Libraries

Memorial Hospital Health Sciences Library www.memorialhospital.com	Colorado Springs	719-365-5182
Mental Health Center of Boulder County Library	Boulder	303-443-8500
Mercy Medical Center www.mercydurango.org	Durango	970-382-1347
Mesa Verde Research Library Museum www.mesaverde.org	Mesa Verde Park	719-529-5079
Metro Wastewater Reclamation District Library	Denver	303-286-3000
Metrum Information Storage Information CenterMile High Center Law Library	Littleton Denver	303-773-4829 303-832-3335
Montrose Memorial Hospital Medical Library www.montrosehospital.com	Montrose	970-240-7394
Museum of Western Colorado www.wcmuseum.org/museum	Grand Junction	970-242-0971
National Archives and Records Admin. www.nara.gov/regional/denver.html	Denver	303-236-0804
National Center for Atmospheric Research www.ncar.ucar.edu	Boulder	303-497-1180
National Indian Law Library www.narf.org/nill/nillindex.htm	Boulder	303-447-8760
National Institute of Corrections Information Center www.nicic.org	Longmont	303-682-0213
National Jewish Medical & Research Center www.nationaljewish.org	Denver	303-398-1483
National Renewable Energy Laboratory www.nrel.gov	Golden	303-275-4215
National Writers Assn. Library	Aurora	303-751-7844
Parkview Episcopal Medical Center Medical Library	Pueblo	719-584-4582
Penrose St. Francis Healthcare System Library	Colorado Springs	719-776-5288
Platte River Power Authority Library	Fort Collins	970-229-5230

Porter Adventist Hospital Medical Library *www.centura.org*	Denver	303-778-5656
Poudre Valley Hospital Library	Fort Collins	970-495-7323
Public Service Company of Colorado Library	Denver	303-571-7084
Raytheon Engineers & Constructors Inc.	Englewood	303-843-2256
Rocky Mountain News Editorial Library	Denver	303-892-2746
Rocky Mountain Philatelic Library	Denver	303-759-9921
Rose Medical Center Medical Library	Denver	303-320-2160
Science Apps International Corporate Library	Greenwood Vill.	303-773-6900
Second Judicial District Law Library	Denver	303-640-2233
Security Life of Denver Corporate Library	Denver	303-860-2338
Sixth Judicial District Law Library	Durango	970-247-2304
S. Metro Denver Small Chamber of Commerce *www.southmetronews.com*	Littleton	303-794-0142
Southeastern Colorado Area Health Education Center	Pueblo	719-544-7833
St. Mary's Hospital & Medical Center Library	Grand Junction	970-244-7509
Stone & Webster Engineering Tech. Info. Center	Denver	303-741-7323
Storage Tech. Corporation Information Center	Louisville	303-673-5867
Swedish Medical Center Medical Library	Englewood	303-788-6197
Tri-County Health Department Library	Englewood	303-220-9200
U.S. Bureau of Land Management Library *www.blm.gov/narsc/library*	Denver	303-236-6648
U.S. Bureau of Mines Library	Denver	303-236-0474
U.S. Bureau of Reclamation Library	Denver	303-445-2072

U.S. Bureau of Census Information Services Program	Lakewood	303-969-7750
U.S. Court of Appeals Tenth Circuit Library	Denver	303-844-3591
U.S. Defense Finance & Accounting/ Denver Center	Denver	303-676-7567
U.S. Dept. of Veterans Affairs Medical Center Library	Denver	303-393-2821
U.S. EPA Nat'l. Enforcemement Investigations Center *http://es.epa.gov/oeca/oceft/neic/library*	Denver	303-236-6136
U S. EPA Region 8 Library *www.epa.gov/region8*	Denver	303-312-6312
U.S. Geological Biological Ecological Science Center *www.mesc.usgs.gov*	Fort Collins	970-226-9403
U.S. Geological Survey Library *www.usgs.gov*	Denver	303-236-1000
U.S. National Park Service Library *www.cr.nps.gov*	Denver	303-969-2534
U.S. Office of Surface Mining Library *www.wrcc.osmre.gov/techlibrary*	Denver	303-844-1436
U.S. Olympic Committee Information Resources Center *www.usoc.org*	Colorado Springs	719-578-4651
U.S. Veterans Affairs Medical	Grand Junction	970-242-0731
U of CO Health Sciences Center Health Resource Service Center Library *www.uchsc.edu*	Denver	303-315-8555
University of Colorado Technical Reference Center	Boulder	303-492-8774
Ute Mountain Tribal Library	Towaoc	970-564-5348
Wayne Bond Memorial Technical Library	Denver	303-452-6111
Weld County District Court Law Library	Greeley	970-351-7300
YWCA of Boulder County Resource Center	Boulder	303-443-0419

This Must Be The Place

STATEWIDE STATISTICS

General Statistics

Employment

Health Care

Taxes

If you like reading books on world records, technical computer manuals, or actuarial charts, you're going to love this chapter. I have attempted to take a large hodgepodge of data and edit it into a small hodgepodge of data. I have also attempted to integrate narrative material so as not to put the average reader to sleep. This chapter is loosely divided into the four sections shown above. You should keep in mind that many of the charts and figures are based on data that may be several years old and therefore may not provide an accurate picture. The data used is the most recent available from any source; however, due to the explosive growth Colorado has experienced during the last several years, the information provided should only be used as a basis for general trends or historical reference.

General Statistics

Population Growth

Growth! From the smallest rural newspaper to the largest international magazines, the tremendous growth of Colorado is still making headlines. Regardless of which side of the debate you are on—that growth is a blessing or a curse—one thing is undeniable: the boom is not over. Recently released figures from the U.S. Census Bureau show that from 1990 to 2000 the state's population grew over 30%. Some counties experienced growth of more than 30%. Douglas County was in the lead with a total population increase of 191.0%. As a state, Colorado's population grew from 3,294,473 to 4,301,261. That is over one million new residents!

Many lists of subjects like "The Fastest Growing Counties," "The Largest Counties," and related summaries are available from various sources. No such list should be considered definitive. In addition to the problem of "old" data concerning a rapidly changing subject, there is also the problem of statistical manipulation. This section contains three charts concerning the population growth in Colorado based on the 2000 Census. The first shows Colorado's largest counties based on population. The second shows percentage change and the third shows numerical change. If one county had a numerical change of 37,000 new residents up from a base of 370,000 it would have a net 10% increase. However, if a small rural county with a base of 1,000 residents gained 110 new residents it would top the list with an 11% increase. You decide which has more growth.

10 Largest Counties (2000)

Growth Rate County	Population 1990	Population 2000	Annual % Change
Denver	467,610	534,636	1.8%
Jefferson	438,430	527,052	2.0%
El Paso	397,014	516,929	3.0%
Arapahoe	391,511	487,967	2.4%
Adams	265,038	363,857	3.7%
Boulder	225,339	291,288	2.9%
Larimer	186,136	251,494	3.5%
Weld	131,821	180,936	3.7%
Douglas	60,391	175,766	19.6%
Pueblo	123,051	141,472	1.5%

10 Fastest Growing Counties Based on Percentage Change 1990-2000

County	1990 Population	2000 Population	Change
Douglas	60,391	175,766	191.0%
Elbert	9,646	19,872	106.0%
Park	7,174	14,523	102.4%
Eagle	21,928	41,659	90.0%
Archuleta	5,345	9,898	85.2%
Summit	12,881	23,548	82.8%
Custer	1,926	3,503	81.9%
San Miguel	3,653	6,594	80.5%
Hinsdale	467	790	69.2%
Teller	12,468	20,555	64.9%

10 Fastest Growing Counties Based on Numerical Change 1990-2000

County	1990 Population	2000 Population	Increase
El Paso	397,014	596,929	119,915
Arapahoe	391,511	487,967	96,456
Douglas	60,391	175,766	115,375
Jefferson	438,430	527,032	88,626
Adams	265,038	363,857	98,819
Denver	467,610	554,636	87,026
Boulder	225,339	291,288	65,949
Larimer	186,136	252,464	65,358
Weld	131,821	180,936	49,115
Mesa	93,145	116,255	23,110

Substate Population Projections

Colorado is divided into five substate regions (see table in chapter 1). The population projections below are an aggregation of all the counties within each region.

Region	2005	2010	2015
Front Range	3,443,236	3,739,198	4,059,766
Western Slope	445,963	511,363	576,208
Eastern Plains	159,552	174,945	190,235
San Luis Valley	47,702	51,103	54,572
Eastern Mountains	153,556	176,645	204,686
Colorado Total Population Projections:	4,250,110	4,653,254	5,085,467

These projections show that the state's population, which has increased by over 80,000 persons per year in the past three years, will continue to increase, but at a slower rate over the next several years.

Growth along the Front Range in the next several years will be due to the continued increases in certain base industries that have grown in the past three or four years. The largest increases have been in the communications, engineering and business services, chemicals manufacturing, trucking, and warehousing. Other industries that have increased or remained strong in the region have been in electrical machinery and instruments manufacturing, the federal government, air transportation, and construction. Increases are expected to continue over the next ten years but in most of these industries, especially construction, at slower rates than have occurred in the last several years.

On the Western Slope, which is actually the fastest growing part of the state, growth is occurring for several reasons. The most obvious is the resort areas in Summit, Eagle (Vail), Pitkin (Aspen), San Miguel (Telluride) and Routt (Steamboat Springs) Counties. Here the new construction boom in second homes and resort facilities has created construction and service jobs for new permanent populations, many of whom are forced to reside in neighboring counties such as Lake, Grand, Garfield, and Montrose. In addition, the attractiveness of the Western Slope cities to small businesses and telecommuters who want to get away from large metropolitan areas has spawned considerable growth in La Plata (Durango), Montezuma (Cortez), Mesa (Grand Junction), Delta, Montrose, and Chaffee (Salida) Counties. The appeal of all of these areas and others (Archuleta, for example, to retirees) is also adding population to the region. All of the factors behind these types of growth—the growing number of tourist dollars as the baby-boomers reach middle-age, the desire of many small businesses to move to smaller areas, and the overall number of retirees—are expected to continue or increase throughout the projection period.

Five counties elsewhere in the state have grown or will grow because of the location of new prisons and the effect they have in rural areas of solidifying a local economic base and creating a market for new housing. Fremont County (Cañon City), with its large state and federal (Florence) facilities, will continue to provide a very large number of prison-related jobs (as well as house a large number of inmates) for residents of not only Fremont County but also Pueblo, El Paso, and Chaffee Counties. In the past five years the economies of Logan (Sterling), Lincoln (Limon), Crowley (Ordway), and Bent (Lamar) Counties have been boosted by the addition of new prisons.

The remainder of the state—largely agricultural counties—will grow at slower rates, but this growth is in contrast (in many of these counties) to the declines they have experienced for more than four decades. Growth along the Front Range, elsewhere in the West, and new ties to the Pacific Rim generally will increase the markets for their agricultural goods. In addition, many of these non-metropolitan counties and communities will continue to attract small businesses (some related to agriculture, some not) and new retirees—as they have in the recent past—as part of the overall growth in the multi-state region.

In a broader national context, above-average growth is occurring in Colorado because of above-average growth in the West and because of new decentralization tendencies away from California, which is the primary destination for an ever-increasing number of immigrants. According to the 2000 Census, the fastest growing states in the country have been Nevada, Idaho, Arizona, Utah, and Colorado, with Nevada and Arizona adding the most population—40% and 66.3% respectively.

Colorado's potential for gain from these general trends in the West is reinforced by the special appeal of the state to businesses and their employees. Denver, Colorado Springs, and other metropolitan areas of the Front Range are ideally situated in the newly emergent international economy. They sit halfway between the trading centers of Chicago, St. Louis, Texas and the Gulf of Mexico and those of the West coast. They are also favorably juxtaposed between the growing trading centers of Mexico and those of Northwestern Canada. One reason for the growth of the cable television industry in Denver is its central position for satellite relay between Europe and the Pacific Rim.

The Denver International Airport has secured the Front Range's role as a national and international trading center as well as the airport's own role as a transportation hub. The expansion of the Colorado Springs Municipal Airport along with presence of a strong community-based university will also enable that metropolitan area to take advantage of the state's beneficial location and quality of life. Airports in other parts of the state will also be critical in supporting the growth potentials in those areas.

Employment

The Colorado Department of Labor and Employment has released its report, *Colorado Occupational Employment Outlook 1998-2008*, containing data on the growth expected in virtually every occupation. This information is helpful for those contemplating a move to Colorado and to those deciding on educational and career goals. A summary of this report appears below.

Over 60% of the jobs created by growth over the next decade is expected to come from three major occupational categories: Professional/Para-Professional/Technical, Services, and Blue Collar. There will also be many opportunities in Executive, Administrative and Managerial positions, which will average slightly more than 7,000 jobs per year. Sales and Clerical/Administrative Support will add about 8,500 jobs per year. The remaining jobs will come from Agriculture/Forestry/Fishing.

Professional/Para-Professional/Technical (including Education and Computer Sciences), and the Services Sector are anticipated to continue their dominance as the generator of the largest number of new positions. Business services alone will contribute almost 20% of all new jobs in this ten-year period. Other sectors expected to generate a significant number of new jobs are Engineering, Accounting, Research, Management and Related Services, Health Services, Social Services, Amusement and Recreation Services, and Membership Organizations

The Trade Sector is expected to produce jobs at just over half the rate of the Services sector. The largest increase will be in Eating and Drinking Places and Miscellaneous Retail.

Transportation, Communications, and Public Utilities are expected to slow half a percentage point from the pace of the previous decade. Communications will contribute the most new positions, almost 60%, and Motor Freight Transportation and Warehousing will contribute another 28%.

The Finance, Insurance and Real Estate Sector has a predicted growth rate of 2.7% annually, generating 2,000 positions each year. The highest rate is predicted for the Security and Commodity Brokers and Credit Agencies other than banks.

Although **Manufacturing** is expected to grow faster in this ten-year period than it did previously, it will lose approximately one percent of its share of overall employment. The largest increases are projected in Industrial and Commercial Machinery and Computer Equipment, Printing, Publishing and Allied Industries, and Electronic Equipment and Components.

Overall, the **Mining** industry is expected to continue its decline of several years, losing approximately 1,600 positions. However, Nonmetallic Minerals mining is expected to add about 800 new jobs.

Construction is expected to add 1,700 positions each year.

Educational Services is expected to gain 2,400 new jobs annually and **Hospitals** another 1,200.

Local Government is expected to provide over 2,000 new jobs annually, far exceeding new jobs in state government. Federal government jobs are actually expected to decrease within the ten-year period.

Additional Resources
Colorado State Department of Labor and Employment
1515 Arapahoe St.
Denver, CO 80202
303-620-4718
www.cdle.co.state.us/

Key Colorado Employers

I once interviewed for a high-paying position with an "International Corporation." The interview was conducted in an expensively furnished office and the offers were very generous—too generous. Listening to my intuition, I did some checking and discovered I was dealing with a "paper" corporation with questionable resources and intentions. If you are looking for a position and come across one with United Airlines, Hewlett Packard, UPS, or another "household" name, you probably won't have doubts about the offer. Below is a list of many lesser-known regional or statewide companies that employ between 100–16,000 people in Colorado. If you like the security of working for a "large and stable" company, this list may help you sort through the classifieds.

ACX Technologies	Exabyte Corp.	MCI Communications
Adolph Coors Co.	Fischer Imaging Corp.	MDC Holdings Inc.
ARA Services	Forest Oil Corp.	New Century Energies
AT&T Cable Services	Frontier Airlines	Newmont Mining Corp.
Ball Corporation	Good Times Restaurants	OEA Inc.
Bank One Colorado	Grease Monkey	PCL Construction
Basin Exploration	Hensel Phelps Const.	Qwest Communications
BI Incorporated	Hunter-Douglas	Raytheon Company
Big O Tires Inc.	Window Fashions	Safeway
Celestial Seasonings	ICG Communications	Samsonite Corporation
CH2M Hill	Information Handling	Southland Corp.
CommNet Cellular Inc.	Services	Storage Technology
CSG Systems	J.D. Edwards	Synergen Inc.
Cyprus Amax Minerals	Johns-Manville Corp.	Vicorp Restaurants Inc.
Eastman Kodak	Jones Intercable Inc.	Wells Fargo Banks
EchoStar	King Soopers/Kroger	Western Gas Resources
Communications Corp.	KN Energy Inc.	Wild Oats Markets, Inc.

Health Care
www.cdphe.state.co.us

Deaths, accidents: . . . . 39.7 per 100,000 residents

Deaths, cancer: . . . . 136.3 per 100,000 residents

Deaths, cerebrovascular diseases: . . . . 42.9 per 100,000 residents

Deaths, diabetes mellitus: . . . . 14.5 per 100,000 residents

Deaths, heart disease: . . . . 141.9 per 100,000 residents

Deaths, homicide: . . . . 3.5 per 100,000 residents

Deaths, motor vehicle accidents: . . . . 16.5 per 100,000 residents

Deaths, respiratory diseases: . . . . 67.9 per 100,000 residents

Deaths, suicide: . . . . 14.2 per 100,000 residents

Health Care Facilities

To describe every health care facility in Colorado would take 257 pages. Suffice it to say, for most of us having a hospital within an hour of home is good enough. Knowing most ski resorts have some type of emergency facilities and air rescue/ambulance can reach all but the most rugged mountain terrain should ease our fears of injury or serious illness. But what if you or a family member has special medical needs or you are planning a rural move and would like to know what facilities are nearby? There are a number separate directories available from the Colorado Department of Public Health and Environment (4300 Cherry Creek Dr. South, #A200, Denver, CO 80222-1530, 303-692-2800) which contain complete data. Below is a list of the directories offered. Call the CDPHE for the most current pricing and availability. These directories are also available on the Internet at www.cdphe.state.co.us/hf/hfd.asp

Ambulatory Surgical Centers

Community Clinics

Community Mental Health Centers

Community Mental Health Clinics

Comprehensive Outpatient
    Rehab Facilities

Elderly, Blind, Disabled Facilities

End Stage Renal Dialysis Units

Home Health Agencies

Hospices

Hospitals—Alphabetic

Intermediate Care Facilities

Long Term Care

Outpatient Physical Therapy/
    Speech Pathologists

Personal Care Boarding Homes/
    Assisted Living

Portable X-ray Units

Residential Care Facilities for
    Developmentally Disabled

Rural Health Clinics

Swing Beds

Taxes

In addition to federal income taxes, Coloradans are subject to Colorado state income taxes, state sales tax and as well as some county and city sales taxes and various special taxes.

State Income Tax

Colorado's personal income tax in 2000 was 4.63% of what you claim as your federal taxable income (after all deductions and adjustments). If you work for someone else, you will notice state withholding from every paycheck. If you are self-employed, you are responsible for estimated payments and collections just as with federal income tax. This tax rate also applies to corporations. Residency determines whether 100% or some lesser proportion is allocated to Colorado. Residents are allowed credit for tax payments to another state.

State/County/City Sales Tax

The State of Colorado has a flat 2.9% sales tax on the purchase price of retail sales of tangible personal property. This tax also applies to used vehicles and certain services such as telephone. Many counties and cities also have sales taxes that vary and can be as high as 4% for counties and 5% in cities. In addition, certain districts have special taxes for public transportation, cultural facilities, highway construction, and the like. The bottom line is this: in some counties you will pay only 2.9% sales tax on everything you buy and in others it can be three times that amount. But don't bother going to another county to buy your new $60,000 Range Rover to save the extra $2,000 in taxes. Taxes on such purchases are based on your address of record, not where you purchase the vehicle. And if you buy all new furniture in a county without extra taxes and pick it up yourself you are fine. However, if you have it delivered to a county or city with extra taxes, and the retailer has a store there, you pay. The same applies to mail orders when the company has a store in your county or city. Real simple, eh?

Hidden Taxes

As mentioned above, you will pay the appropriate amount of sales tax on all vehicle purchases. You can also expect to pay additional taxes when you register and title your vehicle. This is explained in chapter 5. Every time you have an alcoholic beverage you are paying a hidden tax imposed on the manufacturer. This tax ranges from 8 cents a gallon on beer to 60.26 cents per liter on liquor. If you smoke you pay 20 cents tax per pack and 20% of list price on all other tobacco products. Every time you bet on a horse or tell the dealer to "hit me," you are paying special taxes. And let's not forget about the 22 cents per gallon on gasoline. Call the Department of Revenue with any specific questions, or visit the Department's website at http://www.revenue.state.co.us.

Behind
The
Wheel

5

Registration/Titles

Tags

Insurance

Emissions

Driver's Licenses

On April 25, 1901, New York became the first state to require auto-mobile license plates; the fee was $1. Today, if you are a resident in the City and County of Denver and purchase a new sport utility vehicle (the current vehicle of choice in Colorado) for around $25,000, it will cost you approximately $2,500 for title, taxes, and tags. In addition, you can expect to pay approximately $600 the following year to renew those tags. This fee is gradually reduced over the first four years of ownership, then again in the tenth year.

That is probably why I kept both my Florida driver's license and the Florida tags on my vehicle for almost five years after I moved to Denver (which, contrary to what I may state elsewhere in this book, was many, many years ago and I'm sure the statute of limitations for my heinous offense has since expired). I was lucky to get away with it as long as I did. This was before the Department of Revenue initiated its Violator Hotline. This hotline was established so people could call and turn in anyone (noisy neighbors, ex-lovers, or anyone from California) who they believed were living in Colorado yet keeping out-of-state plates or driver's license. The Hotline was flooded with reports and the dreaded "Truant Title and Tag Police" went into action.

It turned out many of the offenders were long-time Colorado residents who registered their $25,000 Chevy Blazers in another neighboring state where the whole shebang only cost about $10 per year. Shame! Shame!

All kidding and serious warnings aside, when I did finally decide to become an officially registered and tagged citizen of Colorado, I found the entire process very confusing and frustrating. I couldn't get my vehicle plates because I did not have an emissions test; I couldn't get an emissions test because my vehicle was titled and tagged in Florida. They wouldn't accept a bill of sale written on a vodka-and-tonic-stained bar napkin and they told me when I went to trade in my Florida driver's license that someone with my name, height, weight, and address was already in possession of a Colorado ID card. OK, maybe it wasn't all that bad, but it can be a very frustrating process if you don't know everything "you should have known" before attempting the big switchover.

Hopefully, this chapter will help prevent a great deal of aggravation by providing you with the basic information "you should have known." *Note:* Everything in this chapter only applies to on-road vehicles. All off-road vehicles (3 or 4 wheel ATVs, boats, snowmobiles, et al.,) that are not required to have a tag, are required to have an annual registration sticker. The State Department of Resources, Division of Parks and Recreation, Registration Division, handles this process. Many county offices carry the proper forms or the entire process can be completed through the mail.

Write or call:
Division of Parks & Recreation
Registration Division
P.O. Box 231
Littleton, CO 80160
303-791-1920

Registrations/Titles

Every citizen of Colorado who owns or drives a vehicle is required to have a Colorado Driver's License, Colorado Vehicle Title and Registration, and Colorado Vehicle License Plates. You establish state residency at the first occurrence of the following: working at any type of job, owning or operating a business in Colorado, obtaining a Colorado driver's license or living in the state continuously for 90 days. In other words, you are a resident almost immediately upon moving here. There are certain exceptions for special employment situations, military personnel, and students.

BEWARE: failure to register your vehicle within 30 days of establishing residency may result in substantial fines! See the section on driver's licenses below.

A vehicle registration is that little piece of white paper you only see after you have been asked for it by a police officer. A vehicle title is the more official-looking document that proves you own the vehicle (with or without liens). Although these are two separate documents, the information, applications, and fees for both are combined into one process in Colorado.

In all counties except Denver, the County Clerk or Motor Vehicle office handles this process. The end of this section provides a list of County Clerk phone numbers for each county. Denver has several locations that are also listed. You must register your vehicle in the county where you reside.

Registration of your vehicle may be denied if you do not have insurance coverage. Every month, insurance companies must notify the Colorado Department of Revenue of who has insurance and whether it has lapsed. You must provide proof of insurance to your county clerk before you can register your vehicle. Proof can be your insurance card, a copy of your policy, or a letter from the insurance company on letterhead.

The requirements for registering and titling a vehicle are covered for three different circumstances: bringing a vehicle in from another state, buying a new or used vehicle from a dealer within Colorado, and buying a used vehicle from a private owner.

Transferring States

To license and register a vehicle from another state, you must have the following:

- Out-of-state certificate of title for the vehicle or current registration
- Vehicle Identification Number (VIN) verification completed by a:
  - Licensed Vehicle Dealer
  - Emissions Testing Station
  - Law Enforcement Agency
- Emissions Test Certificate (where required, see Emissions section below)
- Current odometer reading
- Proof of insurance

Buying From A Dealer

The process here depends on how you pay for your new or used vehicle. If you pay cash, the dealer will issue a temporary tag and hand you the rest of the paperwork. You then have to proceed to the proper office to register the vehicle and obtain your plates. If you have some type of financing, the process is a little different. In this case, the dealer will send the proper information to the lien holder who will take care of the title work. Once the county receives an OK from the lien holder, you will be notified by postcard and will then have to go to the proper office in your county to apply for permanent tags.

Note: Most car dealers are authorized to collect state sales tax, some county and city taxes, and certain fees involved. It's best to make sure you know what taxes and fees are covered in the purchase price so you don't get a rude awakening when you go to apply for tags.

Buying From A Private Owner

Let's say you can't exactly afford the new $25,000 Jeep you want so you settle for a used vehicle from a private owner. In this situation, you will need the following to register your vehicle:

- A signed (and possibly notarized) vehicle title
- A recent (within 120 days) emission test (where required) provided by the seller
- A notarized bill of sale indicating purchase price

Titles: Colorado titles issued after January 1, 1990 do not require a notary seal. There is a space on the back where the purchase price is entered. Titles issued before January 1, 1990 require the seller(s) to sign the title in the presence of a notary public. If the vehicle has an out-of-state title you would be well advised to check with your county clerk to verify the requirements. Also, make sure the current title is in the name of the individual selling the car and that nothing has been filled-in or "whited-out" on the back. The powers that be frown upon third party title transfers and white-out.

Bill of Sale: Although not required, especially for titles issued after January 1990, it is well worth the effort to obtain a notarized bill of sale showing the vehicle make, model, year, and VIN along with the purchase price. The amount of sales tax the state, county or city collects is based on your purchase price and they have the option to collect taxes based on the current Blue Book value of the vehicle if the purchase price you declare is in doubt and you do not have a notarized bill of sale as proof.

Taxes and fees: There are many taxes and fees involved in transferring a title and getting tags. These include title fee of $5.50, registration fee, license fee based on the weight of the vehicle, ownership taxes based on the age and original value, sales taxes (state and possibly county and city), and depending on the county in which you reside, additional miscellaneous fees. When buying from a private owner, you will have to pay all this when you transfer title and register your vehicle.

Phone List For County Clerks

Adams	303-654-6010	Bent	719-456-2009
Alamosa	719-589-6681	Boulder	303-441-3510
Arapahoe	303-795-4500	Chaffee	719-539-4004
Archuleta	970-264-5633	Cheyenne	719-767-5685
Baca	719-523-4372	Clear Creek	303-569-3251

Conejos	719-376-5422	Logan	970-522-1544
Costilla	719-672-3301	Mesa	970-244-1667
Crowley	719-267-4643	Mineral	719-658-2440
Custer	719-783-2441	Moffat	970-824-5484
Delta	970-874-2150	Montezuma	970-565-3728
Denver	303-576-2200	Montrose	970-249-3362
Dolores	970-677-2381	Morgan	970-867-5616
Douglas	303-660-7440	Otero	719-383-3020
Eagle	970-328-8710	Ouray	970-325-4961
Elbert	303-621-2341	Park	719-836-4222
El Paso	719-520-6240	Phillips	970-854-3131
Fremont	719-275-1522	Pitkin	970-920-5180
Garfield	970-945-2377	Prowers	719-336-4447
Gilpin	303-582-5321	Pueblo	719-583-6507
Grand	970-725-3347	Rio Blanco	970-878-5068
Gunnison	970-641-1602	Rio Grande	719-657-3334
Hinsdale	970-944-2228	Routt	970-870-5557
Huerfano	719-738-2380	Saguache	719-655-2512
Jackson	970-723-4334	San Juan	970-387-5671
Jefferson	303-271-8100	San Miguel	970-728-3954
Kiowa	719-438-5421	Sedgwick	970-474-3346
Kit Carson	719-346-8638	Summit	970-668-5623
Lake	719-486-1410	Teller	719-689-2951
La Plata	970-382-6280	Washington	970-345-6565
Larimer	970-498-7878	Weld	970-353-3840
Las Animas	719-846-3314	Yuma	970-332-5809
Lincoln	719-743-2444		

License Plates (Tags)

There are 74 different types of plates issued in Colorado. Six are for vehicle manufacturers or dealers, six are government-type plates issued to city, county, and state vehicles, with special plates for State Senators, State Representatives, members of Congress, U.S. Senators and members of the Honorary Consular Corps. Several more are issued to utility companies, farm vehicles, commercial fleets, and tractor/trailer rigs or heavy trucks.

For the rest of us, a wide choice of standard or custom versions is offered. In 1998 House Bill 1075 was passed by the Colorado Legislature requiring a total replacement of all license plates. This process will take effect between January 1, 2000 and December 31, 2003. This bill was passed to improve vehicle identification for law enforcement and to simplify our plated schemes by standardizing coloring and utilizing one configuration.

The new plates will be easy to see and read; our existing plates are manufactured using a "beads on paint" system in which only the numbers and letters are reflective, not the background. Colorado will manufacture the new license plates using reflective sheeting resulting in better visability. There will be a combination of embossed (raised lettering) and flat plates. All personalized and special organization plates will be flat. All sequential plates will be embossed.

The state anticipates during this four-year period, approximately four million license plates will be replaced.

Vehicle Classes

Passenger: Passenger vehicles, station wagons, hearses, ambulances (non-government), passenger vans, buses and motor homes.

Light Trucks: Empty weight less than 16,000 pounds, body designed to transport property with special fees for tow trucks, wreckers, race horse vehicles, veterinary mobile trucks, and special use vehicles.

Recreational Truck: Trucks that do not have an empty weight over 6,500 pounds and are not used exclusively for pleasure (non-commercial).

Trailer: Wheeled vehicle without motor power.

Motorcycle: Motor vehicle designed to travel on no more than three wheels.

Collector Series: At least 25 years old, passenger vehicles and trucks, not for commercial use. Plates are issued for a five-year period.

Street Rod: Issued to passenger and light trucks made in 1948 or earlier.

Horseless Carriage: Manufactured in 1942 or prior. Driving limited to/from auto club functions, to/from repair shops, and occasional leisure drive.

Custom Plates

Special Organizational: Various military affiliations and individuals in various branches of the military, reserves, or National Guard.

"Honorably Discharged Veteran" is available to any person who has received an honorable discharge or is retired from any branch of the U.S. Armed Services. Issued to passenger, light trucks, recreational trucks, farm trucks and motorcycles, as well as motorhomes. (One set only.)

Disabled Veteran: One free set to qualifying applicant (50% or more permanent service connected disability). Issued to passenger, light truck, recreational truck, farm truck or motorcycle; may also be issued to a motorhome with no weight restriction.

Former Prisoner of War: One free set to qualifying applicant (on active duty with the U.S. Armed Forces during a period of armed conflict and was incarcerated by an enemy of the U.S.). Issued to the same vehicles as above.

Persons with Disability: Issued to passenger, light truck or mobile homes. Application must be signed by a Colorado-licensed physician.

Amateur Radio/Commercial Call Letters: Issued to passenger and light trucks with an empty weight of less than 10,000 pounds. One set per amateur call letter, up to 10 sets per commercial call letter.

For additional information concerning special or custom plates, call the State Motor Vehicle Division at 303-205-5607, or visit their web site at: www.mv.state.co.us/titlereg/registration/plates/index. html.

Vehicle Insurance

Vehicle insurance is mandatory in Colorado. In fact, there are over 40 Colorado Revised Statues under Article 7, Motor Vehicle Financial Responsibility Law. When you register your vehicle you must sign a sworn statement indicating you now carry and will continue to carry the proper insurance. The mandatory liability minimum is $25,000 bodily injury, $50,000 per accident, and $15,000 property damage. You are required to have proof of insurance with you at all times when driving and failure to do so can result in a mandatory court appearance and possible fines. The courts in this state tend to go ballistic on people without proper insurance coverage!

The only exception to the above are those who qualify for a certificate of self-insurance. Don't count on it. Section 42-7-501, C.R.S. reads as follows:

"Any person in whose name more than twenty-five motor vehicles are registered may qualify as a self-insurer. . . when the director [of motor vehicles] is satisfied that such person is possessed and will continue to be possessed of ability to pay all judgments which may be obtained against such person."

Emissions Testing

You can save yourself a lot of brain damage by skipping this section unless you plan to, or currently live in *or work* in the following counties:

Enhanced Program Area: Adams, Arapahoe, Boulder, Denver, Douglas, El Paso, and Jefferson Counties.

Basic Program Area: Larimer, Pitkin, and Weld Counties.

Due to several factors (topography, heavy industry, and an increasing number of automobiles), the Front Range of Colorado—especially the greater Denver Metro region—suffers from what is known as the "Brown Cloud." When conditions are right, this cloud of pollutants can easily be seen from miles away. In an attempt to reduce the major source of pollutants (automobile emissions), the state's Air Care Colorado Program has recently intensified its effort to reduce emissions by instituting a more stringent testing program along with the older "tailpipe" test, which has existed for years.

This effort has not been without its difficulties. The new test and testing facilities have been under attack since their inception from both consumers and some state legislators alike. If you live or work in any of the above listed counties, you must have a valid emissions test to register your vehicle and a valid emissions sticker on the windshield of your car or truck. Exceptions are noted below.

Enhanced Program Area

1981 and older vehicles: A tailpipe test is required each year at an Air Care Colorado Facility or an independent test-only station.

1982 and newer vehicles: An enhanced emission test (on a dynamometer under actual driving conditions) is required at an Air Care Colorado facility every two years.

Change of ownership: An emission test is required when a vehicle is sold or its ownership changes. The seller is responsible for obtaining the test.

Commuters: Vehicles registered outside of the region but which are driven into the six-county area 90 or more days a year must also undergo the tests.

Newly manufactured vehicles: Any new, never titled vehicle is exempt from the emissions test for four years, or until a change of ownership.

Cost: $24.25 for 1982 and newer vehicles—two-year sticker.

$15.00 for 1981 and older vehicles—one-year sticker.

$45.00 for diesel powered vehicles—one-year sticker.

Tips to ease the pain:

- Check your emissions sticker for the expiration date and have your vehicle tested promptly.
- Call the Air Care Colorado Hotline at 303-456-7090 (or 719-594-8709 in El Paso County) for the best time an most convenient locations (see map).
- Standard hours of operation are Monday-Friday, 7:00 A.M. to 7:30 P.M., and Saturday, 8:00 A.M. to 3:00 P.M. Closed Sundays and holidays.
- Avoid the busiest times—the first three days and the last three days of each month, as well as any time during the noon hour.
- Make certain your vehicle has a gas cap.
- Cash and checks are accepted, but NOT credit cards.
- Warm up your engine thoroughly for at least 15 minutes before testing.
- All-wheel and four-wheel drive vehicles must use specially marked testing lanes. Make sure you don't wait in the wrong lane.

- If your vehicle fails the test you can have it retested free after repairs within 10 days of the initial test.

- In the Enhanced Program Area, test and repairs are not done at the same facility.

Now, if that's not confusing enough, there are certain parts of Adams and Arapahoe counties that are completely exempt from any testing. In general, if you live east of Kiowa Creek you are exempt. However, as stated above, if you work west of Kiowa Creek, you need the test. The same degree of confusion applies to the Basic Program Area covered next.

Basic Program Area

In the basic program area (Larimer, Pitkin, and Weld Counties), all vehicles, regardless of age (except new, never been titled) are re-quired to have an annual tailpipe test only. There are independent inspection and repair facilities and inspections and repairs *can be* performed at the same facility.

The cost for this test is $15.00. 1982 and newer vehicles receive, a two-year sticker and 1981 and older a one-year.

Now, all of Pitkin County participates, a large portion of Larimer County including Loveland, Fort Collins and Poudre Park participates, yet Estes Park, Rustic, and Virginia Dale areas are completely exempt. As far as Weld County is concerned, only the city of Greeley is involved; the remainder of the county is exempt from all testing. But remember the Commuters Regulation about working in a covered area. If in doubt, call the Air Care Colorado Hotline at 970-225-2328 (Larimer and Weld Counties) or 970-920-5075 (Pitkin County).

A map showing enhanced testing station locations appears at the end of this chapter.

Driver's Licenses

Colorado law states you must obtain a Colorado driver's license and vehicle plates immediately upon establishing state residency. The state considers you a resident upon the first occurrence of the following: you work at any type of gainful employment, you own or operate a business in Colorado, you obtain a Colorado driver's license, or you live here continuously for 90 days.

The information presented in this section is intended as a guideline. For complete information please obtain a copy of the *Colorado Drivers' Manual and Supplemental Motorcycle Drivers' Manual* available online from the Colorado Department of Revenue, *www.mv.state.co.us/driverforms.html*.

Any person 16 years of age or older who operates a motor vehicle or motor driven cycle (including mopeds) on the public streets and highways is required to have a valid license. The only exceptions to this are as follows:

Special Employment: Any resident who is employed in another state where the laws of that state require licensing to drive in order to engage in a regular trade or profession, does not need a Colorado driver's license as long as such other license to drive is in force and the employment is not terminated. This exemption applies only if the other state is a member of the Interstate Driver License Compact Agreement.

Other Exemptions: The following need not obtain a Colorado license provided they are 16 years of age or older and possess a valid license from their home state or state of last assignment.

- **Military:** Anyone who is serving as a member of the Armed Forces of the U.S. on active duty, including the spouse and children of such member.
- **Foreign Military:** On duty or assigned to temporary duty with the U.S. Armed Forces to include the spouse and children of such member.
- **Students:** Any non-resident who is temporarily residing in Colorado for the principal purpose of furthering his/her education and who is considered a non-resident for tuition purposes. If a student, regardless of the above, also works (even part-time) in Colorado, he/she needs both a Colorado driver's license and plates.
- **Trainees/Instructors:** Any employee of a Colorado licensed company, corporation, organization, school or business who

is assigned temporarily in Colorado for the principal purpose of receiving or teaching special training relative to his trade, profession, or employment.

- **Non-Resident Aliens:** Foreign tourists, instructors, and business persons may drive up to one year with their own personal driver's license. Such foreign driver's licenses and/or permits issued by foreign countries are recognized when the holder has a valid U.S. Immigration Form 1-94, Arrival/Departure Record, and is driving any private (non-commercial) vehicle including rental vehicles.

Colorado Issues Five Classifications of Driver's Licenses

The Class R (basic license) applies to any vehicle with a GVWR of less than 26,001 lbs., as a single unit or in combination, manufactured to transport 15 or fewer passengers including the driver, and not used to transport hazardous materials. The Class R license is valid for chauffeur purposes and for motorized bicycles.

The Class M (motorcycle) license is valid for any vehicle designed to travel on not more than three wheels in contact with the ground except any such vehicle as may be included within the term farm vehicle or motorized bicycle. Effective October, 1999 no *new* class M Licenses will be issued. The M will appear only as an endorsement on regular or commercial licenses.

Commercial Driver's License: There are three classes of commercial driver's licenses that are covered in the Colorado Drivers' Manual.

Note: If you drive both automobiles and motorcycles, you do not need two licenses. For qualified applicants, a motorcycle endorsement is added to the Class R license.

New Residents With A Valid License

If you are 16 years of age or older and have a valid license in your possession which was issued by another U.S. state, territory, or possession, you will normally not be required to take the road performance test or written examination if the out-of-state license is similar to the Colorado classified driver's license and you surrender the valid out-of-state license.

The driver examiner has a responsibility to require a road performance test—even if you turn in a valid license—if there appears to be a problem with your Physical Aptitude Analysis (obvious disabilities), your Driving Record Analysis, or your Visual Screening (required in all cases).

Should you fail the road performance test, you will be issued an Instruction Permit. When you return to complete the test, both the Instruction Permit and any driver's license must be surrendered.

Fees: $15.60 for adults 21–60, valid for 10 years; $8.10 for adults 61 and older, valid for 5 years; $15.60 for minors* age 16–21, valid until 20 days after 21st birthday. A $1.00 surcharge if motorcycle endorsement was part of old licenses. Add $16.60 for new motorcycle endorsements.

*Effective July 1, 2001: For drivers licenses, the minor age group now includes age 16 to age 21. Minor licenses issued on or after July 1, 2001 will expire 20 days after the 21st birthday. Minor (under 18) and Provisional (under 21) licenses issued before July 1, 2001, will expire 20 days after the 18th or 21st birthday.

Note: If you plan to drive a motorcycle in Colorado and you do not have a motorcycle endorsement on your previous license you will be required to take both the written and motorcycle driving skills test.

Renewal of A Colorado License or Instruction Permit: Once you obtain a Colorado Classified Driver's License or Instruction Permit, you will not normally have to repeat the written or driving test unless:

- You apply for a different class of license or endorsement
- Points from tickets within a 12-month period result in suspension
- You are driving when a fatality has occurred
- The license or permit is canceled, revoked, or denied
- You let the license or permit expire

You Can Lose Your License. All reports of traffic accidents and traffic law violations committed in Colorado are posted to your driving record. A poor record may be cause for suspension or revocation of your driving privilege. Suspension may be for any period up to one year. Revocation must be for at least one year.

Colorado Point System

There are a specified number of points assigned for most traffic law violations. If you accumulate a certain number of points, your license may be suspended for up to one year. Points assessed against your record are not erased when you get a new license.

A driver's license may be classified as a chauffeur license; however, the vehicle must be a public or common carrier. To qualify as chauffeur points, all violations must have been received as a chauffeur of a motor vehicle in use as a public or common carrier of persons or property.

The point accumulations for suspension are as follows:

Minor Driver under 18 years old: More than 5 points in any 12 consecutive months or more than 6 points for period of license.

Minor Driver 18 to 21 years old: 9 points in any 12 consecutive months or 12 points in any 24 consecutive months or 14 points for the period of the license.

Regular Driver: 12 points in any 12 consecutive months or 18 points in any 24 consecutive months.

Chauffeur Points: 16 points in any 12 consecutive months or 24 points in any 24 consecutive months or 28 points in any 48 consecutive months.

Points Assessed

12 Points: Leaving scene of accident, DUI or under the influence of drugs, speed contests, eluding or attempting to elude a police officer

8 Points: Driving while ability is impaired by alcohol, reckless driving

6 Points: Failure to stop for a school bus, failing to yield right-of-way to disabled person

4 Points: Careless driving or following too closely, driving on wrong side of road, improper passing, failure to observe

traffic sign or signal, failure to yield to emergency vehicle, failure to maintain or show proof of insurance, failure to yield right-of-way to pedestrian

3 Points: Failure to yield right-of-way, improper turn, driving through safety zone, driving in wrong lane or direction on one-way street, conviction of violations not listed

2 Points: Failure to signal or improper signal, improper backing, failure to dim or turn on lights, operating an unsafe vehicle, failure to wear seatbelt

1 Point: Operating a vehicle with defective headlights

Speeding over posted limit

0 Points   1-4 m.p.h. (fine only)
1 Point   5-9 m.p.h.
4 Points   10-19 m.p.h.
6 Points   20-39 m.p.h.
12 Points   25 or more m.p.h.

Your Driving Privilege My Be Suspended/Revoked/Canceled If You:

- Are convicted of driving under the influence of alcohol or drugs
- Refuse to be tested for alcohol or drug content
- Leave the scene of an accident without stopping, exchanging information, and rendering aid
- Fail to report an accident to the Colorado Motor Vehicle Division according to the requirements of the financial responsibility law
- Give false information on your driver's license application
- Fail to settle a judgment against you as a result of an accident while operating a vehicle
- Lend your license to someone else or misuse it in any way
- Alter or deface your license
- Fail to appear for a special reexamination requested by the Motor Vehicle Division

- Use a motor vehicle in committing a felony
- Are convicted of manslaughter as a result of a motor vehicle accident

If you are convicted of driving "while under restraint," your driving privilege will be suspended again effective for one year from the date you would have been reinstated.

Re-examination of Drivers

You may be required to submit to a re-examination if the Motor Vehicle Division has good cause to believe you are incompetent or otherwise not qualified to be licensed. After you have taken the examination, your license may be returned, suspended, revoked, or you may be issued a restricted license. Refusal to submit to this test is grounds for suspension or revocation of your license.

Expressed Consent Law (Alcohol & Drugs)

The Expressed Consent Law provides that if a law enforcement officer suspects that a person is driving under the influence of alcohol or other drug substance and the driver refuses to take the required test, or if the result of such test indicates a blood alcohol concentration (BAC) of .10 or more, the officer will confiscate the driver's license and issue a "Notice of Revocation or Denial," which becomes a seven-day driving permit. A request must be made at a driver's license office, or in writing, within the seven days allotted on the driving permit or the revocation of the license and driving privilege becomes effective automatically. If you do not have a valid driver's license the "Notice of Revocation or Denial" issued by the officer does not become a seven-day driving permit and only allows the person to request a hearing within the seven-day period.

Identification Cards

To obtain a Colorado ID card you must appear in person at any driver's license office. You must present at least two (2) documents of identification to support your true name and correct birthday, such as a state-certified birth certificate, marriage certificate, or other legal documents. Documented proof of a Social Security number is required. If you are under 60 years of age you will be required to pay the ID card fee of $4.10. Effective July 1, 2001, you cannot be issued an identification card if you hold a valid driver license.

The Driver Examination

There are five separate tests to take in order to receive a driver's license: Driving Record Analysis, Physical Aptitude Analysis, Vision Screening, Basic Written Test, and Driving Test.

Office Locations

Main Office

1881 Pierce Street, Lakewood, CO 80214, 303-205-5600

Express Offices (No testing)

Arvada 303-425-4638: 7450 W. 52nd Ave., Unit O (offers written test)

Aurora 303-337-5872: Buckingham Square Mall, 1307 S. Joliet

Aurora S.E. 303-693-4652: 13736 E. Quincy Ave. (offers written test)

Colorado Springs 719-598-2929: Chapel Hills Mall, 1520 Briargate Blvd.

Colorado Springs 719-328-0082 (offers written test, drive tests by appointment)

Denver 303-839-1829: 8:30-4:30, M-F, 1560 Broadway

Denver 303-292-9310: 8:30-4:30, M-F, 2736 Welton St.

Littleton 303-973-2926: Southwest Plaza Mall, 8501 W. Bowles Ave.

Westminster 303-426-9683: Westminster Mall, 5433 W. 8th Ave.

Branch Offices (Hours/days vary, call for details and location)
Location given if phone number unavailable

Akron	970-345-2484	Alamosa	719-589-4274
Aurora	303-344-8400	Avon	970-949-3156
Bailey	303-838-4280	Boulder	303-442-3006
Brighton	303-659-5055	Buena Vista	Senior Center
Burlington	719-346-8638	Cañon City	719-275-5617
Castle Rock	303-688-4625	Cheyenne Wells	719-767-5685
Colorado Springs	719-594-8701	Conejos	719-376-5919
Cortez	970-565-9779	Craig	970-824-5447
Creede	719-658-2440	Del Norte	719-657-2708
Delta	970-874-9795	Denver	303-937-9507
Dove Creek	970-677-2283	Durango	970-247-4591
Eads	719-438-5421	Estes Park	970-577-1491
Evergreen	303-674-4152	Fort Collins	970-223-3648

Fort Morgan	970-867-2647	Fowler	City Hall
Frisco	970-668-5015	Fruita	970-249-5426
Georgetown	303-569-2005	Glenwood Springs	970-945-8229
Granby	970-887-3875	Grand Junction	970-248-7010
Greeley	303-352-5845	Gunnison	970-641-1052
Holyoke	970-854-3131	Hotchkiss	Town Hall
Hugo	719-743-2796	Julesburg	970-474-3346
Kiowa	303-621-3125	Kremmling	Public Library
La Junta	719-384-2801	Lake City	970-944-2223
Lakewood	303-986-2742	Lamar	719-336-2670
Las Animas	County Courthouse	Leadville	719-486-0888
Littleton	303-795-5954	Longmont	303-776-4073
Loveland	303-667-6497	Meeker	970-878-5548
Montrose	970-249-5426	Northglenn	720-929-8636
Norwood	1565 Grand Ave.	Nucla	970-864-7531
Ordway	311 Main Street	Ouray	970-325-4323
Pagosa Springs	970-264-6088	Parker	303-627-0985
Pueblo	719-543-5164	Rangely	970-675-2881
Rifle	970-625-2044	Saguache	719-655-2512
Salida	719-539-2802	San Luis	719-672-3372
Security-Widefield	719-392-6101	Silverton	970-387-5671
Springfield	719-523-4372	Steamboat Springs	970-879-0715
Sterling	970-522-5982	Strasburg	County Building
Trinidad	719-846-4348	Walden	970-723-4334
Walsenburg	719-738-2807	Westcliffe	Town Hall
Woodland Park	719-687-2447	Wray	970-332-5855
Yuma	970-848-3878		

Air Care Colorado Centers

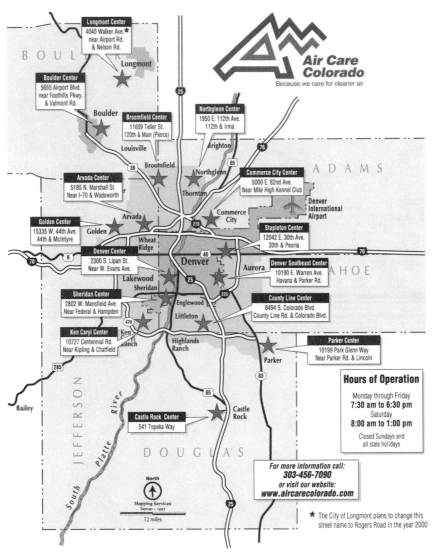

Longmont Center
4040 Walker Ave. ★
near Airport Rd.
& Nelson Rd.

Boulder Center
5655 Airport Blvd.
near Foothills Pkwy.
& Valmont Rd.

Broomfield Center
11609 Teller St.
120th & Main (Pierce)

Northglenn Center
1950 E. 112th Ave.
112th & Irma

Arvada Center
5185 N. Marshall St.
Near I-70 & Wadsworth

Commerce City Center
5000 E. 62nd Ave.
Near Mile High Kennel Club

Golden Center
15335 W. 44th Ave.
44th & McIntyre

Stapleton Center
12042 E. 30th Ave.
30th & Peoria

Denver Center
2300 S. Lipan St.
Near W. Evans Ave.

Denver Southeast Center
10190 E. Warren Ave.
Havana & Parker Rd.

Sheridan Center
2802 W. Mansfield Ave.
Near Federal & Hampden

County Line Center
8494 S. Colorado Blvd.
County Line Rd. & Colorado Blvd.

Ken Caryl Center
10727 Centennial Rd.
Near Kipling & Chatfield

Parker Center
10199 Park Glenn Way
Near Parker Rd. & Lincoln

Castle Rock Center
541 Topeka Way

Air Care Colorado
Because we care for cleaner air

Hours of Operation

Monday through Friday
7:30 am to 6:30 pm
Saturday
8:00 am to 1:00 pm

Closed Sundays and
all state holidays

For more information call:
303-456-7090
or visit our website:
www.aircarecolorado.com

★ The City of Longmont plans to change this
street name to Rogers Road in the year 2000

North
Mapping Services
Denver - 1997
12 miles

BOULDER
ADAMS
JEFFERSON
DOUGLAS
ARAPAHOE

Longmont
Boulder
Louisville
Broomfield
Brighton
Northglenn
Thornton
Commerce City
Denver International Airport
Arvada
Golden
Wheat Ridge
Denver
Stapleton
Aurora
Lakewood
Sheridan
Englewood
Littleton
Ken Caryl Ranch
Highlands Ranch
Parker
Bailey
Castle Rock
South Platte River

Send Lawyers, Guns, and Money

Laws

Rules

Regulations

You just got married a month ago to your 15-year-old cousin who now wants a divorce and half of your winning Lotto ticket. So you go out to buy some liquor at the nearest drive-through using a check you know you can't cover, and while having a few belts in the parking lot you get busted for DUI. On top of that, your landlord served you an eviction notice and the transaction on your new "For Sale by Owner" house is null and void because of bad paperwork. Maybe you should have read this chapter first. As the saying goes, ignorance of the law is no excuse.

DUI/DWAI

This section won't be a lecture on drinking and driving, though a word of warning is warranted. In addition to the legal implications, DUI in Colorado can be quite hazardous to your health. A great number of people tend to drink and drive while on a weekend get-away to the mountains. Don't! Imagine driving down unfamiliar, unlit, very narrow, and slick mountain roads. Now imagine it after a couple of drinks.

In Colorado, a driver with a Blood Alcohol Content (BAC) between 0.05% and 0.09% is, by law, driving with ability impaired (DWAI). If a driver's BAC is 0.10% or higher, they are, by law, driving under the influence (DUI). The penalties for DWAI/DUI are tough. First offense DWAI can result in eight points on your license, a $500 fine, up to 180 days in jail, and 48 hours of community service. You can be arrested for DWAI/DUI if you are in your car sitting in a parking lot, in an alley, or parked on the street. Unlike some states, Colorado does acknowledge DUI offenses on private property.

Liquor Laws

Colorado has some unique liquor and beer codes. In California, I can walk into a 7-Eleven and buy liquor and munchies too. In Colorado, the only alcoholic beverage you can buy outside a liquor store or bar is 3.2% beer. Conversely, liquor stores can't sell food, snacks or anything else not directly related to the consumption of alcoholic beverages. The legal drinking age is 21; however, someone at least 18 years old can handle, dispense or sell drinks if acting as an employee for a liquor licensee.

Liquor and drug stores may sell alcoholic beverages from 8:00 A.M. until midnight but may not sell on Sundays or Christmas. All bars, restaurants and taverns may sell drinks from 8:00 A.M. until 2:00 A.M. 365 days a year.

Bad Checks

Colorado is not the place to write a bad check—intentionally or unintentionally. (More information may be found in Section 18-5-205 of the Colorado Criminal Code.) In essence, the law states that if any person, knowing he has insufficient funds, issues a check for the payment of services, wages, rent, property, etc., that person commits fraud by check. Depending on the amount of the check, the charge can range from a Class 3 misdemeanor to a Class 6 felony. Even if you bounce a $5.00 check, you are subject to a fine of $100 or three times the amount of the check, whichever is greater.

Evictions

Colorado has very clear laws and procedures in regard to evictions, although technically, there is no such thing in the state. None of the courts or legal forms uses the term "eviction." All such actions are re-ferred to as "Unlawful Detainer," and are covered under the Forcible Entry and Detainer (FED) Statute (13-40-101 et seq. C.R.S.).

Whether you are a landlord or a tenant, it pays to know the laws if you are faced with a possible eviction. There are state statutes in place to protect the rights of both parties. Landlords need to know how to give proper notice, complete, file, and serve the necessary forms and avoid violating any tenant rights. Tenants should know the legal defenses to an eviction, how to file an answer or counter-claim, and the laws regarding security deposits.

A written lease is of utmost importance to both parties. In almost all situations where there is a conflict between the common law and lease provisions, the lease will control. This is particularly impor-tant in regard to notice, security deposits, and rental liability issues.

The factual and legal issues involved in an eviction are far too complicated to cover in this section. Before you lease property as a landlord, or, as a tenant you find yourself on the receiving end of a possible eviction (for any reason), I highly recommend the *Landlord and Tenant Guide to Colorado Evictions*. I have seen cases won in court by a wrongful party simply because they knew the laws and the in-nocent party did not.

Marriage

Requirements for a legal marriage vary widely from state to state. Below are the basic requirements for marriage in Colorado.

Marriage License Requirements: Licenses can be issued in any county seat and are valid throughout the state. There is no waiting period after the license is issued; the license must be used within 30 days of issuance. The fee for the license is $10 cash; checks are not accepted.

Age Requirements: The legal age without parental consent is 18 years of age. Ages 16-17 require a notarized consent form from both parents, a parent having sole custody, or a guardian having legal cus-tody, of the minor. If these do not apply then judicial approval is re-quired. Applicants 15 years of age and under must obtain a both notarized consent and court-granted judicial approval in the county where residency has been established.

Identification: Acceptable forms of identification and proof of age are driver's license, passport, birth certificate, military ID, or a state-issued ID card.

Blood Test: No blood test is required in Colorado.

Application Form: Both applicants must complete and sign the license application. At least one of the parties must apply for the license in person. If one party cannot appear due to illness, travel, or incarceration, he or she must obtain an absentee application in a county seat. This form must be completed, notarized and returned before a license will be issued. Applicants do not need to be residents of Colorado.

Ceremonies: A judge or public official who is authorized to perform a marriage ceremony may do so. Also, a person recognized by a religious denomination, Indian tribe or nation, may perform the marriage. Clergy from out of state need not be registered in the state to perform the ceremony. Couples may also solemnize their marriages themselves (in accordance with C.R.S. 14-2-109).

Witnesses: Witnesses are not required in the state of Colorado, although some judges or public officials may request them.

Prohibited Marriages: A person may not remarry unless a divorce is absolutely final. Proof of divorce is required if it has been granted within 30 days prior to application for marriage license. Marriage between ancestor, descendent, brother, sister, uncle, aunt, niece, or nephews is prohibited, whether the relationship is by half or whole blood. Marriages between first cousins and further relations are permitted. Contact your county clerk for additional information.

Divorce

Although everyone would like to think his or her marriage was made in heaven and will last forever, statistics beg to differ. Over half of all marriages end in divorce in Colorado. Depending on issues such as financial assets and children, there are four ways you can handle the process. You can do it all yourselves, do it yourselves with limited assistance from a legal center or attorney, do it yourselves with mediation, or have an attorney do it for you. Regardless of method, I recommend *The Friendly Divorce Guidebook for*

Colorado. In Colorado, whether and how you use a lawyer in your divorce is up to you, but having the proper information is invaluable.

Before running to the courthouse, you may want to consider the options in Colorado. Marriage counseling, marital mediation, physical or trial separation, legal separation, annulment, and finally the legal dissolution of marriage (divorce) are all available.

For a legal separation or divorce, the process begins by filing a petition with the clerk of the district court. You must have been domiciled in Colorado for at least 90 days before filing your first papers. A waiting period of 90 days, required by law, begins once you have filed the petition. The 90-day waiting period is mandatory as a "cooling off" time so both parties can give the action serious consideration before making it final.

Couples usually use the 90 days to work out their final divorce plan which, when written, is called the separation agreement. A separation agreement must cover all the following: property division, payment of debts, maintenance (alimony), custody and support of children, taxes, and medical and life insurance. A separation agreement must be presented to the court at the time you ask for a final decree. A final decree can be obtained by affidavit without appearing before the court if there are no undecided issues between the parties, no minor children are involved, or, if there are children, both parties must be represented by counsel. Those who do not qualify for divorce by affidavit, and those seeking a decree of legal separation, must appear at a final hearing in court.

After your divorce or legal separation has been granted, the court retains continuing jurisdiction over your children in matters of custody, support, and higher education.

One final note: Colorado recognizes common law marriages. You have a common law marriage if you have lived together while "holding yourselves out" as being married, meaning that you acted as though you were married. Typical proof of this is you introduced each other as wife and husband, used the same last name, or filed married/joint tax returns and neither of you was still married to someone else, either by a marriage license and a ceremony or by common law. A common law marriage and a marriage with a license and a ceremony are legally equal and subject to the same requirement for divorce.

Real Estate

Almost all aspects of real estate transactions are regulated by the Division of Real Estate (303-894-2166). The Division administers the Real Estate Recovery Fund, which can be used by persons to recover sums lost because of the actions of a licensee. Persons who obtain a final judgment against a broker or salesperson can regain their actual loss suffered in a transaction up to $15,000 per claimant and up to $50,000 in the aggregate against any one licensee. The Division also regulates all time-share projects sold in Colorado and regulates developers of subdivisions consisting of 10 or more residential sites, tracts or lots.

Real estate brokers in Colorado are required to "declare their allegiance" in any transaction. They must state up front whether they are working for a seller or a buyer. This law was put in to place to protect consumers from being misled by agents claiming to be on their side while they were actually looking out for the best interest of someone else.

Finally, if you are looking to buy rural property (acreage), there are many considerations that may not be apparent: water rights, well permits, test for septic permits, mineral rights (especially in Colorado), mining patents, legal access, road maintenance, zoning restrictions, utilities, and drastic changes in seasons to list a few. My wife and I looked at a beautiful six-acre plot for $36,000. However, it would have cost at least $10,000 to install electricity, $10,000 for well/septic, and $25,000 to grade the dirt road. Now the price was over $80,000 before we laid the first brick. If you are serious (or just not sure) about moving out of the city, get copies of *Discover the Good Life In Rural America (The City Slicker's Guide To Buying Country Real Estate Without Losing Your Shirt)*, and *Country Bound! (Trade Your Business Suit Blues for Blue Jean Dreams)*, both published by Communication Creativity.

Lottery

www.coloradolottery.com

Colorado has scratch card Lottery, Lotto & Cash 5 games. The prizes for Cash 5 are preset with a maximum of $20,000 for matching 5 out of 32 numbers. Lotto has a progressive pot that starts at

$1.5 million. If you win the Lotto jackpot, you must choose a payment option of either a 25-year annuity or the Cash Value (40% before taxes).

You can check with any Lottery retailer for the previous day's drawing results. Winning numbers for games are also available by calling the Lottery Luck Line at 303-759-LUCK (5825) in Denver, 719-542-LUCK in Pueblo and toll-free at 1-800-283-LUCK outside of the Denver Metro area, or at the Colorado Lottery website. These numbers also appear in local newspapers and at your Lottery retailer. You may begin claiming winning tickets the morning following the drawing.

If you win, immediately sign the back of your ticket if you haven't already done so. To claim scratch game prizes up to $50 and Lotto prizes up to $150, simply present your ticket at any Lottery/Lotto retailer within 180 days of the winning drawing. Retailers may redeem any ticket up to $599, but are not required to do so. To claim prizes $600 and over, you must visit one of the Lottery offices in Pueblo, Denver, Fort Collins, or Grand Junction, or mail the signed ticket and a completed claim form (available at all Lottery retailers) to the Colorado Lottery, P.O. Box 7, Pueblo, CO 81002-0007 for payment by mail. Lotto jackpot winners (all six numbers matched) will be paid only at Denver or Pueblo Lottery offices.

Every time you play, Colorado wins. Since the Lottery's inception in 1983, over $1 billion has been distributed for local and state park and recreation projects, outdoors and wilderness projects, and for state public buildings and facilities.

You must be 18 or older to purchase tickets. Tickets may be given as gifts to anyone and winners are entitled to claim their prizes regardless of age. All prize claims are subject to validation. Federal and state laws require a minimum 32% tax withholding on individual winnings over $5,000.

In November 2000, Colorado voters approved the multistate lottery, Powerball. The first drawing in Colorado was August 4, 2001. Proceeds are to benefit parks and schools. Drawings are every Wednesday and Saturday. Information at *www.powerball.com*.

Changes In Latitudes, Changes In Attitudes

THE TEN FASTEST GROWING COUNTIES IN COLORADO

Explosive growth! I have used that term numerous times in this book. I can't think of a better way to describe it. Growth in Colorado has been sudden, unexpected, uncontainable and, in some respects, devastating to the state's natural, economic and social resources.

I was drawn to Colorado more than a decade ago. The natural beauty, wide-open spaces, uncrowded cities (for the most part), and friendly, laid-back attitudes of Colorado's residents were all factors in my move from Florida.

Since then I have been an eyewitness to some dramatic changes in the state. When I arrived in the mid-eighties, the state was in an economic bust. Downtown Denver's business district was nearly vacant, LoDo (Lower Downtown) was a place you did not want to be after dark, traffic in and out of Denver was congested only on rare occasions, mountain land could be had for a song, and there were distinct, natural divisions between one city and the next—all a memory now.

The state's population increased by over a million people—over 30% a year—in the last decade. While most of the increase was centered in the six-county Denver metro area, many of the rural and mountain communities have also seen tremendous growth. There

have been numerous news reports lately concerning the unwanted effects this growth has had in many areas. Several of the state's one-time
wildlife areas no longer have much wildlife due to a constant onslaught of hikers, campers, hunters, and the like. The long-time residents of some smaller, rural areas are up in arms because newcomers
are destroying the assets and beauty of their home turf. Many small
areas have been populated by affluent new arrivals that, once situated,
demand improvements in roads, utilities, and conveniences so their
new home will be more like the one they couldn't wait to leave.

For those considering a move, this chapter contains basic information about the ten fastest growing counties in the state. The
counties appear alphabetically, not in order of growth.

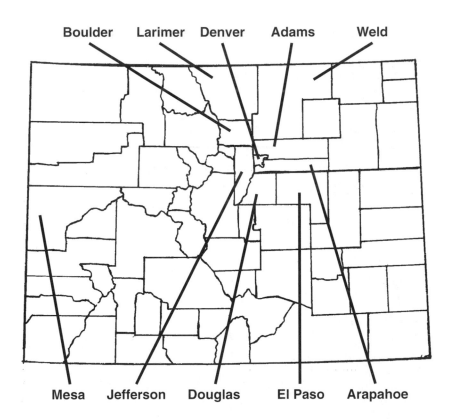

Adams County
www.co.adams.co.us

Address:	450 South 4th Avenue, Brighton, CO 80601 303-659-2120
Date of Incorporation:	1902
County Seat:	City of Brighton

Largest Cities/Towns/Communities

Aurora, Bennett, Brighton, Broomfield (to become its own City/County in November 2001), Commerce City, Federal Heights, Northglenn, Thornton, and Westminster

Population Estimates By Age Groups, 2001-2010

Age group	2001	2005	2010
0 to 4	28,595	31,223	35,833
5 to 19	87,584	92,447	101,279
20 to 34	81,415	91,692	107,857
35 to 64	133,845	162,300	184,831
65 to 89	28,430	33,516	41,129
90 and over	574	691	890
Total	360,443	411,869	471,919

Local Community Description

Adams County stretches from the foothills of the Rockies to the eastern Colorado plains, making up the northern tier of the six-county Denver metropolitan area. Western urbanized Adams County includes portions or all of the cities of Arvada, Aurora, Brighton, Commerce City, Federal Heights, Northglenn, Thornton, and

Westminster. Situated in a fast-growing area, Adams County is a diverse, cosmopolitan county supported by a broad base of business and industry. A wide price range of housing is available for the county's diverse work force.

Local Emergency Services — Call 911

Law enforcement:	Adams County Sheriff Department
Phone:	303-654-1850

Climate

January temperature	30°F
July temperature	73°F
Annual precipitation	15"
Annual snowfall	54"
Area (in square miles)	1,192

Selected Major Employers

Adams County, the cities of Brighton, Commerce City, Westminster, Northglenn, and Thornton, Sundyne Corporation, Whirlpool Corporation, Fischer Imaging, APS Medical, Silver Engineering Works, Barber Poultry, JC Penney, Kmart, King Soopers, NAPA, Conagra, Inc., Target, North Suburban Medical Center, Frederic Printing, Melco Industries

Adams County has a diverse economy but major segments are services, manufacturing (electronics), and government.

Public School Information

http://reportcard.cde.state.co.us/reportcard/CommandHandler.jsp

There are 176 school districts in Colorado, with 1568 schools. The state's website has valuable information about any public school in Colorado. You can learn about a school's academic performance, CSAP results, safety and discipline incidents, class size, teacher/student ratios, teacher quality, and how taxpayer dollars are spent. The site's search function allows you to find a school by district, city, county, or zip code, and even has maps to help you locate a school geographically.

Nearest four-year college: University of Colorado
(Denver, Boulder)

Nearest community college: Community College of Aurora

Nearest vocational center: Pickens Technical Center
(Aurora)

Local Transportation

Nearest Scheduled Air Service
Denver International Airport
Jeffco Airport

Local Buses and Trucks
Greyhound, Alpine Charter, RTD, Grayline of Denver, variety of truck lines providing local, interstate, and intrastate service

Freight Trains: Colorado Southern, Denver and Rio Grande, Chicago Rock Island Pacific, Union Pacific, Burlington Northern

Passenger Trains: Amtrak

Arapahoe County
www.co.arapahoe.co.us

Address: 5334 South Prince St.,
Littleton, CO 80166
303-795-4400

Date of Incorporation: 1861

County Seat: City of Littleton

Largest Cities/Towns/Communities
Aurora, Centennial, Englewood, Greenwood Village, and Littleton

Population Estimates By Age Groups, 2001-2010

Age group	2001	2005	2010
0 to 4 years old	32,877	32,713	34,161
5 to 19	105,934	106,649	105,313
20 to 34	99,502	106,925	114,411
35 to 64	213,016	223,532	231,451
65 to 89	44,199	48,839	58,868
90 and over	1,106	1,338	1,724
Total	496,644	529,996	545,928

Local Community Description

Arapahoe County is a rapidly growing area with several cities including Aurora, Englewood, Greenwood Village, Littleton, and the newly created city of Centennial. It was one of the original 17 counties in the Colorado Territory and today has the highest number of upscale communities in the greater Denver metro area. Arapahoe County has its own business airport and contains a great portion of the Denver Technological Center.

Local Emergency Services — Call 911

Law Enforcement:	Arapahoe County Sheriff Department
Phone:	303-794-101

Climate

January temperature	34°F
July temperature	79°F
Annual precipitation	15"
Annual snowfall	52"
Area (in square miles)	803.2

Selected Major Employers

Stearns-Rogers, Inc., IBM, United Airlines, Honeywell, Inc., Amoco Product Co., Allstate Insurance

The leading source of income is office/light-industrial near Centennial Airport.

Public School Information

http://reportcard.cde.state.co.us/reportcard/CommandHandler.jsp

There are 176 school districts in Colorado, with 1568 schools. The state's new website has valuable information about any public school in Colorado. You can learn about a school's academic performance, CSAP results, safety and discipline incidents, class size, teacher/student ratios, teacher quality, and how taxpayer dollars are spent. The site's search function allows you to find a school by district, city, county, or zip code, and even has maps to help you locate a school geographically.

Nearest four-year college:	Metropolitan State College of Denver, University of Colorado (Auraria Campus-Denver)
Nearest community college:	Community College of Aurora
Nearest vocational center:	Pickens Technical Center (Aurora)

Local Transportation

Nearest Scheduled Air Service
Denver International Airport
Centennial Airport

Local Buses and Trucks
Continental Trailways, Greyhound, RTD. All major truck lines serve Arapahoe County and the surrounding metropolitan area

Freight Trains: Union Pacific, Denver and Rio Grande Western, Burlington Northern

Passenger Trains: Amtrak (in Denver)

Boulder County
www.co.boulder.co.us

Address:	P. O. Box 471
	Boulder, CO 80306
	303-441-3131
Date of Incorporation:	1861
County Seat:	City of Boulder

Largest Cities/Towns/Communities

Boulder, Broomfield (to become its own City/County in November 2001), Lafayette, Longmont, Louisville, Nederland, and Superior

Population Estimates By Age Groups, 2001-2010

Age group	2001	2005	2010
0 to 4 years old	18,078	18,404	20,161
5 to 19	63,598	65,728	67,231
20 to 34	66,291	71,153	80,040
35 to 64	125,136	133,383	141,363
65 to 89	23,611	26,530	32,820
90 and over	821	881	959
Total	297,535	316,079	351,574

Local Community Description

Boulder County houses the University of Colorado's main campus, with an enrollment of 26,000 undergraduate and graduate students. In addition, the county is the center for research and high technology manufacturing. Nestled against the foothills of the Front Range, Boulder County is also a prime recreation area for activities including backpacking, hiking, cycling, water sports, and skiing.

The territory within Boulder County first became part of the United States in 1803 with the Louisiana Purchase. Today the county remains diversified, with both rural and urban settings. It is situated on the eastern slope of the Rocky Mountains, with varying elevations from the 5,000-foot level of the plains to the 14,000-foot peaks of the Continental Divide.

Local Emergency Services — Call 911

Law Enforcement:	Boulder County Sheriff Department
Phone:	303-441-4444

Climate

January temperature	31°F
July temperature	73°F
Annual precipitation	16"
Annual snowfall	93"
Area (in square miles)	742.5

Selected Major Employers

IBM, Rockwell, Storage Technology Corp., Ball Aerospace, NCAR, Valleylab, Dieterich Standard, Flatiron Companies, University of Colorado, St. Vrain Valley School District, Boulder County, US Department of Commerce, City of Boulder, City of Longmont, FAA, NOAA, Celestial Seasonings, Inc., Boulder Beer, Longmont Foods, Boulder Community Hospital

The leading sources of income are manufacturing, services, tourism.

Public School Information

http://reportcard.cde.state.co.us/reportcard/CommandHandler.jsp

There are 176 school districts in Colorado, with 1568 schools. The state's new website has valuable information about any public school in Colorado. You can learn about a school's academic performance, CSAP results, safety and discipline incidents, class size, teacher/student ratios, teacher quality, and how taxpayer dollars are spent. The site's search function allows you to find a school by district, city, county, or zip code, and even has maps to help you locate a school geographically.

Nearest four-year college: University of Colorado (Boulder)

Nearest community college: Front Range Community College (Westminster)

Nearest vocational center: Boulder Valley Vo-Tech (Boulder)

Local Transportation

Nearest Scheduled Air Service
Fort Collins-Loveland Municipal Airport
Denver International Airport

Local Buses and Trucks
Continental Trailways, RTD, BDT, Consolidated Freightways, Globe Truck Line, Yellow Freight, American Freight

Freight Trains: Burlington Northern, Union Pacific

Passenger Trains: Amtrak in Denver (30 miles)

City And County Of Denver
www.Denver.gov.org

Address: 1437 Bannock Street
Denver, CO 80202

Date of Incorporation: 1902

County seat: Denver

Largest Cities/Towns/Communities
This county consists of the City of Denver.

Population Estimates By Age Groups, 2001-2010

Age group	2001	2005	2010
0 to 4 years old	48,790	48,491	51,378
5 to 19	124,684	135,921	143,110
20 to 34	102,063	102,378	114,154
35 to 64	223,512	225,743	221,549
65 to 89	59,337	59,324	62,510
90 and over	2,601	2,705	2,822
Total	560,987	574,562	595,523

Local Community Description

The heart of Colorado is the six-county Greater Metropolitan Area around the City and County of Denver. Denver is a mix of the downtown business district, neighborhood businesses, residential areas, industrial parks, and the new Denver International Airport. The capital city of Colorado, with a very rich historical background, Denver is home to many amenities and recreational and cultural facilities including the Denver Center for the Performing Arts with nine theaters seating nearly 10,000 people, the Denver Art Museum, the Denver Museum of Nature & Science, the Denver Zoo, and the Denver Botanical Gardens. Its revitalized LoDo (lower downtown) area includes many restaurants, brewpubs, Coors Field, and Six Flags Elitch Gardens.

Local Emergency Services — Call 911

Climate

January temperature	30°F
July temperature	73°F
Annual precipitation	15"
Annual snowfall	60"
Area (in square miles)	153.3

Local Economic Development Contacts

The downtown business district alone has 7,000 employers.

Public School Information

http://reportcard.cde.state.co.us/reportcard/CommandHandler.jsp

There are 176 school districts in Colorado, with 1568 schools. The state's new website has valuable information about any public school in Colorado. You can learn about a school's academic performance, CSAP results, safety and discipline incidents, class size, teacher/student ratios, teacher quality, and how taxpayer dollars are spent. The site's search function allows you to find a school by district, city, county, or zip code, and even has maps to help you locate a school geographically.

Nearest four-year college:	Metropolitan State College of Denver, University of Colorado-Denver, (Auraria Campus)
Nearest community college:	Community College of Denver (Auraria Campus)
Nearest vocational center:	Several schools in Denver

Local Transportation

Nearest Scheduled Air Service
Denver International Airport

Local Buses, Trucks, and Trains
All major carriers serve the greater Denver Metropolitan Area.

Douglas County
www.douglas.co.us

Address:	101 Third Street
	Castle Rock, CO 80104
	303-660-7400

Date of Incorporation: 1861

County Seat: Town of Castle Rock

Largest Cities/Towns/Communities
Castle Rock, Highlands Ranch, Lone Tree, Parker

Population Estimates By Age Groups, 2001-2010

Age group	2001	2005	2010
0 to 4 years old	16,607	19,089	22,878
5 to 19	43,382	52,487	62,593
20 to 34	45,021	53,481	62,609
35 to 64	74,322	90,401	111,868
65 to 89	7,237	10,522	1,600
90 and over	81	130	202
Total	186,650	226,110	261,750

Local Community Description
Located between the Denver and Colorado Springs metropolitan areas on Colorado's Front Range, Douglas County is experiencing significant development. In fact, from 1990 to 2000, Douglas County had a total population increase of 190.1 percent, making it the fastest growing county in the nation. Offering open terrain ranging from rolling grasslands on the east, to pine forests and rock canyons, the county has a wide potential for growth. There are 21 planned communities in the County offering a choice of lifestyle from remote rural to adult condominium and suburban neighborhoods. Elevation of the county ranges from 6,300 to 9,800 feet. One third of the county is in federal, state and local public lands.

Local Emergency Services — Call 911
Law Enforcement: Douglas County Sheriff Department
Phone: 303-660-7505

Climate

January temperature	28°F
July temperature	73°F
Annual precipitation	14"
Annual snowfall	57"
Area (in square miles)	840.2

Selected Major Employers

Douglas County School District, Douglas County, Racquet World-Inverness, Industrial Textiles, Denver Brick, E.I. DuPont, Ensign-Bickford, Information Handling Systems, Honeywell, Hewlett-Packard, Hartford Insurance, Mercy Medical Center

The leading sources of income are technology and communications services, and construction.

Public School Information

http://reportcard.cde.state.co.us/reportcard/CommandHandler.jsp

There are 176 school districts in Colorado, with 1568 schools. The state's new website has valuable information about any public school in Colorado. You can learn about a school's academic performance, CSAP results, safety and discipline incidents, class size, teacher/student ratios, teacher quality, and how taxpayer dollars are spent. The site's search function allows you to find a school by district, city, county, or zip code, and even has maps to help you locate a school geographically.

Nearest four-year college:	Metropolitan State College of Denver, University of Colorado (Auraria Campus)
Nearest community college:	Arapahoe Community College (Littleton)
Nearest vocational center:	Several schools in Denver

Local Transportation

Nearest Scheduled Air Service
Denver International Airport

Local Buses and Trucks
Continental Trailways-5 buses/day, RTD to Parker. All truck lines
that service Denver and Colorado Springs

Freight Trains: Santa Fe, Rio Grande, Burlington Northern

Passenger Trains: Amtrak available in Denver (25 miles).

El Paso County
www.co.el-paso.co.us

Address:	27 East Vermijo
	Colorado Springs, CO 80903
	719-520-6400
County seat:	City of Colorado Springs

Largest Cities/Towns/Communities

Colorado Springs, Fountain, Manitou Springs, Monument, Palmer Lake

Population Estimates By Age Groups, 2001-2010

Age group	2001	2005	2010
0 to 4 years old	39,759	42,119	45,709
5 to 19	118,829	124,166	129,021
20 to 34	128,915	135,866	146,014
35 to 64	195,200	212,142	230,435
65 to 89	45,809	49,813	58,418
90 and over	1,183	1,368	1.731
Total	528,975	565,474	611,328

Local Community Description

Primarily rolling plains, El Paso County is located south of the Palmer Divide, which separates it from Douglas County. The Federal government owns most of the southwestern part of the county for use by the U.S. Army located at Fort Carson. The largest city in the county is Colorado Springs, which also has the second largest population in the state.

Local Emergency Services — Call 911

Law enforcement:	El Paso County Sheriff
Phone:	719-520-7100

Climate

January temperature	27°F
July temperature	78°F
Annual precipitation	16"
Annual snowfall	59"
Area (in square miles)	2,126.7

Selected Major Employers

Ft. Carson, Peterson/NORAD/Space Command, Air Force Academy, City Governments, School District 11, County Governments, Harrison School District, Academy School District, Widefield School District, Hewlett-Packard Co., Digital Equipment Corp., TRW Inc., Current Inc., Ampex Corp., Inmos Corp., Honeywell Inc., Ford Aerospace, Kaman Corp., Texas Instruments Inc., Penrose Hospitals, Memorial Hospital, St. Francis Hospital, King Soopers, Safeway, Sears, Schoollage Lock Co., Farmers Insurance Group

The leading sources of income are high tech and military.

Public School Information

http://reportcard.cde.state.co.us/reportcard/CommandHandler.jsp

There are 176 school districts in Colorado, with 1568 schools.

The state's new website has valuable information about any public school in Colorado. You can learn about a school's academic performance, CSAP results, safety and discipline incidents, class size, teacher/student ratios, teacher quality, and how taxpayer dollars are spent. The site's search function allows you to find a school by district, city, county, or zip code, and even has maps to help you locate a school geographically.

Nearest four-year college: University of Colorado (Colorado Springs)
Colorado College

Nearest community college: Pikes Peak Community College (Colorado Springs)

Nearest vocational center: Several schools in Colorado Springs

Local Transportation

Nearest Scheduled Air Service
Colorado Springs Municipal Airport

Local Buses and Trucks
Greyhound, Continental Trailways, AANDA, ABF, ANR, American Freight, Consolidated Freightways, Edson, Ellis, McLean, Yellow Freight

Freight Trains: Santa Fe and Rio Grande

Jefferson County
www.co.jefferson.co.us

Address: 100 Jefferson County Parkway
Golden, CO 80419
303-271-8512

Date of Incorporation: 1861

County Seat: City of Golden

Largest Cities/Towns/Communities

Arvada, Bow Mar, Broomfield (to become its own City/County in November 2001), Conifer, Edgewater, Evergreen, Golden, Lakewood, Morrison, Wheat Ridge

Population Estimates By Age Groups, 2001-2010

Age group	2001	2005	2010
0 to 4 years old	33,004	33,981	35,642
5 to 19	110,551	108,624	106,499
20 to 34	104,920	113,427	120,879
35 to 64	229,939	235,360	240,178
65 to 89	54,541	55,425	69,915
90 and over	1,498	1,723	2,073
Total	534,453	548,546	575,186

Local Community Description

Jefferson County is situated in the north central portion of the state where the eastern plains rise to meet the Rocky Mountains. The County forms the western and southwestern extension of Colorado's principal urban center, the six county Denver metropolitan area. Prairies, valleys, mountains and forests offer a varied physical appearance to the county whose chief landmark is the rock formation near Morrison that forms Red Rocks Amphitheater. Jefferson County's growth has led to increases in small business and professional services, the expansion of industrial operations, the creation of shopping centers, and the enlargement of the regional operations of many federal government agencies. Economic expansion has created the opportunity for diverse lifestyles among the county's residents and has resulted in one of the nation's finest public education systems and a nationally acclaimed program for the preservation of open space. Golden, the county seat, was the state's first capital.

Local Emergency Services — Call 911

Law Enforcement:	Jefferson County Sheriff Department
Phone:	303-271-0211

Climate

January temperature	29°F
July temperature	75°F
Annual precipitation	16"
Annual snowfall	50"
Area (in square miles)	772.2

Selected Major Employers

Lockheed-Martin, Rockwell International, Cobe Laboratories, Ball Metal Container, International Business Machines, Rocky Mountain Energy, Amax Inc., Mobile Premix, Jolly Rancher, Adolph Coors Co., Federal Government, Jefferson County, R-1 School District, Federal Center, King Soopers, United Airlines

Public School Information

http://reportcard.cde.state.co.us/reportcard/CommandHandler.jsp

There are 176 school districts in Colorado, with 1568 schools. The state's new website has valuable information about any public school in Colorado. You can learn about a school's academic performance, CSAP results, safety and discipline incidents, class size, teacher/student ratios, teacher quality, and how taxpayer dollars are spent. The site's search function allows you to find a school by district, city, county, or zip code, and even has maps to help you locate a school geographically.

Nearest four-year college:	Colorado School of Mines (Golden)
Nearest community college:	Arapahoe Community College (Littleton)
Nearest vocational center:	Columbine Beauty School Mile Hi College (Lakewood)

Local Transportation

Nearest Scheduled Air Service
Denver International Airport

Local Buses and Trucks
Greyhound, Continental Trailways, RTD. A full array of truck lines serve the Denver Metro area and Jefferson County.

Freight Trains: Denver and Rio Grande Railway, Great Western Railway.

Passenger Trains: Amtrak

Larimer County
www.co.larimer.co.us

Address:	200 W. Oak Street
	Fort Collins, CO 80521
	970-498-7000
Date of Incorporation:	1861
County Seat:	City of Fort Collins

Largest Cities/Towns/Communities

Berthoud, Estes Park, Fort Collins, Loveland, Timnath, Wellington

Population Estimates By Age Groups, 2001-2010

Age group	2001	2005	2010
0 to 4 years old	15,717	16,704	18,186
5 to 19	57,000	58,795	60,548
20 to 34	59,481	65,616	72,301
35 to 64	102,340	113,227	124,679
65 to 89	23,012	24,588	28,733
90 and over	842	946	1,060
Total	258,392	279,876	305,507

Local Community Description

Larimer County is located on the eastern edge of the Rocky Mountains in northern Colorado. Major urban areas in the county are arranged along scenic foothills, with a backdrop of spectacular mountain peaks. The county extends to the Continental Divide and includes several mountain communities and Rocky Mountain National Park. Lifestyle opportunities in Larimer County are as varied as the terrain and include sophisticated urban areas with established cultural facilities, productive agricultural lands, small-town environments, and a wealth of outdoor recreation areas enjoyed by urban and rural residents alike. The area benefits from its proximity to the Denver metropolitan area, but has retained its own identity and unique quality of life. Colorado State University is located in Larimer County, which together with University of Colorado in adjacent Boulder County has established the area as a center of advanced research and learning. The unique environment has attracted a variety of businesses, both large and small, which have generally prospered, so growth of existing business is a more important source of new jobs than those created by new industry.

Local Emergency Services — Call 911

Law Enforcement:	Larimer County Sheriff
Phone:	970-498-5108

Climate

January temperature	23°F
July temperature	71°F
Annual precipitation	14"
Annual snowfall	58"
Area (in square miles)	2,601.4

Selected Major Employers

Woodward Governor, Teledyne Water Pik, Hewlett Packard, Eastman Kodak, Anheuser Busch, Colorado State University,

Poudre Valley Schools, Larimer County, City of Fort Collins, Poudre Valley Hospital

The leading source of income is high tech manufacturing.

Public School Information

http://reportcard.cde.state.co.us/reportcard/CommandHandler.jsp

There are 176 school districts in Colorado, with 1568 schools. The state's new website has valuable information about any public school in Colorado. You can learn about a school's academic performance, CSAP results, safety and discipline incidents, class size, teacher/student ratios, teacher quality, and how taxpayer dollars are spent. The site's search function allows you to find a school by district, city, county, or zip code, and even has maps to help you locate a school geographically.

Nearest four-year college: Colorado State University (Fort Collins)

Nearest community college: Aims Community College (Greeley)

Nearest vocational center: Front Range Community College (Fort Collins)

Local Transportation

Nearest Scheduled Air Service
Fort Collins-Loveland Municipal Airport

Local Buses and Trucks
Continental Trailways, TWX, American Freight Systems, Consolidated Freightways, Chandw Transportation Co., Ryder

Freight Trains: Union Pacific, Colorado and Southern

Mesa County

www.co.mesa.co.us

Address: 720 Main Street
                        Grand Junction, CO 81502
                        (970) 244-1602

Date of Incorporation: 1883

County Seat: Grand Junction

Largest Cities/Towns/Communities

Grand Junction, Fruita, Palisade, Clifton, Fruitvale, DeBeque, Colbran, Mesa, Mack, and Loma

Population Estimates By Age Groups, 2001-2010

Age group	2001	2005	2010
0 to 4 years old	7,758	8,781	9,993
5 to 19	17,092	26,989	29,681
20 to 34	24,968	29,245	32,869
35 to 64	36,630	43,369	55,056
65 to 89	16,161	16,054	16,715
90 and over	627	711	817
Total	103,236	125,149	145,131

Local Community Description

Located on the western border of Colorado, Mesa County is surrounded by many natural landmarks such as the Colorado National Monument, Grand Mesa National Forest, and the colorful Bookcliffs. Grand Junction is the largest city in Mesa County and in western Colorado, and is the medical hub between Denver and Salt Lake City, Utah.

The Grand Valley is noted for its agricultural produce and mild climate and is a popular place for recreation and relocation. Mesa County is home to more than 100,000 people in 15 towns. Besides agriculture, the area is home to a number of light manufacturing and service industries, three hospitals, and a regional airport.

Local Emergency Services — Call 911

Law Enforcement: Mesa County Sheriff Department

Phone: (970) 244-3500

Climate

January temperature	35°F
July temperature	90°F
Annual precipitation	13"
Annual snowfall	37"
Area (in square miles)	3,309

Selected Major Employers

Mesa County, City of Grand Junction, Mesa County Valley School District, Mesa State College, City Market, St. Mary's Hospital

Public School Information

http://reportcard.cde.state.co.us/reportcard/CommandHandler.jsp

There are 176 school districts in Colorado, with 1568 schools. The state's new website has valuable information about any public school in Colorado. You can learn about a school's academic performance, CSAP results, safety and discipline incidents, class size, teacher/student ratios, teacher quality, and how taxpayer dollars are spent. The site's search function allows you to find a school by district, city, county, or zip code, and even has maps to help you locate a school geographically.

Nearest four-year college: Mesa State College (Grand Junction)

Local Transportation

Nearest Scheduled Air Service
Walker Field, Grand Junction

Passenger Trains: Amtrak

Weld County
www.co.weld.co.us

Address:	915 10th Street
	Greeley, CO 80631
	970-356-4000
Date of Incorporation:	1861
County Seat:	City of Greeley

Largest Cities/Towns/Communities

Greeley, Evans, Fort Lupton, Gilcrest, Platteville, Windsor

Population Estimates By Age Groups, 2001-2010

Age group	2001	2005	2010
0 to 4 years old	14,241	16,309	19,011
5 to 19	43,841	48,245	55,270
20 to 34	45,030	52,642	60,923
35 to 64	68,489	79,815	78,069
65 to 89	15,761	17,820	21,562
90 and over	562	613	689
Total	187,924	215,444	235,524

Local Community Description

Weld County represents a highly diversified economy with excellent growth potential. Weld County offers an outstanding quality of life. Within a 60-mile radius are located four major universities with their attendant cultural and athletic events. The Denver metro area forms the county's southern boundary and six major ski areas are located within a two-hour drive. The county is home to the largest performing arts center in northern Colorado.

Local Emergency Services — Call 911

Law Enforcement:	Weld County Sheriff Department
Phone:	970-356-4015

Climate

January temperature	29°F
July temperature	75°F
Annual precipitation	13"
Annual snowfall	37"
Area (in square miles)	3,992.8

Selected Major Employers

Eastman Kodak, Monfort of Colorado, Hewlett Packard, ConAgra, School District #6, University of Northern Colorado, Aims College, Weld County, City of Greeley, Federal Government, State of Colorado, School District #8, School District #4, North Colorado Medical Center, Qwest, Golden Recycling (Coors), State Farm Insurance, Safeway, Toddys, Kmart, Hensel Phelps (contractor), Steinbecker Brothers (motor freight transport.), Northwest Publishing, Greeley Publishing.

The leading sources of income are agriculture, oil and gas, meat products, film, computers.

Public School Information

http://reportcard.cde.state.co.us/reportcard/CommandHandler.jsp

There are 176 school districts in Colorado, with 1568 schools. The state's new website has valuable information about any public school in Colorado. You can learn about a school's academic performance, CSAP results, safety and discipline incidents, class size, teacher/student ratios, teacher quality, and how taxpayer dollars are spent. The site's search function allows you to find a school by district, city, county, or zip code, and even has maps to help you locate a school geographically.

Nearest four-year college: University of Northern Colorado (Greeley)

Nearest community college: Aims Community College (Greeley)

Nearest vocational center: Front Range Community College (Fort Collins)

Local Transportation

Nearest Scheduled Air Service
Greeley-Weld County Airport

Local Buses and Trucks
Greyhound, Estes Park Bus Company, Greeley Bus, Weld County Mini-Van System, Continental Trailway, Airport Shuttle. Most major trucklines.

Freight Trains: Great Western, Union Pacific, Burlington Northern

Passenger Trains: Amtrak

Money For Nothing

Small and Home-Based Business Start-Up

I have been self-employed since I turned in my parachute, beret, and uniform and became a civilian again in 1979. I can tell you from experience, the "American Dream" of owning your own business is not always what it's cracked-up to be. It takes a special type of person to make it. There is the hard work, the uncertain financial return, the responsibility, and the ever-increasing burden of rules, regulations, and laws.

This chapter is designed to help you determine if starting your own small or home-based business is really what you want to do and to give you as much information and as many resources as space permits. While all federal laws concerning this subject are uniform throughout the country, most states have unique laws, rules and regulations of which you need to be aware. The simple self-quiz below should help you decide whether to skip this chapter or not.

So You Want To Be An Entrepreneur?

There is no way to eliminate all the risks associated with starting a small business. However, you can improve your chances of success with good planning and preparation. A good starting place is to evaluate your strengths and weaknesses as the owner and manager of a small business. Carefully consider each of the following questions.

Are you a self-starter? It will be up to you, not someone else, to develop projects, organize your time, and follow through on details.

How well do you get along with different personalities? Business owners need to develop working relationships with a variety of people including customers, vendors, staff, bankers, and professionals such as lawyers, accountants, and consultants. Can you deal with a demanding client, an unreliable vendor, or cranky staff person in the best interests of your business?

How good are you at making decisions? Small business owners are required to make decisions constantly, often quickly, under pressure and independently.

Do you have the physical and emotional stamina to run a business? Business ownership can be challenging, fun, and exciting. But it's also a lot of work. Can you face 12-hour work days six or seven days a week? How well do you plan and organize? Research indicates many business failures could have been avoided through better planning. Good organization—of financial inventory, schedules, and production—can help avoid many potential pitfalls.

Is your drive strong enough to maintain your motivation? Running a business can wear you down. Some business owners feel burned out by having to carry all the responsibility on their shoulders. Strong motivation to make the business succeed will help you survive slowdowns as well as periods of burnout.

How will the business affect my family? The first few years of business start-up can be hard on family life. The strain of an unsupportive spouse may be hard to balance against the demands of starting a business. There also may be financial difficulties until the business becomes profitable, which could take months or even years. You may have to adjust to a lower standard of living or put family assets at risk.

Is it worth it? For many, yes! While there are numerous reasons not to start your own business, there are many advantages that, for the right person, far outweigh the risks. For starters, you get to be your own boss. Your hard work and long hours directly benefit you, rather than increasing profits for someone else. Your earnings and growth potential are far less limited. A new venture—your new venture—is exciting and running a business will provide endless variety and challenge and won't settle into a dull routine.

Assuming you have seriously considered each of these questions and have decided to go for it, the next step is to plan your new venture using the checklist below.

Check-List For New Business Start-Up

You should be fully aware of the implications of owning your own business. The best advice for anyone starting or operating a business is to *educate yourself.* This chapter is only a first step. It outlines only the basic information you will need to start your business. To obtain complete information, there are dozens of books available, many specific to Colorado business operation. Highly recommended is the Colorado Business Start-up Kit available free of charge from the Colorado Business Assistance Center.

- Decide upon the legal structure of your business and register your business and tradename with the appropriate state and/or federal agencies. **If you plan to open a business checking account you must have a tradename registration.** Refer to the Legal Structure and Registration section of this chapter.

- If your business will have employees, you must open federal, state and local wage withholding and payroll tax accounts. See the Employers Responsibilities section of this chapter.

- If your business will be selling, renting, or leasing tangible personal property, obtain state and local sales tax licenses. If you rent accommodations for less than 30 days, a sales tax license is also required. Refer to the Colorado Sales Tax Licenses section.

- Be aware of the personal and business tax implications of starting your own business. Refer to the Income and Property Taxes section.

- Define the products or services you will provide. Is there actually a need for what you will provide in today's marketplace? Is the demand great enough to be profitable!? What is your competitive advantage? Develop your marketing strategy first!

- Are there any special licenses required for the business you are starting? The Colorado Business Assistance Center has information on federal, state, and local business licensing.

- Find the best location for your business. The Colorado Department of Transportation has information on traffic patterns on state highways. Some local governments have information on city and county roads. They may also have information on local population demographics. Observe pedestrian movement during business hours to estimate walk-in potential.

- Check with the local city and county government regarding any special business regulations, sales taxes, personal property taxes and zoning restrictions.

- Seek management advice and counseling. Assemble your team of professional advisors—an accountant, an attorney, an insurance broker, a real estate agent, etc. Business organizations, business consultants, your local Small Business Development Center, the Small Business Administration, trade associations, and your local Chamber of Commerce are good resources. Refer to the Additional Resources section.

- Develop a sound business plan with specific goals and objectives. A business plan should show where you are, where you want to go and how you will get there. There are numerous books and software packages designed to assist you in every step of formulating a business plan-well worth the investment!

- Develop a financial plan. Include profit and loss projections, cash flow analysis and capital requirements.

- Obtain adequate insurance coverage. Protect your business activities for enough in advance to cover your growth. See the Business Insurance section.

- Protect your ideas, products, symbols and logos through the proper registration and maintenance. The Colorado Business Assistance Center has information on Trademarks, Patents, and Copyrights.

New, Established, or Franchise

There are typically three avenues available to start a new business: starting a new venture from scratch, buying an existing business, or buying a franchise.

Starting a new venture

A new start-up is typically pursued when you have a unique idea that requires special equipment, specialized talents or a new way of doing things. A new venture may also be pursued when there is a customer base you can serve, or you are aware of an unfilled market. Factors you need to consider when forming a new venture include legal structure, location, facilities, equipment, employees, taxes, marketing and advertising, a records system, and capital. *Be warned: estimates suggest investors lose $500 million annually in franchise and work-at-home schemes.* There are several free brochures available from the Federal Trade Commission including *Job Ads*, *Job Scams and '900' Numbers*, *Work At Home Schemes*, and *Telemarketing Fraud*.

Buying An Established Business

Buying an existing business can have its advantages. By purchasing a business that is already established, you may eliminate some of the problems associated with starting a new business. However, when you acquire an existing business, you may also acquire the business' debts. Purchasing an existing business can be fairly complex. The following is a brief summary of some of the concerns of which you should be aware to avoid commercial fraud.

- Do you know why the seller is selling the business? If the business has not been profitable, find out why. Do you have a plan to make it profitable?

- Does your purchase agreement include the sale of the business name? The property? The equipment and inventory? The debts? Be sure the exact terms of the sale are explained clearly before you buy. It is highly recommended you have your own attorney review all parts of the agreement.

- Ask the seller about outstanding claims on inventory, equipment and fixtures. Whose responsibility is it to settle these claims? Are there liens against the property you are buying? Check with the seller and the county clerk and recorder's office in the county where the business and the seller are located. Also check with the Colorado Secretary of State, Uniform Commercial Code Section for records of any security interests that may have been filed as liens against the property or assets of the business.

- Will the owner of the building transfer the lease to you? What are the terms and restrictions of the lease?
- Review the business's past and current financial statements. Are they in good order? Also, examine any existing contracts that affect the business's operations.
- Can you transfer the existing phone number(s)? The phone service may require information from both you and the seller. See the Qwest heading under the Additional Resources Section.

If there are employees in the business, you will be responsible for withholding tax, unemployment insurance, workers' compensation and social security (FICA). You must open new employee payroll accounts unless you buy out the stock of an existing corporation and do not set up a new corporation. In every case the unemployment history established under the former owners will transfer to your account. When you purchase the business, the former owner should file form UILT-2 to report the change in ownership. For more information on payroll tax requirements see the Employer Responsibilities section.

Tax Liabilities
If you purchase a retail business you may be liable for sales tax debts of the business. As a precaution, you should get a tax status letter from the Department of Revenue before buying. The current owner using form DR0096 must request the tax status letter. Tax status letters may be requested on all state collected tax accounts including sales tax, wage withholding and corporate income tax accounts. There is a charge for each tax status record requested. If you purchase a corporation, you may have the option of keeping the

same sales tax account with the Department of Revenue. If you purchase a sole proprietorship or a partnership, you are required to open a new sales tax account.

When you purchase tangible property as part of a business, such as furniture, fixtures or equipment (new or used) for which you have not paid sales tax, you must pay a state use tax. For further information about state tax liabilities when purchasing a business contact the Colorado Department of Revenue.

Many cities and counties also collect a *use* tax. Most of the use tax is collected by the state. Large home rule cities may collect use taxes directly. There may be additional liabilities for personal property taxes imposed by the county. Contact the local city clerk, the county assessor and/or the county treasurer's offices for more information regarding local use and personal property taxes.

Buying a Franchise

Franchising offers a unique opportunity for individuals interested in operating a business. It allows you to both own and operate a business while drawing from the resources of the parent company. This arrangement may reduce some of the risks of going into business for yourself depending upon the quality and stability of the franchiser. It should be noted that while a franchise is a method for going into business it is *not* a form of legal structure. The franchiser—the business with the plan and structure—and the franchisee (you) must determine the appropriate form of legal structure. See the next section on Legal Structure and Registration for more information.

Once you have decided you are able to meet the requirements for purchasing a franchise, you may want to shop around for the best investment. There are various publications and franchise directories available from bookstores and public libraries. Many times the classified sections of your local newspaper or magazines have listings of franchise offers.

Exercise Caution

Before you agree to invest in a company that promises you large financial returns, you should exercise some caution. *Colorado lacks specific laws to protect you should you need recourse.* There are, however, general provisions governing "good business practices." These protections against deceptive and unfair trade practices are stated in the *Colorado Consumer Protection Act and the Uniform Consumer Credit Code*. The Federal Trade Commission's Franchise Rule requires franchisers to provide prospective buyers with a detailed disclosure statement regarding the company's history, background and operations. This document should also describe the costs and responsibilities of both the franchiser and the franchisee and must be made available to you at least ten days before any agreements are signed, or at the first face to face meeting, whichever comes first.

For more information on franchising opportunities, go to the International Franchise Association website at www.franchise.org. *The Franchise Opportunities Handbook*, published by the U.S. Department of Commerce, is out of print but may still be available at local libraries.

Disclosure Requirements and Prohibitions Concerning Franchising and Business Opportunity Ventures (The Franchise Rule) is available free from the Federal Trade Commission by calling 303-844-2271.

Legal Structure And Registration

Choosing The Right Legal Structure

When starting your own business you must carefully choose the appropriate legal structure for your business. You should examine the characteristics of each structure as well the needs of and desires you have for your business.

A **Sole Proprietor** is a single individual who owns and operates the business. There is no legal separation between the individual and the business. She or he benefits from 100% of the profits and is personally responsible for 100% of all the debts and liabilities of the business.

A **General Partnership** is similar to a sole proprietorship except there are two or more individuals who own the business. A general partnership offers the means for pooling all resources and sharing control of a business. There is relatively little formality required to establish and run the business, and control remains with the partners. However, all partners remain 100% responsible for all the debts and liabilities of the business, regardless of any partnership agreement outlining work responsibilities and shares of profit.

A **Limited Partnership** is one in which some of the partners have given up their right to manage the business. In return, their liability is limited. They are "limited" partners, as opposed to "general" partners.

A **Corporation** is a legal entity separate from the owners of the business and there are significant formalities that must be observed to properly operate a corporation. The corporation provides a wall of liability protection between the business and the owners. It also has the ability to raise capital by issuing stock.

While the limited liability enjoyed by shareholders may appear attractive, most lenders will probably require a personal guarantee as collateral anyway. The corporation must pay its own taxes and the owners who work in the business are normally classified as employees. A corporation must comply with the Colorado Corporation Code. Among the requirements of the Code are the following:

- *Articles of Incorporation* must be filed with the Secretary of State

- The corporation must adopt bylaws

- A corporation must adhere to certain corporate formalities including procedures for shareholder meetings, the election of the board of directors, maintenance of corporate records and proper filings with the Secretary of State

A **Subchapter S Corporation** is not actually a separate form of legal structure, but rather a special tax status granted by the IRS to tax a company's income more like that of a partnership or a sole proprietorship. While an S corporation is not subject to double taxation as is a regular corporation, it may lose the ability to deduct the full cost of medical insurance as a business and business losses are treated differently. A competent tax advisor should be consulted before applying for S Corporation tax status. It is important to note the corporation must file the Articles of Incorporation with the Secretary of State before it can apply to the IRS for Subchapter S status.

For more specific information about qualifying and applying for filing as a Subchapter S Corporation, contact the IRS.

Non-Profit Corporations are not covered in this chapter. If you are interested in forming an NPO, all information can be obtained through the office of the Secretary of State. It should be noted that an individual can form a not-for-profit corporation in Colorado for approximately $50.

A **Limited Liability Company** (LLC) allows you to combine the benefits of liability protection such as a corporation provides with the more simplified tax structure that a partnership can employ.

A **Limited Liability Partnership** (LLP) is basically the same as an LLC except it is for use by partnerships.

As you decide upon your legal structure, you should carefully evaluate both your present and future needs for operating your business. To avoid duplication of legal expenses, licensing and paperwork, analyze your various options and choose the business structure that will meet your long-term needs rather than choosing a business structure solely for its short-term convenience.

Where To Register Your New Business

Department of Revenue

If you are a sole proprietor or general partnership and will be doing business under a name other than your own legal name(s), you must register a trade name with the Department of Revenue. Registration of the trade name does not grant exclusive rights to the use of that name. Sole proprietors and general partnerships gain exclusive rights to the use of a trade name only through the use of the name over a period of time. If you want to find out if a name is already being used, call the Department of Revenue.

There are two forms that you may use to register a trade name. If your business will not have any sale of tangible products or any employees you may use form DR0592, *Trade Name Registration.* If you will have employees or sales of taxable goods, you should use the *Colorado Business Registration* form. This form will register your trade name as well as open your sales tax license, state wage withholding, and unemployment insurance accounts. The appropriate form can be obtained from the Department of Revenue or through the Small Business Hotline. Completed forms may be filed via mail or in person. Please note that if forms are mailed you will receive confirmation in approximately 4-6 weeks. In person, accounts will be established immediately.

Secretary of State

If your business will be a Limited Partnership, Limited Liability Company, or Corporation, you must file with the Secretary of State. You should not register trade names for these businesses with the Department of Revenue. If you do business under an additional name, you must file a *Certificate of Assumed or Trade Name* with the Secretary of State. If you are outside the Denver metro area, you can obtain the original filing paperwork and trade name forms for the Secretary of State through the Small Business Hotline.

Internal Revenue Service

All forms of legal structure, except sole proprietors with no employees, must obtain a Federal Employer Identification Number. The FEIN is your federal tax ID number and you can obtain yours by filing the SS-4 form with the IRS in Ogden, UT 84201. If it is necessary to obtain your FEIN immediately, complete the form and call 801-620-7645. This form can be obtained from the IRS or through the Small Business Hotline. If you fax your form you will receive your FEIN in approximately 10-14 days. A sole proprietor with no employees may use their Social Security number as their Federal Tax ID number.

Colorado Sales Tax Licenses

If you sell, rent, or lease tangible personal property in Colorado, you must obtain a sales tax license. The type of license you need and the amount of tax you are required to collect depends upon to whom you are selling and where and how you are doing business. A license is also required to rent accommodations to others for periods of less than 30 days.

Retailer License

A retailer license is required if you are selling, renting, or leasing your product to the end user. If you will be generating wholesale and retail sales you need only a retailer license. A retailer license costs $16 for a two-year period plus a one-time $50 deposit. The deposit will be automatically refunded to you once you have collected and remitted a total of $50 in state sales tax to the Department of Revenue. 501(c)(3) charitable organizations are not required to pay the $50 deposit when they obtain their license.

Wholesaler License

A wholesaler license is required if you are selling to another business that will resell your product or use it as an ingredient in another product to be resold. A wholesaler license costs $16 for a two-year period. If your business is primarily wholesale, you may have up to $1,000 in retail sales per year and will not be required to obtain a retailer license. If you will have more than $1,000 in retail sales per year, you should get a retailer license and record your wholesale sales under your retail license.

Single Event

If you plan to attend a single event as a vendor somewhere other than your regular business location, you must obtain a single event license. This costs $8.00 unless you already have a wholesaler or retailer license, and there is no charge.

Multiple Event License

If you attend more than one event during a two-year period, you should obtain a multiple event license. This costs $16, unless you already have a wholesaler or retailer license, and then there is no charge.

Local License

Most city sales taxes are collected for the city by the state. However, there are 43 home rule cities in Colorado that have their own city sales tax license for retail sales conducted within their jurisdiction (see Collecting Sales Taxes below).

Fees

All state sales tax licenses are $16 and are issued for the same two-year period. Each two-year period is divided into four six-month "quarters." The actual cost of your initial license will be prorated depending upon the quarter in which you start your business.

Collecting Sales Taxes

If you will be selling a product to the end user, you must collect sales tax. The amount of sales tax you collect depends upon the taxing districts where your business is located, the type of business you are in, and how the transaction is completed. To determine the amount of tax you must collect, check with the Department of Revenue.

You may also be required to collect county, city, Regional Transportation District, and other special taxes. You should obtain a retail sales tax license to collect all state taxes and you may need several city sales tax licenses from the home rule cities where you do business. Department of Revenue Publication DRPl002 (Colorado Sales/Use Tax Rates), lists all state, county and city sales tax rates as well as addresses and phone numbers for home rule cites with separate licensing and collection procedures. Also note special situations below:

Mail Order and Delivery
When you have a mail order business or you sell a product contingent upon delivery to another location within the state, you must collect the taxes you have in common with the delivery location. Check with the Department of Revenue for details.

Mobile Businesses
If your business involves sales at your client's address or is mobile, you must collect the appropriate tax for each sales location. This applies to such businesses as mobile locksmiths, mobile dog grooming, interior decorators and the like. If this situation applies, you will not have a principal place of business and must collect the appropriate tax for each point of sale.

Craft Shows
If you will be selling at events you must have a state multiple events license. If the event is held in a city that collects its own city sales tax,

you may be required to obtain an additional city sales tax license.

Flea Markets
Flea markets that operate more than three times per year are considered to be a retail location. If you sell at a flea market, you may not use an event license. All vendors should obtain retail licenses.

Multiple Permanent Business Locations
If your business has multiple permanent branch locations, each branch must have its own license and collect the appropriate tax. **Exception:** Vending machine operators are only required to have one state license and report the appropriate tax collection under a single license. Each machine is required to display a sales tax decal and may still be subject to local licensing requirements.

Small Home Businesses
If you operate a small business from your home and your total annual sales are less than $1,000 per year, you do not have to obtain a state sales tax license. You must, however, collect all applicable sales taxes and file a *Combined Annual Retail Sales Tax Return* (DRO1OOA), at the end of each year. In addition, you will not be able to purchase inventory or supplies at wholesale without a license. If you are located in a home rule city, contact your city officials regarding the local sales tax requirements.

Employer Responsibilities

As your business grows you may ask, "Should I hire full- or part-time employees or should I hire subcontractors to perform specific jobs on an as-needed basis?" If you hire contract labor, your paperwork is much easier. But just calling someone contract labor doesn't make her/him so and if you incorrectly classify those working for you, you may end up paying substantial penalties and back taxes to the IRS and the State of Colorado.

Most individuals who work for you will be considered either common law employees or independent contractors. Unfortunately, there are many state and federal laws that are used to define an employment relationship and to determine whether an individual who performs services for you is an "employee" or an "independent contractor." The following are general definitions for common law employees and independent contractors.

Common Law Employees

Common law employees are individuals who perform services subject to the control of an employer, regarding what, where, when and how something must be done. It does not matter if the employer gives the employee substantial discretion and freedom to act, so long as the employer has the legal right to control both the method and results of service. Employers are responsible for withholding all state and federal taxes and all common law employees must be covered by workers' compensation insurance.

Independent Contractors

Persons in a trade, business, or profession such as law, accounting, or construction who offer their services to the general public are usually considered independent contractors. The most important characteristics of independent contractors are freedom from control and financial risk. An independent contractor is responsible for his or her own self-employment taxes and any necessary insurance.

The IRS uses a list of 20 factors to determine whether a worker is a common law employee or an independent contractor. The Colorado Unemployment Insurance-Liability Unit and the Division of Worker' Compensation use similar guidelines.

Statutory Employees

Commissioned delivery drivers, insurance agents, full-time commissioned sales agents, and individuals who do piece work with materials supplied by the employer are considered to be statutory employees by the IRS. The employer is not required to withhold federal income tax from payments. However, if the contract states an individual must perform the services personally, that the individual will perform the service on a continuing basis and that the equipment will be supplied by the employer, then the payments are subject to FICA. Payments to commissioned delivery drivers and sales agents are subject to unemployment insurance tax. Because statutory employees are similar in some respects to both common-law employees and independent contractors, you should contact the Colorado Division of Workers' Compensation directly regarding your workers' compensation liability.

Children and Spouses

If your business is a sole proprietorship, your children who work for your business are not considered to be employees by the IRS and are not subject to FICA and Medicare taxes until age 18. If a child is paid for domestic work in the parent's home, wages are not subject to Social Security and Medicare taxes until the child reaches age 21. Federal unemployment insurance does not cover services performed by children under the age of 21 who work for their parents. It is not necessary for the children to be claimed as dependents. All wages paid to children may still be subject to income tax withholdings. Wages paid by a sole proprietor to a spouse are subject to income tax withholding and social security taxes (FICA), but not to federal unemployment insurance taxes. All wages paid to a child or a spouse are subject to withholding taxes, FICA and state and federal unemployment insurance taxes if the parent/spouse's business is a partnership or a corporation, unless each partner is parent of a child. Workers' Compensation insurance must be provided for family member/employees.

Corporate Officers

Generally, working corporate officers are considered employees by the IRS and may not be paid through a distribution of dividends only. They must be paid a "reasonable wage or salary." All wages are subject to federal and state wage withholding, FICA, and unemployment insurance taxes. Corporate officers who own more than a 10% share of the business may elect to reject workers' compensation coverage. These rules apply to the corporate officers in both C and S corporations.

Leased Employees

An alternative to hiring your own employees is to contract for workers from a temporary employment agency or an employee-leasing agency. You pay the agency a fee to provide the number and type of employees you need and specify the conditions they must work under, but the individual workers remain employees of the agency. The agency is responsible for all payroll taxes, unemployment insurance, and workers' compensation. However, if a leasing company defaults in payment of unemployment insurance, the client company is then responsible for payment of unemployment insurance. A temporary agency is used when workers are needed for a short period of time. Leasing agencies provide employees under contract on a permanent basis.

Household Employees
If you hire someone to work in your own home, you may have responsibilities as a household employer. If the employee earns over $50 during a quarter, you are responsible for Social Security and Medicare taxes. If the employee earns over $1,000 during a quarter, you will also be responsible for unemployment insurance. The law does not require that you withhold federal or state income taxes for your employee; however, you may do so voluntarily if requested by your employee and she or he completes Form W-4. Workers' compensation insurance must be obtained for household employees who work 40 or more hours per week or five or more days per week. For additional information regarding your responsibilities as a household employer, call the IRS to request Publication 926, *Employment Taxes for Household Employers.*

Payroll Tax Filing Requirements And Forms

Wage Withholding and Social Security/Medicare Taxes
If you have employees, you will be responsible for withholding income taxes and Social Security/Medicare taxes from your employees' wages. As the employer, you must pay an equal share of Social Security/Medicare taxes. Also, you must withhold Colorado income tax from all employees working in Colorado, including non-residents.

Unemployment Insurance
Unemployment insurance is a fund established by law to provide benefits to employees who lose their jobs through no fault of their own. As an employer, you will be required to pay both state and federal unemployment insurance taxes.

Employee W-2s
At the end of the year you are responsible to report wage and tax withholding information with W-2 forms. Copies of the W-2 must be sent to your employee no later than January 31. Copy A of form W-2 must be sent to the Social Security Administration (SSA) by

February 28 with form W-3. For your Colorado employees, you must file DR 1093, Transmittal of State W-2s.

Independent Contractor 1099s

If you have determined your workers are independent contractors, you are not required to withhold or pay any taxes on their behalf, though you must keep track of how much you pay them and file form 1099 for each person you paid over $600 during the year. The independent contractor must be sent her/his form 1099 by January 31. Copy A of form 1099 must be sent to the IRS by February 28 with form 1096.

Payroll Records And Audits

It is important to keep complete and accurate employee/payroll records and to retain the records for at least five years. The IRS, the Immigration and Naturalization Service, the Colorado Department of Revenue and the Colorado Department of Labor & Employment all have the authority to audit your records. Remember that your liabilities begin as soon as you hire an employee.

Workers' Compensation

Workers' Compensation is mandatory insurance that provides coverage for medical expenses and lost wages due to a job-related injury or occupational disease. The employer must pay the cost of coverage for employees and all employees must be covered beginning with the very first employee. Corporate officers who actively work in a Corporation and members who work in a Limited Liability Company must be covered unless they own at least 10% of the business and they formally elect in writing to reject coverage. The election to reject coverage is filed with the insurance carrier. If there are no other employees, the election to reject coverage should be filed using form WC43 with the Division of Workers' Compensation. According to state law, sole proprietors and partners in a partnership have the option of electing coverage for themselves although a prime contractor may require it. However, this election may significantly affect health insurance coverage. Carefully discuss this election with your insurance agent before making your decision.

Business Insurance

Before starting your business you should be aware of the potential liabilities that may be incurred. You should look into what types of insurance may be required or may be in your best interest.

General Business Liability

This is the broadest form of coverage that can protect you against losses when injury, damage or even death result to another person or her/his property because of business negligence. Your obligations may even extend beyond the general liability for which you assume you are responsible. Read the terms of the insurance contract carefully.

Product Liability Insurance

If you manufacture a product, product liability insurance can also cover the goods you produce. Insurance coverage typically relates to the product itself but may also protect you, as the manufacturer should someone experience personal injury or property damage from the use of your product.

Completed Operations Insurance

If you are a contractor, you can become insured for events that may occur after you leave the job site. Problems that may be covered include personal injuries or damage to property due to something on which you worked going wrong. This is called Completed Operations Liability Insurance.

Health Insurance

Employers are not required by federal or state law to provide health coverage to their employees. However, if you do provide health benefits, certain laws will determine the nature of the plan and how it is administered. Colorado health insurers in the small group market (employers with 1-50 employees) must at least provide a basic or standard health benefit plan to an entire small group, regardless of the health status of its employees. Other consumer protections that apply to small group policies include guaranteed renewals, underwriting restrictions, and stringent premium rating rules. All of the above applies to even one-person businesses.

Property Insurance
This coverage is especially important if you own the property or building where your business is located. As the mortgagee, you can be protected against losses and a loss of income in the event your business experiences damage as a result of natural disaster, fire, burglary, or vandalism that may destroy all or part of your property.

Business Interruption Insurance
(Also referred to as "Specific Time Element Coverage") can pay losses of income as a result of personal property damage that might occur to your business from either environmental factors, natural disasters, or destruction by others until you are able to begin operating again.

Errors and Omission/Professional Liability Insurance
E & O insurance is often recommended for employees, owners, and directors of the business. E & O and professional liability coverage offer protection for employees and owners of the business against lawsuits that many arise as a result of their actions, or the failure to act for duties performed during the course of business.

Bonding
Bonding is not an insurance contract, but there are several types of surety bonds you can purchase which cover a wide range of losses. Fidelity bonds are designed to protect a business or employer from losses due to the dishonesty of employees, partners, or officers in the business. Performance bonds guarantee a business' performance because of an obligation or contractual agreement. Colorado law requires certain occupations (such as construction work or motor vehicle dealers) post a bond before they can be licensed or before they are awarded a state contract. Bonding is usually not a mandatory requirement; however, many companies do require that you post a bond before beginning work.

Income and Property Taxes

Corporations
If your business is a corporation located in or doing business in Colorado, it is subject to state and federal corporate income taxes. If

you will be filing as an S corporation, your company's income will be taxed as a partnership and will be exempt from corporate income taxes, although a corporate income tax return must still be filed. Working corporate officers are still treated as employees, even in an S corporation, and must be paid a reasonable wage that is subject to all payroll taxes.

Every corporation, including S corporations, doing business in Colorado or deriving income from Colorado sources, must file a corporate income tax return with Colorado.

If you expect your federal tax liability to be $500 or more and/or your state tax liability to be $5,000 or more, you are required to file and pay estimated taxes during the year. A corporation that owes more than $500 in federal income tax or $5,000 in state income tax may be subject to penalties and interest.

Partnerships

If your business is a partnership, you must file state and federal partnership income tax returns. The partnership as a whole is not required to pay income tax. Each partner is responsible for her or his own self-employment taxes as an individual. If you and your spouse run your business together and share in the profits, your business may be considered a partnership. You should record your respective shares of partnership income or loss separately for self-employment taxes. Doing this will usually not increase your total tax, but will give each spouse credit for Social Security earnings on which retirement benefits are based. The IRS Publication Tax on Partnerships is a useful guide regarding filing requirements and the allocation of income to the partners.

Self-Employment Taxes

If you are a sole proprietor or a partner in a partnership, you must file your own estimated self-employment taxes. When you work for others as an employee, your employer withholds your taxes from your paycheck. As an employee, your employer pays half of your Social Security taxes and you pay half. When you are self-employed, you must pay the entire amount. Estimated taxes are normally paid quarterly on actual income. If you do not have taxable income, you do not have to pay estimated taxes. If you expect to owe the IRS more than $500 in federal taxes, you must make federal estimated tax payments. IRS Publication 533, Self-Employment Tax, is a useful guide in determining your estimated federal tax liability. If you expect to owe Colorado more than $1,000 in state taxes, you must pay state estimated tax payments. Estimated payments are made using federal form 1040-ES and Colorado form 104-ES.

Property Taxes
These taxes are assessed on any real and/or personal property (land, buildings, furniture, equipment, etc.) that directly or indirectly produce income within your business. The County Assessor will mail a declaration schedule for property taxes after January 1st. Taxes must be paid by April 15th unless an extension has been obtained. The County Treasurer is responsible for mailing and collecting the actual property tax bill. Agricultural and natural resources are treated somewhat differently

Enterprise Zones
An Enterprise Zone is defined as an economically depressed area of Colorado in which special tax incentives are offered to businesses that expand or locate in the zone. There are currently 16 Colorado enterprise zones. An individual zone may include all of several counties in rural areas or small portions of a single county in urban areas. You should call the Department of Revenue for more information regarding tax incentives.

Additional Resources
The Business Assistance Center was established to serve as an ombudsman for the small business community in Colorado. The Center helps identify and work to eliminate unnecessary, duplicative, and burdensome regulation. It maintains a database of comprehensive (federal, state and local) regulatory requirements. The Center assists over 6,000 new, expanding and existing Colorado businesses each month.

DBE Certification
A service provided by the Department of Certification is Disadvantaged Business Enterprise (DBE) certification. The certification process determines the eligibility of minority and women owned

businesses to participate as DBEs on projects for the Colorado Department of Transportation, the Regional Transportation Distinct and the Denver Water Board.

Office of Business Development
The Office of Business Development (OBD) works with companies starting, expanding or relocating in Colorado. The Colorado First training program provides job training assistance as an incentive for companies to expand within Colorado or relocate to the state. OBD manages a Revolving Loan Fund that serves existing businesses in rural areas.

Small Business Office
The Small Business Office coordinates start-up and existing small business programs and activities that include the Colorado Leading Edge Training Program that teaches new and existing businesses how to develop a comprehensive business plan during a 10-12 week intensive education program.

Minority Business Office
The Minority Business Office provides assistance to ethnic minority-owned businesses in areas of procurement, marketing, training, and technical assistance programs. The office works as an advocate for minority businesses and is a point of contact for current bid information and maintains a database of ethnic minority-owned businesses.

Small Business Development Centers
Small Business Development Centers (SBDC) offer free one-on-one counseling services in the areas of business financing information, research and marketing, business plan preparation and other small business subjects, as well as specialized seminars on many small business topics. There are 21 community-based SBDC branches co-sponsored by OBD. Services are provided for new and existing businesses. In addition to general services listed above, local SBDCs also specialize in international trade, government procurement, home-based business, and technology resources. The SBDCs are a cooperative venture of the U.S. Small Business Administration, the State of Colorado Community Colleges and Chamber of Commerce.

Local Small Business Development Centers

Alamosa	719-587-7372	Aurora	303-341-4849
Boulder	303-442-1475	Cañon City	719-275-5335
Colorado Springs	719-592-1904	Craig	970-824-7078
Delta	970-874-8772	Denver	303-620-8076
Douglas County	303-814-0936	Durango	970-247-7009
Fort Collins	970-498-9295	Fort Morgan	970-542-3263
Glenwood Springs	970-928-0120	Grand Junction	970-243-5242
Greeley	970-352-3661	Lakewood	303-277-1840
Lamar	719-336-8141	Pueblo	719-549-3224
Trinidad	719-846-5644	Westminster	303-460-1032

For more information regarding the programs administered by the offices previously described call 303-892-3840.

Colorado Community Colleges and
Occupational Educational System

Colorado offers a wide variety of education and training programs for youth and adults through the Colorado Community College and Occupational Education System. The system provides training in more than 400 specific occupations ranging from basic entry-level skills to highly technical positions and develops industry specific training programs for employers for entry-level employees or upgrading of current employees.

Access Colorado Library and Information Network
www.aclin.org.

Access Colorado Library and Information Network is a project of the Colorado library community in partnership with Colorado Supernet—a Colorado access point to the information superhighway. ACLIN provides access to the information resources of the libraries in the state to support education, business, health, social services, and personal growth activities of the residents of Colorado. It creates a statewide library computer network that links the automated systems and online catalogs of participating libraries in a single network including academic, public, private and specialized (medical, legal, and others) library participants. The service also provides free access to over 130 library catalogs, listing over 11 million books, as well as over 35 other information databases. ACLIN connects users via a single phone call, local or toll-free, using a computer and a modem from home, office, school or library. For additional information about ACLIN, contact your local public library.

Note: if you attempt to use the 800 number from an area with a local number, your call will be blocked. At the first two prompts (user name and annex) type "ac" then follow the on-line instructions.

ACLIN Phone Numbers
Toll Free within Colorado 1-800-748-0888

Alamosa	719-589-0505	Boulder	303-440-9969
Colorado Springs	719-575-0200	Denver	303-294-7260
Durango	970-385-4949	Fort Collins	970-212-0077
Glenwood Springs	970-928-0055	Grand Junction	970-243-4441
Greeley	970-353-2225	Gunnison	970-641-4446
Pueblo	719-543-8811	Salida	719-530-0365
Steamboat Springs	970-870-0926	Sterling	970-521-0713
Summit County	970-968-2267	Telluride	970-728-4448

Small Business Administration
The Small Business Administration (SBA) is a federal agency that offers a wide variety of services for new and expanding businesses, including an all-day business seminar on advertising/marketing, financial sources, record keeping, insurance needs, legal considerations and computers. Reservations may be required and there is usually a nominal charge. The SBA also offers free counseling to small businesses through SCORE (Service Corps of Retired Executives) and ACE (Active Corps of Executives). For more information on these and other programs please contact the Small Business Administration at 303-844-3985 or SCORE toll-free 1-800-634-0245.

Colorado Department of Labor & Employment

Colorado Department of Labor & Employment operates a statewide network of Work Force Centers providing a number of employer services including Screening and Referral, Mass Recruitment, Affirmative Action Hiring, Layoff Assistance, and the Interstate Job Bank.

Local Work Force Centers

Alamosa	719-589-5118	Aurora	303-752-5820
Basalt	970-927-3825	Bear Valley	303-922-2450
Black Hawk	303-582-5444	Boulder County	303-441-3985
Brighton	303-659-4250	Broomfield	303-439-8161
Burlington	719-346-5331	Cañon City	719-275-7408
Castle Rock	303-688-4825	Colorado Springs	719-444-8024
Commerce City	303-227-2000	Cortez	970-565-3759
Craig	970-824-3246	Delta	970-874-5781
Denver	303-376-6700	Dumont	303-567-4357
Durango	970-247-0308	Edwards	970-926-4440
Fort Collins	970-223-2470	Fort Morgan	970-867-9401
Frisco	970-668-5360	Glenwood Springs	970-945-8638
Golden	303-271-4700	Granby	970-887-1857
Grand Junction	970-248-7560	Greeley	970-353-3800
Gunnison	970-641-0031	Idaho Springs	303-567-3135
La Junta	719-383-3191	Lakewood Youth	303-987-4866
Lamar	719-336-2256	Leadville	719-486-2428
Limon	719-775-2387	Littleton	303-738-5636
Longmont	303-678-8103	Loveland	970-667-4261
Meeker	970-878-4211	Monte Vista	719-852-5171
Montrose	970-249-7783	Pagosa Springs	970-264-4133
Pueblo	719-253-7800	Rangely	970-675-5071
Rifle	970-625-5627	Rocky Ford	719-254-3397
Salida	719-539-6523	Steamboat Springs	970-879-3075
Sterling	970-522-9340	Thornton	303-452-2304
Trinidad	719-846-9221	Walsenburg	719-738-2372
Yuma	970-848-3760		

Governor's Job Training Office

www.state.co.us/gov_dir/gjto/gjtohmpg.html
720 S. Colorado Blvd., Suite 550
Denver, CO 80222
303-758-5020
Fax: 303-758-5578
Director: Vickey Ricketts

The Governor's Job Training Office provides opportunities for both employees and employers by offering programs through the Job Training Partnership Act. The goal is to prepare unemployed individuals, youths and adults, for entry into the labor force and to assist with job training for those individuals who require this assistance to prepare them for productive employment. To achieve this goal, local service areas develop training programs that meet the needs of local employers as well as eligible clients. Employers may receive financial reimbursement for hiring and helping train eligible participants.

Local GJTO service areas:

Arapahoe/Douglas Counties	303-752-5820	Boulder County	303-441-3985
Denver County	303-893-3382	Larimer County	970-223-2470

Local Economic Development Offices

www.state.co.us/gov_dir/oed.html
Local Economic Development Offices (LEDO) provide variety of different services to the businesses in their area, including permitting assistance; relocation, demographics, and site location information; and counseling and support services. A few offices administer small loan programs. Some are agencies of local city or county governments and others are independent nonprofit organizations that receive funding from local governments and/or chambers of commerce. Check with your local chamber of commerce office to locate the LEDO nearest you.

Chambers of Commerce

www.state.co.us/business_dir/chambers.html
Chambers of commerce provide a number of opportunities for busi-

ness owners. Primarily, your local chamber is where you can meet and network with other business owners from your community. Some chambers provide additional services including counseling, training programs and guest speakers on useful business topics.

Minority Chambers of Commerce:

Asian 303-595-9737
www.asianchambercommerce.org.

Gay & Lesbian 303-595-8042

Black-Colorado Springs 719-260-6821

Black 303-341-1296
www.coloradoblackchamber.org

Hispanic 303-534-7783
www.chcc.com

American Indian 303-446-2422
www.rmicc.org

Latino-Pueblo 719-542-5513
www.nclcc.org

Women's 303-458-0220
www.cwcc.org

Geographic Chambers of Commerce:

Akron 970-345-2342

Antonito 719-376-5475
www.coloradodirectory.com/antonitochamber

Aurora 303-344-1500
www.aurorachamber.org

Basalt 970-927-4031
www.toski.com/basalt

Berthoud 970-532-4200
www.berthoudcolorado.com

Brighton 303-659-0223

Brush area 970-842-2666
www.brushchamber.org

Burlington 719-346-8397

Carbondale 970-963-1890
www.carbondale.com

Colorado Springs 719-635-1551
www.coloradospringschamber.org

Alamosa County 719-589-3681
www.alamosachamber.com

Aspen 970-925-1940
www.aspenchamber.org

Avon/Beaver Creek 970-949-5189

Bayfield area 970-884-7372
www.bayfieldcochamber.org/index.html

Boulder 303-442-1044
www.boulderchamber.com

Broomfield 303-466-1775
www.broomfieldchamber.org

Buena Vista 719-395-6612
www.vtinet.com/buenavista

Cañon City 719-275-2331
www.canoncitychamber.com

Castle Rock 303-688-4597
www.castlerock.org

Conifer 303-838-0178
www.coniferchamber.com

Cortez 970-565-3414

Crawford area 970-921-3018

Crested Butte 800-545-4505
www.crestedbuttechamber.com

Crowley County 719-267-3572

Del Norte 719-657-2845
www.delnortechamber.com

Denver, Greater 303-534-8500
www.denverchamber.org

Denver, NW Metro 303-424-0313

Divide 719-687-7375

Dove Creek 970-677-2245

Eads 719-438-5595

Elizabeth 303-646-4287

Erie 303-828-3440
www.eriechamber.org

Evans area 970-330-4202

Florence 719-784-3544

Fort Lupton 303-857-4474

Fountain 719-390-4066

Fruita 970-858-3894

Gilpin County 303-582-5077

Golden 303-279-3113

Grand Junction 970-242-3214
ww.gjchamber.org

Craig 970-824-5689
www.craig-chamber.com

Creede-Mineral 800-327-2102
www.creede.com/cmccc

Cripple Creek 719-689-2169
www.cripple-creek/co.us

Custer County 719-783-9163
www.custerguide.com

Delta 970-874-8616
www.deltacolorado.org

Denver, N. Metro 303-288-1002
www.metronorthchamber.com

Denver, S. Metro 303-795-0142
www.bestchamber.com

Dolores 970-882-4018

Durango 800-525-8855
www.durango.org

Eagle Valley 970-328-5220
www.villageprofile.com/colorado/eaglevalley/main

Englewood 303-789-4473
www.greatenglewoodchamber.com

Estes Park 970-586-4431
www.estesparkresort.com

Evergreen area 303-674-3412
www.evergreenchamber.org

Fort Collins 970-482-3746
www.fcchamber.org

Fort Morgan 800-354-8660
www.fortmorganchamber.org

Fowler 719-263-4461

Georgetown 303-569-2888

Glenwood Springs 970-945-6589
www.glenscape.com

Granby 970-887-2311
www.granbychamber.com

Grand Lake 970-627-3402
www.grandlakechamber.com

Greeley/Weld 970-352-3566
www.greeleychamber.com

Haxtun 970-774-6600

Hotchkiss 970-872-3226

Idaho Springs 303-567-4383
www.idahospringschamber.com

Johnstown-Milliken 970-587-4661

Keenesburg 970-732-4246

La Junta 719-384-7411
www.lajuntacochamber.com

Lafayette 303-666-9555
www.chamber.lafayette.co.us

Lakewood 303-233-5555

Las Animas 719-456-0453
www.trinidadco.com/chamber

Limon 719-775-9418
www.limonchamber.com

Longmont 303-776-5295
www.longmontchamber.org

Loveland 970-667-6311
www.loveland.org/index

Manitou Springs 719-685-5089
www.manitousprings.org

Monte Vista 719-852-2731
www.monte-vista.org

Monument/Tri-Lakes 719-481-3282

New Castle 970-984-3167
www.newcastlechamber.org

Olathe 970-323-5601

Pagosa Springs 800-252-2204
www.pagosa-springs.com

Paonia 970-527-3886

Plateau Valley 970-487-3457

Gunnison 970-641-1501
www.gunnison-co.com

Holyoke 970-854-3517
www.holyokechamber.org/community

Huerfano County 719-738-1065

Jefferson-West 303-233-5555
www.westchamber.org

Julesburg 970-474-3504

Kremmling 970-724-3472
www.rkymtnhi.com/kremmling

La Veta 719-742-3676
www.ruralwideweb.com/lvcc

Lake City 970-944-2527

Lamar 719-336-4379
www.lamarchamber.com

Leadville 800-LEADVILLE
www.leadvilleusa.com

Logan County 970-544-8609
www.logancontychamber.com

Louisville 303-666-5747
www.louisvillechamber.com

Lyons 303-823-5215
www.lyons_colorado.com

Meeker 970-878-5510
www.meekerchamber.com

Montrose 970-249-5000
www.montrosechamber.org

Nederland 970-258-3650

North Park 970-723-4600
www.northparkcoc.com

Ouray County 800-228-1876
www.ouraycolorado.com

Palisade 970-464-7458
www.palisadecoc.com

Parker 303-841-4268
www.parkerchamber.com

Platteville 970-785-2265

Pueblo 800-233-3446
www.pueblochamber.org

Rico Bus. Assn. 970-967-2871

Rifle 970-625-2085
wwwriflechamber.com

Salida 719-539-2068
www.salidachamber.org

Snowmass 970-923-2000
www.snowmassvillage.com

Springfield 719-523-4376
www.springfieldchamber.com

Summit County 800-530-3099
www.summitchamber.org

Trinidad 719-846-9285
www.trinidadco.com/chamber

Vallecito Lake 970-884-9782
www.vallecito.com

Windsor 970-686-7189

Woodland Park 719-687-9885
www.woodlandparkchamber.com

Rangely 970-675-5290
www.rangely.com

Ridgway 970-626-5181
www.ridgwaycolorado.com

Rocky Ford 719-254-7483
www.rockyfordchamber.com

Silverton 800-752-4494
www.silverton.org

South Fork 800-571-0881

Steamboat Springs 970-879-0882
www.steamboat-chamber.com

Telluride 800-525-3455
www.telluride.org

Vail 970-949-5189
www.vailvalleychamber.com

Victor 719-689-4044
www.tellercounty.com

Winter Park 970-726-4118
www.winterpark_info.com

Yuma 970-848-2704
www.yumachamber.com

Colorado Small Business Incubators

Small business incubators are designed to assist business start-ups during the most critical formative years (embryo stage). These incubators provide workshops to teach business skills and to improve knowledge of business operations and management. Other benefits of utilizing an incubator include formal and informal networks of business assistance, consulting services, multi-tenant office space, shared office services and improved access to financial resources. Call the following incubator sites for more information:

Denver Enterprise Center *www.thedec.org*	303-296-9400
Jefferson County Business and Innovation Center	303-238-0913
Western Colorado Business Development Corporation *www.state.co.us/gov_dir/obd/gjincubator*	970-243-5242

Fremont County EDC and Business Development Center   719-275-8601

Colorado Bio-Venture Center   303-237-3998
www.directory.bigexchange.com/academic_detail

Qwest Home Office Consulting Center   800-898-9675
http//my.qwest.net/crossroads_bus.html

Virtually all local phone service in Colorado is handled by Qwest Communications. They have created a Home Office Consulting Center that offers free advice and service from consultants who are specially trained to provide creative, cost-efficient ideas for work-at-home professionals and entrepreneurs. I can tell you that from experience they really know their stuff. With so many new services available it really pays to have one of these professionals work out the best system for your home office.

AT&T Home Business Resources
www.att.com/business/

Same as above except for long-distance services. Call 800-473-7687 and ask for an information package and a free subscription to AT&T Powersource, a quarterly magazine loaded with useful and up-to-date information.

Rocky Mountain Home-Based Business Association
www.rmhba.org

This nonprofit association offers networking opportunities, educational seminars, a quarterly newsletter, and special events designed specially for those with home-based businesses. Call 303-367-1918 for more information, or e-mail *asboc@henge.com*.

Additional Resources

Census Bureau
303-231-5050
www.census.gov

Colorado Business Assistance Center
303-592-5920 or 800-333-7798
www.state.co.us/oed/sbdc/bac.html

Colorado Department of
Business Development
303-892-3840
www.state.co.us/oed/sbdc

Colorado Department of Revenue
303-866-3091
www.revenue.state.co.us

Colorado Department of
Revenue-Income Tax Information
303-232-2446
www.revenue.state.co.us

Colorado Department of Revenue-Sales
Tax Information
303-232-2416
www.revenue.state.co.us

Colorado Department of Transportation
303-757-9011
www.dot.state.co.us

Federal Employer I.D. Numbers
801-625-7645

Federal Wage & Hour Division
303-844-4405
www.dol.gov/dol/esa/public/contacts/
who/america2.html

Front Range Community College
Small Business Development
303-404-5345
www.frcc.cc.co.us/institute/sbdc

Government Printing
Office Bookstore
303-844-3964
www.ota.nap.edu/bkstores.html

Immigration and Naturalization
Service
303-371-3041
www.ins.usdoj.gov

Internal Revenue Service-
Recorded Tax Information
800-829-4477
www.irs.ustreas.gov/

Internal Revenue Service-Tax
Form & Publication Assistance
800-829-3676
www.irs.ustreas.gov/

International Trade
303-844-6623
www.state.co.us/gov_dir/oed/ITO/
intl_trade_gov.htm

Minority Business
Assistance Office
303-892-3840
www.state.co.us/oed/mbo/

Occupational Safety and
Health Administration
303-844-5285
www.osha.gov

Red Rocks Community College
Small Business Development
303-277-1840
www.state.co.us/gov_dir/oed/sbdc

Secretary of State
303-894-2200
www.sos.state.co.us

Service Corps of Retired
Executives (SCORE)
303-844-3985
www.scoredenver.org

U. S. Department of Commerce
303-497-3000

U. S. Department of Labor
303-844-1256
www.cdle.state.co.us/default.asp

U. S. Postal Service-Requirements
and Permits
303-853-6120
www.usps.gov

U. S. Small Business
Administration Services
303-844-3985
www.sbaonline.sba.gov

University of Colorado
Business Advancement Center
303-554-9493
http://outreachdb.colorado.edu/paout/

Get Out Of Denver

9

STATE-WIDE RECREATION, ENTERTAINMENT AND CULTURE

Communing With Nature

Winter Activities

Water Sports

Bicycling

Sky-High Adventure

Weekend Getaways

Tours

Professional Sports

Downtown Denver

Leisure

Fun & Unusual Things To Do

The Arts & Culture

Looking for something to do in Colorado? Try: Arts, Amusement Parks, Archaeological Tours, Ballet, Ballooning, Bed & Breakfasts, Bicycle Touring, Boating, Brewpubs, Camera Safari, Camping, Concerts, Cross-country Skiing, Dog Sledding, Downhill Skiing, Festivals, Flying, Four-Wheel-Drive Trips, Gambling, Glider Rides, Gold Panning, Golf, Hang Gliding, Hiking and Backpacking, Historic Tours, Horseback Riding, Hot Springs, Ice Climbing, Ice Skating, Kayaking, Llama Trekking, Mine Tours, Mountain Biking, Mountaineering, Museums, Narrow-gauge Train Rides, Nature Walks, Opera, Paragliding, Plays, Planetariums, Professional Baseball, Basketball, Football, or Hockey, River Rafting, Rock Climbing, Running, Sailing, Scenic Drives, Scuba Diving, Skydiving, Sleigh Rides, Snowshoe Walks, Snowboarding, Snowmobiling, Swimming, Tennis, Trail Walks, Water Skiing, Weekend Getaways, Windsurfing, Winery Tours, Zoos.

As you can see, there are unlimited options when it comes to things to do in Colorado. You might also guess it would be impossible to adequately cover all these options in this book. The intent of this chapter is to provide an overview of the possibilities and direct you to sources of more complete information. In fact, there are dozens of books available on Colorado's cultural and recreational activities. If you are interested in a particular activity, I recommend the books listed throughout this chapter.

When you think of New York City, you imagine skyscrapers, crowded streets, and rude taxi drivers. When you think of Florida, you imagine vast stretches of beach, palm trees, and water sports. When you think of Colorado, you imagine thousands of square miles of wilderness and all the activities that go with them. Colorado has 3 national parks, 7 national monuments, 12 national forests, 40 state parks, 1 national recreation area, dozens of ski areas/resorts, and dozens of large lakes and reservoirs. These areas offer a multitude of things to do during all four seasons.

Communing With Nature

Camera Safaris, Nature & Trail Walks, Camping, Hiking, Backpacking Horseback Riding, Llama Trekking, Mountaineering, or Rock Climbing

Please observe the following rules while visiting or camping in any national park, national monument, or national forest, and check with each location for additional rules and regulations:

www.nps.gov   *www.fs.fed.us*

1. Leash laws for pets vary from location to location. Check any posted signs pertaining to containment.
2. Do not feed or touch wild animals and do not keep food in tents.
3. Hunting is allowed in designated areas by permit only.
4. Picking wildflowers and plants is allowed by permit only.
5. Harassment of wildlife is prohibited.
6. Fishing requires a valid Colorado state fishing license.
7. Camping is restricted to designated areas in national parks; however, most national forests are considered open area.
8. A permit is required for all overnight stays in national parks but not in national forests.
9. Fires may be built only in picnic areas and campsites with grates in national parks, though most national forests are considered open area. Be sure to check the fire danger signs where posted.
10. Vehicles must remain on designated roadways or in parking areas.
11. Trail bikes, snowmobiles, and all other vehicles are restricted to designated trails.
12. Remove all your own trash from picnic areas and campsites.

National Parks (NP)

Mesa Verde National Park

www.nps.gov/meve   *www.mesa.verde.national-park.com*
Entrance Fee: $10/private vehicles good for 7 days
Annual National Parks Pass — $50
Over 600 cliff dwellings and nearly 3,900 sites have been found
MVNP has 55,121.93 acres total.

MVNP is located in southwestern Colorado. Established in 1906, the park contains ancient cliff dwellings dating back to 1200 A.D. The most notable of the cliff dwellings are Cliff Palace in Cliff Canyon, which contains more than 200 rooms and 23 kivas (ceremonial chambers), Spruce Tree House in Spruce Tree Canyon, with 114 rooms and 8 kivas, and Balcony House in Soda Canyon, a small cliff dwelling of at least 30 rooms. The Park covers 81.4 square miles and includes two museums and a 494-unit campground. For additional information call 970-529-4465.

Rocky Mountain National Park

www.nps.gov/rmno/

RMNP is located 62 miles (as the crow flies) northwest of Denver. Covering 415.3 square miles, the park includes 113 named peaks above 10,000 feet including Longs Peak at 14,255 feet. The park has 57 miles of paved road (including Trail Ridge Road), 14 miles of gravel road, and 346 miles of hiking trails. RMNP has 5 campgrounds with a total of 500 sites. For additional information call 970-586-1206.

Black Canyon of the Gunnison National Park

www.nps.gov/blca/

BCGNP is located near Montrose in southwestern Colorado. Its spectacular landscape, with 2,000-foot canyon walls dropping almost vertically to the Gunnison River, was formed slowly by the action of water. No other canyon in North America combines the narrow opening, sheer walls, and startling depths of the Black Canyon of the Gunnison. The park covers 53 square miles, 27,705 total acres, has 115 campsites and attracts 230,000 visitors per year. For visitor information call 970-641-2337, ext. 205.

National Monuments (NM)
www.therenback.com

National Parks & Monuments	Main Number	303-969-2500
Canyons of the Ancients	Dolores	970-882-4811
Colorado	Fruita	970-858-3617
Dinosaur	Dinosaur	970-374-3000
Florissant Fossil Beds	Florissant	719-748-3253
Great Sand Dunes	Mosca	719-378-2312
Hovenweep	Cortez	970-562-4282
Yucca House	Mesa Verde NP	970-529-4465

National Forests (NF)
www.therenback.com

Rocky Mountain Region National Forest Service		303-275-5350
Arapaho National Forest	Fort Collins	970-498-1100
Grand Mesa National Forest	Delta	970-874-7691
Gunnison National Forest	Delta	970-874-7691
Pawnee National Grassland	Greeley	970-353-5004
Pike National Forest	Pueblo	719-545-8737
Rio Grande National Forest	Monte Vista	719-852-5941
Roosevelt National Forest	Fort Collins	970-498-1100
Routt National Forest	Steamboat Springs	970-879-1722
San Isabel National Forest	Pueblo	719-545-8737
San Juan National Forest	Durango	970-247-4847
Uncompahgre National Forest	Delta	970-874-7691
White River National Forest	Glenwood Springs	970-945-2521

National Historic Site

Bent's Old Fort	La Junta	719-383-5010

www.nps.gov/beol

National Recreation Area

Curecanti National Recreation Area   Gunnison   970-641-2337
www.nps.gov/cure

Wilderness Areas

www.wilderness.net

Wilderness	+- Acres	Management
Black Canyon/Gunnison	15,599	Black Canyon of the Gunnison NP
Black Ridge Canyons	75,550	Grand Junction BLM
Buffalo Peaks	43,410	Pike, San Isabel NF
Byers Peak	8,913	Arapaho NF
Cache La Poudre	9,238	Roosevelt NF
Collegiate Peaks	166,938	Gunnison, San Isabel, White River NF
Comanche	66,791	Roosevelt NF
Eagles Nest	132,906	Arapaho, White River NF
Flat Tops	235,035	Routt White River NF
Fossil Ridge	31,534	Gunnison NF
Great Sand Dunes	33,450	Great Sand Dunes NM
Greenhorn Mtn	22,040	San Isabel NF
Holy Cross	122,797	San Isabel, White River NF
Hunter-Fryingpan	81,866	White River NF
Indian Peaks	70,374	Arapaho, Roosevelt NF, Rocky Mtn. NP
La Garita	128,626	Gunnison, Rio Grande NF
Lizard Head	41,193	San Juan, Uncompahgre NF
Lost Creek	119,790	Pike NF
Maroon Bells-Snowmass	181,117	Gunnison, White River NF
Mesa Verde	8,100	Mesa Verde NP
Mt. Evans	74,401	Arapaho, Pike NF
Mt. Massive	27,980	San Isabel NF
Mt. Sneffels	16,565	Uncompahgre NF
Mt. Zirkel	159,935	Routt NF
Neota	9,924	Roosevelt, Routt NF
Never Summer	20,747	Arapaho, Routt NF
Platte River	743	Roosevelt NF
Powderhorn	60,510	Bureau of Land Management
Ptarmigan Peak	12,594	Arapaho NF

Raggeds	64,992	Gunnison, White River NF
Rawah	73,068	Roosevelt, Routt NF
Sangre de Cristo	226,420	Rio Grande, San Isabel NF
Sarvis Creek	45,190	Routt NF
South San Juan	158,790	Rio Grande, San Juan NF
Uncompahgre	102,790	Uncompahgre NF
Vasquez Peak	12,986	Arapaho NF
Weminuche	488,200	Rio Grande, San Juan NF
West Elk	176,172	Gunnison NF

Colorado State Parks

www.parks.state.co.us

Fees: A valid parks pass is required on every vehicle entering a state park. A daily pass is $4; an annual pass, good for the entire calendar year at all state parks is $40. Camping permits are $6-$16 per night, depending on the facilities available. Day-use areas are generally open from 5 A.M. to 10 P.M. and campgrounds (when open) are open 24 hours a day.

For additional information call 303-866-3437. For camping reservations call 303-470-1144 or 800-678-CAMP. Before using any of these parks you should request a copy of the State Park Regulations. All state parks are listed below:

Park Name	Location	Phone Number
Arkansas	Salida	719-539-7289
Barbour Ponds	Longmont	970-678-9402
Barr Lake	Brighton	303-659-6005
Bonny Lake	Idalia	970-354-7306
Boyd Lake	Loveland	970-669-1739
Castlewood Canyon	Franktown	303-688-5242
Chatfield	Littleton	303-791-7275
Cherry Creek	Aurora	303-699-3860
Colorado River	Clifton	970-434-3388
Colorado State Forest	Walden	970-723-8366
Crawford	Crawford	970-921-5721
Eldorado Canyon	Eldorado Springs	303-494-3943

Eleven Mile	Lake George	719-748-3401
Golden Gate Canyon	Golden	303-582-3707
Harvey Gap (no pets)	Rifle	970-625-1607
Highline	Loma	970-858-7208
Jackson Lake	Orchard	970-645-2551
Lake Pueblo	Pueblo	719-561-9320
Lathrop	Walsenburg	719-738-2376
Lory	Bellvue	970-493-1623
Mancos	Mancos	970-883-2208
Mueller	Divide	719-687-2366
Navajo	Arboles	970-883-2208
North Sterling	Sterling	970-522-3657
Paonia	Paonia	970-921-5721
Pearl Lake	Clark	970-879-3922
Picnic Rock	Bellvue	970-493-1623
Ridgway	Ridgway	970-626-5822
Rifle Falls/Gap	Rifle	970-625-1607
Roxborough (no pets)	Littleton	303-973-3959
San Luis	Mosca	719-378-2020
Spinney Mountain	Lake George	719-748-3401
Stagecoach	Oak Creek	970-736-2436
Steamboat Lake	Clark	970-879-3922
Sweitzer Lake	Delta	970-874-4258
Sylvan Lake	Eagle	970-625-1607
Trinidad Lake	Trinidad	719-846-6951
Vega	Collbran	970-487-3407
Yampa River Legacy	Hayden	970-276-2061

Additional Activities and Resources

Boulder Mountaineer Climbing School	303-442-8355
Boulder Rock School (Boulder Rock Club)	303-447-2804
American Camping Association (Kids' summer camp)	970-577-0219
www.acacamps.org	or 888-926-2267
	765-342-8456
Bureau of Land Management	303-239-3600
www.co.blm./gov	
CO Association of Campgrounds, Cabins & Lodges	303-659-5252
www.campcolorado.com	

National Park Service   800-365-2267
www.nps.gov

US Forest Service   303-275-5350
www.fs.fed.us   or 800-280-2267

Winter Sports

Cross-country Skiing, Dog Sledding, Downhill Skiing, Ice Climbing, Ice Skating, Snowboarding, Snowmobiling, Snowshoeing, and Sleigh Rides

Colorado is world famous for its winter sports. Many summer sports have their counterparts in winter (hiking/snowshoeing, rock climbing/ice climbing, in-line skating/ice skating). This allows you, with the proper change of clothing, to enjoy your favorite type of activity year-round.

Cross-country Skiing

It's not unusual to see the city parks full of cross-country skiers after the first good snowfall of the season. Many are just warming up for serious treks into the backcountry. Cross-country skiing is becoming increasingly popular with many novices heading straight for the woods, which can be very dangerous. Every year skiers die in avalanches usually caused by their own activity and perfect avalanche conditions. Don't get in over your head (literally) and don't let your enthusiasm override your experience.

Colorado Avalanche Hotlines
www.firstrax.com

Aspen	970-920-1664	Colorado Springs	719-520-0020
Denver	303-275-5360	Durango	970-247-8187
Fort Collins	970-482-0457	Summit County	970-668-0600
Vail	970-479-4652		

Downhill Ski Areas and Resorts
www.skicolorado.org   *www.toski.com*

You won't have any problem finding complete information about the many ski areas in Colorado. Every fall dozens of magazines and directories become available for the new season. One of the best sources is Colorado Ski Country USA (303-837-0793). Many resorts offer special rates, ski schools, and multi-day passes. It can get as confusing as buying discount airline seats so please check with each resort for details. The prices vary at each area.

Ski Area	Reservations	Snow Report
Arapahoe Basin	888-ARAPAHOE	970-468-4111
Aspen Highlands	800-262-7736	888-277-3676
Aspen Mountain	888-452-2409	888-277-3676
Beaver Creek	800-622-3131	888-296-3155
Berthoud Pass	800-283-7458	800-SKI-BERT
Breckenridge	800-221-1090	970-453-6118
Buttermilk	888-452-2409	970-925-1221
Copper Mountain	800-458-8396	800-789-7609
Crested Butte	800-544-8448	970-349-2323
Cuchara	877-282-4272	719-742-3163
Eldora	888-2-ELDORA	303-440-8700
Howelsen	800-525-2628	970-879-8499
Keystone	800-258-9553	970-468-4111
Loveland	800-225-LOVE	800-736-3754 x220
Monarch	888-996-SNOW	800-228-7943
Powderhorn	800-241-6997	970-268-5700 x2065
Purgatory	800-982-6103	970-247-9000
Silver Creek	800-747-7458	800-757-7669
Ski Cooper	800-748-2057	719-486-2277
Snowmass	800-598-2004	888-277-3676
Steamboat	800-922-2722	970-879-7300
Sunlight	800-445-7931	970-945-7491
Telluride	800-854-3062	970-728-7425
Vail	800-427-8216	970-476-4888
Winter Park	800-729-5813	303-572-SNOW
Wolf Creek	970-264-5639	800-SKI-WOLF

Additional Activities and Resources

Colorado Snowmobile Association   800-235-4480/970-667-3191
www.sledcity.com/states/colorado/csa_contact.cfn

Mountain Sports   303-443-6770

NOAA Weather Information	303-494-4221
www.noaa.gov	
http://weather.gov	
Road Conditions (statewide)	303-639-1111
www.dot.state.co.us	

Water Sports

Boating, Kayaking, River Rafting, Sailing, Scuba Diving, Swimming, Water Skiing, and Windsurfing

My last abode before I left Florida was a classic 38' wooden yacht. While driving to Colorado I thought I would never see another boat, windsurfer, or Jet Ski again. I was very wrong. Colorado has over 150 major lakes and reservoirs that provide the water enthusiast with ample opportunities. When you add some of the best rafting rivers in the country, no one should be left unsatisfied. But, before you rush out to hook up the boat trailer or buy a surplus two-person survival raft to hit the rapids, be advised that since most boating areas are "controlled" lakes and reservoirs, they are subject to many rules, regulations, and restrictions. Unless you are a very experienced kayaker or rafter, don't hit the rapids on your own— this can be hazardous to your health. There are numerous outfitters who can provide a fine whitewater experience.

Believe it or not, scuba diving is actually quite a popular sport in Colorado with many lakes and reservoirs in the state that provide interesting dive experiences. You must be certified to dive but there are several metro area centers that provide the training.

Bicycling

Mountain Biking, Bicycle Touring, and Bicycle Races

It seems there are as many bicycles in Colorado as there are automobiles. Many two-car garages have the better car in one side and three to six bicycles in the other. There are literally thousands of miles of designated bike paths in the state. If you were allowed to camp along the way (which you're not), you could spend an entire week touring the greater Denver metro area without ever leaving the bike paths. Home to some of the most beautiful scenery in the country, Colorado also hosts several of the most grueling cycling events in the world.

Probably the best known annual bicycle tour is the week-long "Ride the Rockies" sponsored by The Denver Post. The sponsors provide campsites and transport all gear. This fully supported ride is very strenuous and many of the 2,000 participants spend most of the year training for this one ride. For more information call The Denver Post at 303-820-1338 or visit *www.ridetherockies.com*.

A complete list of Colorado's bicycle organizations is available at *www.bcn.boulder.co.us/transportation/bike.org.html/*.

The downside to this sport's growing popularity is the inevitable conflict between cyclists and automobiles or hikers vying for the same limited spaces. Many of the state's best hiking trails have recently become two-foot-deep ruts due to overuse by mountain bikes. Collisions and other altercations are becoming almost commonplace. Please follow the "Golden Rule," use common sense, and respect the environment while cycling.

Rocky Mountain Cycling Club
www.rmcrides.com

Bicycle Colorado
719-530-0051
www.bicyclecolo.org

Sky-High Adventure

Ballooning, Flying, Glider Rides,
Hang Gliding, Paragliding, and Skydiving

If at times you find yourself in awe at Colorado's natural beauty, you ought to see it from the air (and not from 30,000 feet en route to DIA).

A Balloon Safari Company	Commerce City	303-289-5455
A Real Escape Company	Arvada	303-421-4600
Airtime Above Hang Gliding *www.pilotshack.com/hang_gliders.html*	Evergreen	303-674-2451
Looney Balloons Inc	Littleton	303-979-9476

Parasoft Inc Paragliding School   Boulder   303-494-2820
www.serioussports.com/parasoft/

Sky Fighters, Inc   Denver   303-790-7375
www.skyfighters.com

Weekend Getaways

Bed and Breakfast Accommodations, Cabins,
Cottages and Lodges, Scenic Drives,
RV Parks, and Dude and Guest Ranches

In Colorado almost every portion of the state offers something to do or see that is worth the drive. However, getting up at 4 A.M., driving two to four hours to do something and then driving back the same day is not my idea of fun. Neither is sleeping on the hard ground without running water. Fortunately, there are options. In fact, one of the most popular forms of entertainment in Colorado is the weekend getaway. The best book for planning a getaway is *The Colorado Guide*, published by Fulcrum Publishing. This book lists almost every town and city in Colorado and describes activities, lodging, and dining. The other publishers listed above also produce great books for different aspects of weekend getaways.

Bed & Breakfast Accommodations
There are over 350 bed & breakfast establishments in Colorado spread out among 119 towns, cities, and villages.
http://colorado-bnb.com
www.ibbp.com/obb/colorado/html

Cabins, Cottages, and Lodges
If a cabin, cottage, or lodge is more your style you can choose from over 230.

RV Parks and Campgrounds
Colorado has 400% more RV parks and campgrounds in the mountains than any other state in the country.

Dude and Guest Ranches

They say reservations at dude and guest ranches sharply increased with the release of the movie *City Slickers*. If true, that was good news for the 40 or so operating in Colorado.

Resources

Colorado Association of Campgrounds, Cabins, and Lodges *www.campcolorado.com*	303-659-5252
Colorado Dude & Guest Ranch Association *www.coloradoranch.com*	970-887-3128
Colorado Hotel and Lodging Association *www.coloradolodging.com*	303-297-8335
Colorado Reservation Service *www.reserveusa.com/about*	877-444-6777
Historic Hotels of the Rockies *www.historic_hotels.com*	303-546-9040

Tours

Mines, Wineries, Archaeological, Historical, or Four-Wheel-Drives

The word "tour" usually conjures up visions of being herded around with a bunch of strangers on a pre-planned, packaged, and boring walk or drive through an area that you can look at but not touch. This kind of tour is available in Colorado but that is not what this section is about. Since Colorado has such a rich history (both pre- and modern), sites with historical value and interest literally cover the state. If your interest lies in dinosaur fossils, Indian petroglyphs, or still-active gold mines, you're in luck.

If on the other hand, you are a bit of a wine lover, Colorado wineries always welcome guests for tastings. There is even an annual bicycle tour that can be quite grueling (it's only 30 miles on flat terrain, but it stops at every winery and vineyard along the way). Visit *www.coloradowinefest.com* for information.

Ever wonder what the backcountry of Colorado is really like? Many mountain locations offer four-wheel-drive tours that get you back to where even hikers or horses fear to tread.

Colorado Mining Districts

Old mining districts are great places for prospecting, gold panning, ghost towns, and mine tours. The following cities were once active gold and/or silver mining areas: Alma, Aspen, Bonanza, Breckenridge, Boulder County, Central City, Climax, Creede, Crested Butte, Cripple Creek, Empire-Georgetown-Silver Plume, Fairplay, Garfield, Gilman, Idaho Springs, Lake City, La Plata, Leadville, Montezuma, Ouray, Rico, Silver Cliff, Silverthorne, St. Elmo, Summitville, Telluride, Tincup-Pitkin.

Warning: There are over 23,000 open mine shafts and tunnels in Colorado. Most are unmarked and nearly invisible until it's too late, and some are several hundred feet deep. Use extreme caution while in mining backcountry.

Colorado Wineries and Vineyards

www.thewineman.com/coloradovineyards.htm

Call for hours and directions

Canyon Wind Cellars	Palisade	970-464-0888
Carlson Vineyards	Palisade	970-464-5554
Colorado Cellars	Palisade	970-464-7921
		800-848-2812
Confre Cellars &		
Rocky Mtn. Meadery	Palisade	970-464-7899
Cottonwood Cellars	Olathe	970-323-6224
Grand River Vineyards	Palisade	970-464-5867
Minturn Cellars	Minturn	970-827-4065
Mountain Spirit		
Winery, Ltd.	Salida	719-539-1175
Pikes Peak Vineyards	Colorado Springs	719-576-0075
Plum Creek Cellars	Palisade	970-464-7586
Rocky Hill Winery	Montrose	970-249-3765
St. Kathryn Cellars	Palisade	970-464-9288
Shadow Mountain Cellars	Fort Collins	970-493-7345
Stoney Mesa Winery	Cedaredge	970-856-7572
Trail Ridge Winery	Loveland	970-635-0949
Terror Creek Winery	Paonia	970-527-1175

Professional Sports

www.state.co.us/visit_dir/sports.html

I think it must be a state law to be a sports fanatic if you live here. At least in Denver it seems that professional sports is the unofficial religion. Key players instantly qualify for sainthood and the best are elevated to demigod status. When a home team plays well, sports news takes precedent over any national or international event. The good side is, when a team is playing at home it's a perfect time to go shopping or anything else non-sports related. That being said, Denver is one of only eleven cities in the U.S. with professional sports teams in football, baseball, basketball, and hockey. Over 4.5 million fans attended home games during the 1999 baseball, basketball, and football seasons. The Rockies play at Coors Field, which seats 50,000 and the Broncos play at Invesco Field at Mile High, which seats 76,135. Both the Nuggets and Avalanche use the Pepsi Center, which has 19,000 seats.

Baseball:	Colorado Rockies 303-ROCKIES Tickets: 800-388-ROCK
Basketball:	Denver Nuggets, Pepsi Center 303-893-3865
Football:	Denver Broncos Tickets: 720-258-3335
Hockey:	Colorado Avalanche 303-405-1111
Soccer:	Colorado Rapids Tickets: 303-299-1599

Downtown Denver

Six Flags Elitch Gardens, Brewpubs, and Other Activities

When I first arrived in Denver, the state was in an economic bust, the downtown business district had a high vacancy rate and LoDo (lower downtown) was a collection of abandoned and boarded-up warehouses which was not a safe place after dark. How times change.

Today, 7,000 companies employ over 100,000 people downtown. Many commute to work via mass transportation such as RTD's light-rail service that transports an average of 14,000 riders a day with 8 stops in the downtown area. RTD also operates 20 daily bus routes from downtown to Denver International Airport *(www.rtd-denver.com)*. With so many visitor attractions, downtown Denver offers in excess of 4,100 hotel rooms and in 1990, Denver completed the Colorado Convention Center with almost 300,000 square feet of exhibit space, hosting large conventions and meetings throughout the year.

Once nearly forsaken by full-time residents, downtown now boasts new loft projects that are commanding some of the highest prices in the state. Today the area has roughly 9,000 residents who are surrounded by many of the state's largest-drawing attractions and a vibrant nightlife.

Looking for something different to do? Punt Cherry Creek! A punt is a small boat similar to a gondola, and Punt the Creek offers rides through the central Platte Valley, and a dose of Denver history, during the summer. Reservations are recommended; call 303-893-0750 or visit *www.greenwayfoundation.org/puntcreek.html*.

Bike paths: Denver has one of the most extensive network of bicycle paths in the country, and two of them head right into downtown Denver. Both the Cherry Creek and Platte River paths take you to the heart of the city and offer some incredible views of urban wildlife and landscaping along the way. Where the two paths come together is Denver's Confluence Park (the confluence of Cherry Creek and the South Platte rivers.) Built in the 1970s after flooding destroyed most of the area, the area has recently undergone renovation. Visit on any warm day and you'll see cyclists, walkers, roller-bladers, joggers, and even kayakers. New to the area in the last few years is an REI flagship store, where you can test ride mountain bikes, practice your skills on their indoor climbing wall, or try out a kayak.

Larimer Square is a popular destination. This one block long historic area houses a variety of shops (including Ann Taylor and Cry Baby Ranch), bars, restaurants, and the ever-popular coffeehouse, The Market. It's the perfect destination for an after theater or after dinner cup of coffee and dessert. Check local papers for Larimer Square activities including Oktoberfest and summertime concerts.

Skyline Park is one of Denver's best kept secrets, described by Mayor Webb as "…a gem of downtown Denver." Skyline Park is located between 15th and 18th Streets along side Arapahoe Street. It's a favorite of downtown workers on lunchtime breaks and skateboarding youth, and is slated for renovation in 2002.

Denver Pavillions one of the Metro area's newest shopping centers, located on the 16th Street Mall between Tremont and Welton Streets. With more than 50 stores and restaurants, there is plenty to do. Stores include Nike Town, Virgin Megastore, Talbots, and the locally owned Breaking the Mold Candle Company. Restaurants include Denver's only Hard Rock Café, Maggiano's Little Italy, and Corner Bakery Café. Pavillions also has a 15 screen Universal Artists theater with stadium seating. Visit *www.denverpavillions.com* for more details.

Other annual Denver events not to miss include the AT&T LoDo Music Festival, Denver Blues and Bones, and Downtown Denver International Buskerfest. Information on all of these events is at *www.denverfestivals.com* or write to: Performance International, PO Box 6304, Denver CO 80206.

The most popular area is LoDo. *(www.lodoguide.com* or *www.lodo.org)*. Transformed from Skidrow to the hottest spot in the state in a matter of a few years, LoDo offers a dazzling array of activities and attractions. LoDo is home to art galleries and most of Denver's 20 brewpubs that offer a selection of fine, hand-crafted brews and full menus. But if you don't care to dine at a brewpub, over 80 new restaurants have opened in downtown with 30 or so of these in LoDo. In addition, since the opening of Coors Field, sports bars have popped up by the dozens. Any of the visitor's guides available everywhere contain complete information on what to see and do in this neighborhood.

Six Flags Elitch Gardens, covering 70-acres, is located in the Platte River Valley close to downtown. Open only during the summer, Elitch's has over 100 rides including a huge wooden roller coaster which consumed 500,000 board feet of lumber, 14 tons of nails, 32 tons of nuts, washers, and bolts, and 3,450 gallons of paint (just for the first coat). With 6 entertainment stages, 6 restaurants and 84,000 square feet of gardens, you can plan on spending an entire day there. For more information call 303-595-4386 or visit *www.sixflags.com/parks/elitchgardens/home.asp.*

Leisure, Fun, & The Unusual

Concerts, Festivals, Limited-Stakes Gambling,
Hot Springs, Narrow-gauge & Scenic Train Rides,
Golf, and Tennis

Concerts and Festivals

I can't even attempt to list all the festivals and concerts that take place in this state every year. They literally number in the hundreds. In addition to the hundreds of annual events, there are probably an equal number of one-time, unique gatherings occurring across the state at any given time. Many annual events such as the Renaissance Festival in Larkspur or the People's Fair and Taste of Colorado in Denver's Civic Center Park draw hundreds of thousands. On the other hand, during the summer, it's not uncommon to see a few hundred people sprawled out in a small city park listening to free concerts by a variety of artists. But don't worry about missing anything. There is always a special section in most newspapers highlighting upcoming events for every season.

Limited-Stakes Gambling

In 1991 several historic mining towns decided their economic salvation could be found in gambling. They went through the legal necessities and hence, Black Hawk, Central City, and Cripple Creek have become wall-to-wall casinos. Colorado casinos are limited to slots, blackjack, and several varieties of poker with the maximum bet of $5. However, most allow you to play several hands of blackjack at once and there is an ongoing effort to raise the limit to $25. Driving and parking can be a hassle (especially if you plan to have a cocktail or two), so many casinos and private companies offer shuttle service from different areas including several ski resorts. For more information visit *www.blackhawkcolorado.com,* or contact the Central City Public Information Office at 800-542-2999, or the Cripple Creek Chamber of Commerce at 719-689-2169.

Hot Springs

www.soak.net   www.westernhotsprings.com

Long before the advent of hot tubs, the Ute Indians discovered the almost magical powers of the huge hot springs and vapor caves of Glenwood Springs. Today the enormous hot spring-fed pools are still the major attraction in Glenwood Springs (800-221-0098) but certainly not the only one. Almost all the other activities mentioned thus far in this chapter are available in the area. Other towns with natural hot springs include Alamosa, Buena Vista, Durango, Gunnison, Hot Sulphur Springs, Idaho Springs, Nathrop, Ouray, Pagosa Springs, Ridgway, Salida, and Steamboat Springs. Each town's Chamber of Commerce or Visitor's Center will have additional information. *Colorado's Hot Springs*, *Second Edition* by Deborah Frazier profiles more than 30 hot springs, providing directions, maps, and photos. Available from Pruett Publishing, *www.gorp.com/pruett/cohot.asp.*

Narrow Gauge & Scenic Train Rides

The original narrow-gauge railways were built to supply the mines and export their products. Today many of these railways and trains have been restored and offer some of the most spectacular scenery in Colorado. Most run during summer months only so call before making plans:

Buckskin Joe Park and Railway, Cañon City *www.buckskinjoe.com*	719-275-5149
Cripple Creek/Victor Narrow Gauge Railroad *www.ccvngrailroad.webjump.com*	719-689-2640
Cumbres & Toltec Scenic Railroad, Antonito *www.vivanewmgtico.com/railroad.html*	719-376-5483
Durango-Silverton Narrow Gauge Railroad *www.durangotrain.com*	970-247-2733
Georgetown Loop Railroad *www.gtownloop.com*	303-569-2403
Manitou and Pikes Peak Cog Railroad *www.cograilway.com*	719-685-5401

Golf & Tennis

Two of Colorado's most popular outdoor activities are golf and tennis, and the opportunities for both are too numerous to list here.

Don't be surprised to see people outside enjoying both year round.

Golf & Tennis: Colorado Golf Association   303-366-4653
www.golfwww.housecolorado.org/cga

Colorado Tennis Association   303-695-4116
www.coloradotennis.com/cta.html

The Arts & Culture

Theater, Opera, Dance,
Museums, Planetariums, and Zoos

The capital of Florida is Tallahassee, which is not much more than a small cow-town that happens to house the state government. On the other hand, Denver, the capital of Colorado, is also the state's largest city with most of the better locations for the arts & culture. Some of the best are highlighted below.

The Denver Center for the Performing Arts
www.denvercenter.org
303-893-4100
Located in downtown Denver, this complex is the largest performing arts center under one roof in the world. It contains nine theaters with a total of 9,212 seats. This complex hosts over 1,200 performances a year including many Broadway productions.

Denver Art Museum
www.denverartmuseum.org
720-865-5000
Renovated in 1993 and slated for major expansion, the DAM houses the largest Native American collection in the world.

Denver Botanic Gardens
www.botanicgardens.org
720-865-3500
Located in the center of Denver, the DBG is famous for its award-winning Tropical Conservatory with an extensive collection of orchids, numerous water gardens, the Rock Alpine Garden, and a Japanese Garden complete with teahouse.

Children's Museum

www.cmdenver.org

303-443-444

"Denver's best hands-on experience for children and their grownups..." is located in the central Platte Valley near downtown. The museum has playscapes and programs for newborns through eight-year-olds, and many special events throughout the year.

Denver Zoo

www.denverzoo.org

303-376-4800

Birthplace of the world-famous polar bears Klondike and Snow, the zoo is also well known for its large, naturalistic habitats including the new Tropical Discovery. This exhibit is a complete indoor rain forest with an amazing diversity of tropical plants and animals.

Denver Museum of Nature & Science/
Gates Planetarium/IMAX Theater

www.dhnh.org

303-322-7009

All located in City Park under one roof, this complex has been known to draw immense crowds during the summer months or during the premieres of special exhibits. The Museum of Nature & Science is the fifth largest in the country and can take all day to walk through. Gates Planetarium offers regular laser-light concerts and special events while the IMAX Theater, with its four-story-high screen, is an experience not to be missed.

Colorado's Ocean Journey

www.oceanjourney.org

303-561-4550

Located in the central Platte Valley, this world-class aquarium takes visitors on two journeys, one along the Colorado River from the Continental Divide to the Sea of Cortez, and the other through an Indonesian rain forest. Ocean Journey boasts a large variety of fish and other aquatic life, as well as mammals and birds that rely upon the water.

Outside of Denver

Cheyenne Mountain Zoo

www.cmzoo.org

719-633-9925

This zoo in Colorado Springs is the highest in the country at 6,800' and the country's only mountain zoo. It has over 500 animals, including two of only 75 Mexican wolves alive today. The zoo offers a restored vintage carousel, elephant rides and a nature trail, and is home to "Rocky Cliffs," a naturalistic Rocky Mountain goat habitat, and the most prolific breeding giraffe herd in the world, with 154 births since 1954. Zoo admission includes admittance to the Will Rogers Shrine of the Sun, located on the mountain and dedicated to the humorist and aviator.

Central City Opera

www.centralcityopera.org

303-292-6500

Located one hour west of Denver in a historic mining town, this company, the fifth oldest opera company in the United States, typically produces three shows each summer. The Central City Opera House was built in 1878 and was recently refurbished including new seating.

Greeley Philharmonic

970-356-6406

The Greeley Philharmonic is the oldest symphony orchestra west of the Mississippi, founded in 1911. They perform in the Union Colony Civic Center.

Lincoln Center

www.fcgov.com/lctix

970-221-6735

Lincoln Center is the cultural arts center of Fort Collins. It has three indoor galleries, two indoor performance spaces, and an outdoor sculpture and performance garden. The Center is one of Colorado's largest presenters of theatre, dance, music, visual arts, and children's programs.

Dinosaur Journey
www.dinosaurjourney.org
970-858-7282 or 888-DIG-DINO

Dinosaur Journey is located in Fruita, in the heart of dinosaur country where many fossils have been found. The museum, part of the Museum of Western Colorado, includes a working paleontology laboratory, robotic displays of dinosaurs and many other exhibits.

Aspen Ballet Company
www.aspenballet.com
970-925-7175

Aspen Ballet Company is Aspen's resident dance company and is the only professional ballet company based in and touring out of the Colorado Rocky Mountains. ABC performs and conducts educational outreach throughout the Roaring Fork Valley, the state of Colorado, and the western United States, providing access to professional ballet for many who would not otherwise have this opportunity to understand and appreciate the art of dance.

**For more information about arts and
culture around the state, please call:
Colorado Council on the Arts, 303-894-2617**
www.coloarts.state.co.us/

Eight Miles High

10

High-Altitude Living

Health Precautions

Cooking

Gardening

Colorado may be many things, but sea level is not one of them. Colorado's highest point is Mt. Elbert at 14,433 feet. The lowest point is in the valley created by the Arkansas River at 3,350 feet, with 6,800 feet being the average elevation for the state.

High-altitude living can present unique challenges for the inexperienced lowlander. The air is literally thinner, the atmospheric pressure lower, the sun is a mile or two closer, and the seasonal transitions can be unpredictable. The uninitiated can experience medical maladies, culinary catastrophes, and botanical botcheries. All these, however, can be avoided with a little understanding of how the world works at nosebleed altitudes.

Health Precautions

Newcomers to Colorado may experience a variety of medical problems ranging from shortness of breath or a bloody nose to full-blown altitude sickness. To better understand the causes behind these symptoms we need to start with a little basic physics.

Our atmosphere, containing 21% oxygen by volume, has a normal atmospheric pressure of 760 torrs (14.7 pounds per square inch) at sea level. The pressure decreases with an increase in altitude (12.28 lb/sq. inches at 5,000 feet; 10.2 lb/sq. inches at 10,000). The barometric pressure can sustain human life up to altitudes of approximately 15,000 feet. Keeping in mind the average altitude in Colorado is 6,800 feet, consider that the FAA regulations require airliner cabins to be pressurized to the equivalent of 6,000 feet and that military and private pilots are required to use pressurized oxygen while flying at or above 10,000 feet. Many of Colorado's mountain towns approach this limit.

The human body uses oxygen to cleanse toxins and although muscles can function temporarily without oxygen, a build-up of toxins quickly limits metabolic functions. Oxygen deficiency most directly affects brain and eye tissues, and a decrease in barometric pressure can cause minute blood vessels to swell or rupture. Outlined below are the most common aliments experienced by newcomers and tips on avoidance.

Altitude Sickness and Related Symptoms

Nosebleeds

I was born and raised on the Gulf Coast of Florida. Having spent my entire life at sea level, I was perplexed by having unexplained nosebleeds every time I visited my sister in Denver prior to actually moving here. Within hours of arriving, I would begin the ritual of creating crimson Rorschach inkblots on an endless procession of tissues, paper towels and finally, my newly purchased handkerchiefs. After consulting several experts (bartenders, cab drivers and the like), I determined the nosebleeds were caused by both a decrease in atmospheric pressure, causing the nasal blood vessels to swell, and the remarkably low humidity levels of high altitude. There is not much you can do to prevent this occurrence, although, in most cases the symptoms last only 72 hours or so. However, as we are constantly reminded by the over-the-counter drug companies, "If symptoms persist for more than seven days, consult a physician."

Shortness of Breath

During physical exertion at high altitudes, even the most physically fit athletes experience a degree of breathlessness until acclimatization has occurred. Because the air is thinner here, it contains less oxygen by volume than at sea level. Therefore, even heavy breathing can barely compensate for the lack of oxygen until your body has adjusted. Many professional sports teams arrive in Denver several days before a big game just to allow the players time to acclimatize. Likewise, most seasoned skiers spend a couple of days at mid-altitudes before hitting the 12,000-foot slopes. The best advice is to avoid heavy exertion until you have had time to adjust to new heights.

Eye Irritation

Many people experience varying degrees of eye irritation after arriving in Colorado. This is caused by the same factors as nosebleeds. As mentioned above, brain and eye tissue are most quickly affected by a lack of oxygen and the low humidity tends to dry out the sensitive tissues of the eyes. Also, if you happen to be in the Denver metro area, our infamous "brown cloud" of toxins can aggravate this irritation. The quickest relief comes from lubricating eyedrops.

Altitude Sickness

I have met visitors to Colorado who claim to experience altitude sickness as soon as they climb a flight of stairs in Denver (5,280 feet). I also know a few mountain climbers and hikers who can't wait to reach a 14,000-foot peak so they can have a cigarette, seemingly with no ill effects. I'm not sure why some display symptoms in the foothills and others can climb K2 in the Himalayas without oxygen. The one thing I do know is that altitude sickness is most unpleasant and should be taken very seriously.

The condition itself results from a state of acute oxygen deficiency (hypoxia), which can most definitely occur at altitudes above 12,000-13,000 feet. Symptoms of hypoxia include mild intoxication and stimulation of the nervous system, followed by progressive loss of attention and judgment. If left untreated, unconsciousness will occur and a prolonged lack of sufficient oxygen may cause permanent brain damage.

For newcomers, a mild case of altitude sickness can be combined with the aforementioned conditions to produce light-headedness, nausea, headache, excessive yawning and overall "I wish I were dead" symptoms. It should be noted the consumption of alcohol at high altitudes may increase the effects or likelihood of the above. Take it easy the first couple of nights at the ski lodge and if you think you are experiencing altitude sickness, slow down, descend to lower altitudes, and don't be shy about asking for help.

Sunburn

At higher altitudes, concern also needs to be given to nuclear radiation dangers (sunburn). The earth's atmosphere acts as a filter for the sun's harmful ultraviolet rays, but at higher altitudes, the air is actually thinner than at sea level and thus cannot screen out the same amount of radiation. In fact, at 6,000 feet UV rays are approximately 50-60% stronger than at sea level. Simply put, sunburn can occur more quickly and severely at altitude, especially on snow-covered terrain where the sunlight is reflected. Use sunblock during outdoor activities, even when it's cloudy!

High-Altitude Cooking

Without exception, every time my father visits Colorado, whether he is in my kitchen or my sister's, we can count on the failure of his most prized recipes. Immediately following, we wait for the blame to fall on our "damn ovens" or "!#&*? stoves." Having lived in Florida his entire life and having perfected his recipes through thousands of experiments, my dad refuses to accept the fact that further adjustments are necessary at high altitude. I must admit it took me six years of living here to figure out how long to properly boil an egg. Besides, my dad can scream at my oven all he wants as long as I finally get one of his homemade cheesecakes!

In addition to the basic physics covered in the previous section, we discover the source of most culinary catastrophes experienced by visitors and residents alike. Remembering the relationship between altitude and air pressure, add the following facts. As air pressure drops, water boils at lower temperatures. At sea level, water boils at 212°F. Each 500-foot increase in altitude causes a drop of approximately 1°F in the boiling point. At very high altitudes, water boils at a relatively low temperature and since heat, not boiling, cooks food, more time is required for food to reach the desired internal cooking temperature. Additionally, water evaporates much more quickly than at sea level. Below is a quick reference guide for standard adjustments followed by more detailed directions:

Foods cooked by boiling take more time to reach cooking temperature.

Pressure cookers require an adjustment in pressure within the cooker, or a longer period of processing, since they, too, are affected by altitude.

Sea level temperatures for candies and frostings must be lowered as altitude increases to prevent over-concentration of the sugar mixture from excessive evaporation of the water.

Recipes must be adjusted for flour mixtures that contain considerable amounts of sugar and shortening, and are leavened with carbon dioxide gas from baking powder or soda and acid. When air is used for leavening, as in angel food cakes, or steam is used, as in popovers, few adjustments are necessary.

Since deep-frying vaporizes the moisture in foods, and liquids vaporize at lower temperatures in higher altitudes, temperatures used in deep-frying should be reduced in proportion to the rise in altitude.

When baking, use the following adjustments:

- Reduce each teaspoon of baking powder by ¼
- Decrease each cup of sugar by 2-3 tablespoons
- Increase each cup of liquid by 3-4 tablespoons
- For fats, no adjustments are necessary unless substituting, then 1 cup of shortening equals ¾ cup of butter or oil
- Oven temperature should be increased by 25°F
- Reduce by 25°F when using glass pans
- Slightly increase all cooking times
- And for best results at higher altitudes, grease and flour pans or use parchment paper, especially for cakes, and use smaller pans

Rice, Soups, and Vegetables

Rice, soups, and vegetables all require approximately ¼ cup more water for each cup used and 10-15 minutes of additional cooking time. Vegetables such as green cabbage, potatoes, parsnips, rutabagas, squash, sweet potatoes, and turnips require 4-11% more time at 5,000 feet, 20-25% more time at 7,200 feet, and 55-66% more time at 10,000 feet. Cauliflower, onions, beets, and mature carrots may require at least twice the cooking time at 5,000 feet as at sea level.

High altitudes make little or no difference in temperatures for baking vegetables such as squash, potatoes, and sweet potatoes.

Quick cooking conserves flavor and food value in vegetables. Small vegetables may be cooked whole, but larger ones should be cut up for faster cooking. Add vegetables to rapidly boiling water. Bring temperature back to the boiling point rapidly and maintain it at this point throughout the cooking period. Better flavor and color will result from pressure cooking instead of long boiling. Cook only until tender to save both minerals and vitamin C. Because minerals and water-soluble vitamins C and B dissolve, the cooking water should be used.

Frozen Vegetables

Commercial or home-packed frozen vegetables cook faster than similar fresh products. It is usually sufficient to add only a minute or two to the time designated for sea-level cooking. Dense vegetables, such as cauliflower, will require additional cooking time. Keep your own records as to the time required at your altitude. No hard and fast rules can be applied. Peas, snap beans, and mixed vegetables may be cooked without thawing. Solid pack vegetables, such as greens, should be partially thawed before cooking.

Meat

Simmering or braising meat requires additional time at higher altitudes. In general, one-fourth more time may be required at 5,000 feet than at sea level. Use the sea-level timetable for meats cooked in the oven, because oven temperatures are not affected by altitude change.

Eggs

Boiling eggs at different altitudes requires testing. This means timing the eggs and recording the results. Try to use the same covered saucepan for cooking eggs and note your best results. The "three-minute" egg may take up to six minutes or longer, depending on the altitude and cooking conditions. In Denver, I have found it takes exactly eleven minutes after the water comes to a boil to make perfect hard-boiled eggs. The best thing I recommend is a little egg-shaped plastic gizmo you put in with the eggs. It changes color as the eggs go from raw to hard-boiled and has never failed me at any altitude. But since my four-year old destroyed mine, I haven't found another.

Pressure Cookers

These conveniences may reduce some of the problems of vegetable cookery at high altitude. The temperature of the boiling water is raised because of the pressure built up within the sealed container. The boiling water and steam will cook foods faster than open kettle boiling.

At most altitudes, the cooking time of vegetables in the pressure cooker is no more than 1-2 minutes over sea level timing.

Canning

Non-acid fruits and vegetables should be processed in a pressure cooker, with an increase of one pound of pressure for each 2,000 feet elevation. It is also desirable to increase processing time by one minute for each 1,000 feet above sea level, if indicated time is 20 minutes or less, and by two minutes per 1,000 feet when sea level requirement is more than 20 minutes.

High-acid fruits and vegetables may be safely canned in a boiling water bath.

Frostings and Candies

Just as water boils at a temperature below 212°F at higher altitudes, all other liquids also boil at lower temperatures. Boiling causes loss of moisture through evaporation. The lower the boiling point, the sooner evaporation begins. At high altitudes, when sugar mixtures are cooked at the temperatures suggested in sea level recipes, the faster loss of water causes the mixture to become too concentrated.

Depending on the type of sugar mixture being prepared, the results may be "sugary" (where sugar recrystallizes out), or "hard."

To adjust sugar recipes for altitude, reduce the finished temperature. If you use a candy thermometer, test first the temperature at which water boils. While there will be minor changes from day to day, due to weather conditions, the range is usually slight. At 5,000 feet, water boils at approximately 202°F—ten degrees less than at sea level. Thus, correct the finished temperature for the candy or frosting by subtracting the 10°F. Example: If a sea level recipe for creamy fudge gives a finished temperature for syrup at 238°F, at 5,000 feet the thermometer reading would be 228°F. Cold water tests are reliable when a thermometer is not available.

Cakes

At altitudes above 3,500 feet, increase the oven temperature 25°F over the temperature required at sea level. For example, cakes baked at sea level at 350°F should be baked at 375°F at all altitudes over 3,500 feet. The faster baking "sets" the cell framework within the flour mixture and helps to prevent falling.

In high altitudes, flour may become excessively dry unless it is stored in airtight containers. More liquid than the recipe calls for may be necessary to bring a batter or dough to the correct consistency. Some sea level cakes are delicate and defy adjustment to varying altitudes, in which case, choose a new favorite from altitude-tested recipes. Some other recipes are so well balanced that little if any adjustment may be necessary up to 5,000 feet. This is especially true of some of the commercial cake mixes. Keep a written record of any adjustments you make.

Without fat: Air, incorporated in the beaten eggs, is the leavening agent in cakes without fat. The eggs should be beaten less at high altitudes, so less leavening power is given to the batter. In angel food cakes beat the whites just until they form soft peaks; in sponge cakes beat the eggs only until they are slightly thickened.

With fat: The emulsified shortening available on the market today gives good results in altitude baking. Because the emulsifier enables the shortening to tolerate a larger amount of liquid, it is preferable for the "speed-mix" cakes with high sugar ratio.

Flour: All-purpose flour is preferable in most recipes. Sift before measuring and make the following adjustments: 3,500 to 5,000 feet add 1 tablespoon; 5,000 to 6,500 add 2 tablespoons; 6,500 to 8,000 feet add 3 tablespoons; and 8,000 feet and over add 4 tablespoons.

Eggs: An additional egg may be added to prevent the cake from being too dry and too tender.

Leavening: All types of baking powders and baking soda are treated alike in reductions for increased altitudes. When both baking powder and soda are used in a recipe, make the suggested adjustments in both ingredients. Accurate measurement of leavening is of increasing importance as the altitude increases. The leavening adjustments begin at 2,000 feet elevation. The adjustments are: 2,000 to 3,500 feet, decrease by ¼ to ⅓ teaspoon; 3,500 to 5,000 feet, decrease by ⅓ to ½ teaspoon; 5,000 to 6,500 feet, decrease by ½ to ⅔ teaspoon; 6,500 to 8,000 feet, decrease by ⅔ to ¾ teaspoon; and 8,000 feet, and over decrease by ¾ teaspoon.

Commercial Cake Mixes

Buy only mixes that give directions for adjusting to altitudes, and follow directions given. In most instances, this adjustment comes in the addition of a measured amount of flour to the batter, and in a higher oven temperature. If the resulting cake seems excessively tender, an extra egg added to the batter will strengthen the cell structure and make the cake more easily handled. Bake in pan sizes recommended on the package.

Be sure to store commercial and homemade mixes in airtight containers to avoid excessive loss of moisture.

Cookies

No adjustments are usually needed unless cookies are rich, full of chocolate, nuts, Snickers® bars or the like. In this case, reduce the sugar and the baking powder as for cakes. Baking a sample cookie may prevent ruining an entire batch.

Doughnuts

The sea level recipe is usually too rich for use at higher elevations. The dough will absorb too much fat and crack during the frying. As in the case of some cakes, it is suggested that instead of trying to adapt an old favorite recipe to the altitude, you adopt a new favorite that has been developed and tested to conditions.

Yeast Breads

In short, use less flour per cup of liquid when mixing. Yeast breads rise faster at higher altitude and first rise should not be quite double in size. Final rise should be about 20-30 minutes. Increase oven temperature by 25°F and bake for 10-15 minutes less.

Good basic recipes for yeast breads can be relied on at different altitudes. The fermentation of sugar in the bread is faster and bread may overproof unless it is watched. The general preference seems to be to reduce the proofing time rather than the amount of yeast. One adjustment that applies to all leavened foods is to bake the product "faster" at higher temperatures. At altitudes over 3,500 feet increase the baking temperature 25°F over the sea level temperature.

Biscuits

Any standard recipe can be relied on to give good results at varying altitudes. An additional tablespoon of milk to each cup of flour improves the quality of the product.

Muffins

Slightly less sugar can be used than in a standard sea level recipe. Try reducing sugar by one teaspoon if finished product does not meet your standards.

Quick Breads

Where the amount of sugar is low, little adjustment is needed for increased altitude. Slightly more liquid may be desirable if breads seem to dry excessively in baking. Decrease the temperature in proportion to the rise in altitude—two to three degrees for each 1,000 feet of elevation.

The cookbooks listed in Appendix A are highly recommended. Not only do they contain recipes that are the cream of the crop, all have been adjusted for the average altitude in Colorado.

High-Altitude Gardening

Colorado offers unique challenges and conditions for any type of horticulture (gardening, landscaping, and farming). This is especially true for newcomers to the state who are from lower altitudes with more predictable weather patterns and seasonal transitions. Many folks jump right into gardening and landscaping without considering the subtle, yet major differences in Colorado's growing conditions. There was a story on the news about greenhouses and nurseries dealing with an onslaught of irate customers. It seems the vast majority of these customers were newcomers who purchased and then planted their gardens in late March or April. And why not? We were experiencing warm days and mild evenings with plenty of rain to boot. Besides, it was officially spring and they had always planted this time of year. What they didn't expect was a couple of hard freezes in May. These folks showed up at the greenhouse with trunks full of dead plants demanding refunds.

Due to Colorado's altitude, low humidity, intense sunlight, soil conditions, and totally unpredictable weather, one would be well advised to do a little research before breaking out the shovels and potting soil. This section, as with most in this book, is intended to provide only the basics as a guide. The end of this chapter contains a list of additional resources where complete information can be obtained. Let's look at some basics for the Rocky Mountain region:

Humidity: In Florida, like many coastal areas, it is not uncommon to have both temperature and humidity in the 90s. There is a vast difference between that and temperatures in the 90s with humidity in the teens. Combined with intense sunlight and prolonged heat waves, the evaporation rate of water is tremendous. It is not uncommon for evaporation rates in parts of Colorado to exceed 50 inches of water per year while receiving only 10-20 inches from precipitation. The end result is increased need for supplemental irrigation. In Denver, the average noon humidity during January is 43% while in July it averages 36%.

Sunlight: The effects of sunlight are intensified at higher altitudes. This holds true everywhere, but because of Colorado's latitude and geography, we also get about three additional hours of sunlight per day compared to cloudier regions and on the average have 300 days of sunshine per year. All this combined means many plants that require full sun elsewhere may grow very well in partial shade here.

Growing Seasons: Sheridan, Wyoming has a frost-free growing season of 123 days (May 21-Oct 21), Salt Lake City, Utah's is 202 days (Apr 12-Nov 1), Denver's is 159 days (May 6-Oct 12). There are parts of the country where by mid-May you would be almost ready to harvest your first crop of vegetables. If you came from one of those areas it is hard to adjust to having to wait until May 6th or later to even safely plant. Please take note: 159 days is the season for Denver, not Colorado! Because of the great diversity in altitudes and weather conditions, parts of Colorado have longer seasons and many places have much shorter ones. Check with your local experts before planting. If you simply can't wait until mid-May I highly recommend using "walls-of-water." This product is a teepee-shaped, double-walled, multi-chambered vinyl contraption that you fill with water and place around new plantings. The water traps the heat of sunlight during the day and slowly releases it at night when it gets cold. The manufacturer claims it can jump-start your growing season by six weeks and I have personally had good luck with them. Check with a local garden shop for availability.

Temperature Extremes: Having grown up in Florida, I was accustomed to very mild temperature fluctuations. The temperature and humidity usually ranged from unbearably hot and sticky to almost unbearably hot and sticky. Allowing for the slight change in seasons, the vegetation in Florida knew what to expect. Not so in Colorado! Temperature fluctuations can be drastic and sudden, regardless of season. During spring, we can have stretches of hot weather lasting days or weeks immediately followed by a week of snow and hard freezes. In winter, the temperature can suddenly rise (in a matter of minutes) from below freezing to almost t-shirt weather due to Chinook winds, only to drop again by day's end. This kind of fluctuation is very stressful on many types of plants (not to mention most people). On average, the daily January temperatures in Denver range from 15-42°F, while in July they range from 57-88°F. These are averages, not examples of the very common extremes experienced.

Micro-Climates: Not only do different weather conditions occur throughout various parts of Colorado due to everything discussed so far, but you can also experience very different growing conditions within the boundaries of your own yard. You can have desert-like conditions along a south wall and "Aspen meadow" conditions on the north. The differences between the south and north side of the same house can be equivalent to several thousand feet of mountain elevation change or several thousand miles of latitude change on the plains.

Xeriscape: Xeriscape! Xeriscape! Xeriscape! Simply defined Xeriscape means water-wise gardening. 40-60% percent of clear, cool, drinking water supplied to cities throughout the region is used for landscape irrigation! A Xeriscape approach to landscaping can result in a 50% reduction of needed irrigation. Additional benefits are lower initial cost per square foot and greatly reduced maintenance needs. If done properly, most Xeriscape yards not only save a tremendous amount of water, they also give the yard's owners a lot more time to enjoy other aspects of Colorado's outdoors. The *Xeriscape Flower Gardener* by Jim Knopf is an excellent resource for learning about all the benefits of this environmentally friendly art.

Additional Resources

High-Altitude Recipes
Crème de Colorado Cookbook, C&C Publications
Colorado Cache Cookbook, C&C Publications
Cooking with Colorado's Greatest Chefs, Westcliffe Publishers, Inc.
See publishers listing in Appendix A for details

High-Altitude Gardening
The Xeriscape Flower Gardener: A Waterwise Guide for the Rocky Mountain Region, Johnson Books. See Appendix A.
Successful Gardening for Colorado and the Rocky Mountain Plant Guide
Both available from most nurseries and greenhouses.

Additional information available from:

Colorado Nursery Association 303-758-6672
Associated Landscape Contractors of Colorado, Inc. . 303-830-3781
Colorado Greenhouse Growers 720-887-1926

Public Xeriscape Demonstration Areas:

City of Arvada Parks Department 303-420-0984
Career Enrichment Park, Westminster 303-428-2600
Denver Water Department 303-628-6340
Denver Botanic Gardens 303-331-4000
Longmont Public Library 303-651-8470
Oxley Homestead, Golden 303-526-9463
Fort Collins Xeriscape Demonstration Garden 970-221-6877

Denver Botanic Gardens: DBG offers numerous classes, instruction, and advice about high-altitude gardening and Xeriscape. In addition, they have a complete library with over a dozen books on Xeriscape and their staff includes botanists, horticulturists, landscapers, and professional gardeners.

So Far Away

GETTING FROM THERE TO HERE

Moving Tips

Moving With Children

Temporary Housing/
Relocation Services

We've all been there. The endless lists, the sleepless nights (going over the lists), the packing, the loading, the cleaning, the trip, the unloading and unpacking, the utilities, new bank accounts, etc. Unplanned and unprepared, a major move can put the best of us down for the count. Hopefully, this chapter will assist you in making the most of your next move.

Moving Tips

Moving across town or across the country can be easier if you break it down into three phases: The Preparation Phase, The Work Phase, and The Settling-in Phase. Use the tips below to make a checklist for each.

The Preparation Phase

One Month Prior To Moving: Make all reservations and arrangements for truck rentals or moving companies (see moving company tips below). Start acquiring necessary supplies such as boxes, tape, labels, etc. If you plan to drive to your new home, plan the travel route. Start a special file to save all moving receipts; many moving costs may be tax-deductible. Develop your plan for packing (see Work Phase below). Make sure important records (legal, insurance, and medical) are in a safe and accessible place. Notify the Post Office of your new address.

Moving Company Tips: The Better Business Bureau reports a 38% increase in complaints about moving companies since 1990. *Money* magazine offers the following tips on how to protect yourself from scams and incompetence:

Get a binding estimate before the move and make sure the amount is written into the contract. It costs about $3,500 to move the contents of a three-bedroom house to a different state.

Before signing an agreement, inquire about the company with the local BBB and state or local consumer affairs department. The Interstate Commerce Commission allows interstate movers to give you only 60 cents per pound for lost or damaged goods. To cover potential damage, check your existing homeowner's or renter's policy and buy extra coverage if necessary.

Ask about expected gratuities before hiring and write them into the contract. If your mover demands more money anyway and you're stuck, consider paying but write your protest on the bill as evidence. Specify in the contract that the company will be held responsible for damage to items you packed.

Storage Tips: If you plan to have your possessions in storage for more than a few days, find out how the moving company plans to do this. It is common for companies simply to park the semi-trailer in their lot and leave it until you are ready. In Colorado this can be the wrong thing to do. Due to our intense sunshine, during the summer temperatures inside the trailer can exceed 130° for extended periods. That, combined with our low humidity can play havoc with furniture finishes, glue joints, framed art, music collections, and the like. During the winter, temperatures inside a trailer can fluctuate 50-80° between day and night. Excessive expanding and contracting can also damage furniture. Find another method of storage if possible or get written guarantees about damage from the companies who will, of course, deny any of the above is true.

Two Weeks Prior To Moving: Notify all utility companies of your move and sign up for necessary services at your new location. Completely service your car if it will be used or driven. Start recruiting help for the move (this is the test of true friendship). Confirm all reservations made previously. Confirm payment requirements from any moving companies. Make arrangements to close or transfer all bank accounts.

The Work Phase

Packing: Have all packing supplies in one place (boxes, bubble wrap, marking pens, tape measure, furniture pads, rope, tools and knife, tape and scissors). Label boxes with the contents and the room where they belong in your new home. Number each box and keep a list of the contents. Make sure fragile items are clearly marked. Designate certain boxes or suitcases for personal items you'll need during the move. Keep a medical kit handy.

Cleaning: Cleaning is 90% planning and 10% effort, so make a plan! Start with all necessary cleaning supplies so your momentum isn't broken. Do a preliminary job on the bathroom and kitchen, but expect them to be used up until the last time you close the door to your old home. It's easy to become immersed in your work so keep child safety rules in mind around cleaning supplies.

The Settling-In Phase

Physical: Make sure your new home—especially the bathroom and kitchen—is perfectly clean (you'll never go back and do it right once they are full of stuff). Check off every numbered box from your list as it comes into the house. The first box in should be your tool kit of unpacking supplies (knife, tape measure, large trash bags, and necessary tools for reassembly). The second thing in should be a radio or portable stereo. Get all boxes and used packing out of the house as soon as they are emptied.

Emotional: The following suggestion applies to all phases of moving: without fail, schedule some time to relax and enjoy yourself (a movie, a bike ride, pizza and wine on the balcony). Allow yourself to grieve the loss of moving (friends, family, favorite places). Look forward to meeting new friends, starting your new job, and finding new favorite places. Accept the fact moving is a major thing. Take it easy, you don't have to adjust to everything at once.

Moving With Children

If you're a parent you already know children do not think, feel, or react as adults. What may seem like a logical, well-planned, checklisted sequence of events to you may be traumatic for children. While tending to the million details of a move, it's easy to overlook how it might affect your children. *Moving With Children* is an outstanding book published by Gylantic Publishing, covering every aspect of the moving process in general, and offering the following information.

Preparation Phase Stress Factors For Children: The unpredictability of the moving schedule, the presence of strangers in the house, the disruption of familiar family routines and activities, reduced time and attention and possible periods of separation from parents, unaccustomed travel to visit a new neighborhood or community prior to the move and the process of having to break the news and answer questions about the move to friends, classmates, and neighbors.

Work Phase Stress Factors For Children: The disruption of a comfortable family structure, the physical demands of packing and cleaning, the necessity of giving away or leaving behind familiar belongings, physically leaving friends and neighbors, the excitement, disruption and physical labor of moving day and the possible rigors of traveling to a new house.

Settling-In Phase Stress Factors For Children: The possible delay, loss of or damage to possessions during the move; the physical demands of unpacking, storing and decorating, the work of making home comfortable, the reestablishment of familiar family routines and schedules, the absence of a familiar support group, the process of becoming acquainted with a new community and meeting new neighbors.

If ignored or improperly handled, the tremendous amount of

stress placed on children during a move can result in a wide range of emotional and physical symptoms. If you are planning a family move and don't have a Ph.D. in child psychology, I recommend the book mentioned above.

Temporary Housing/ Relocation Services

If you find yourself here before your belongings or will have an extended wait while your new home is finished, you will need temporary housing. There are numerous companies in Colorado that specialize in matching people with apartments, condos, or rental homes. Most of their clients are making a permanent move but these companies also work with newcomers who need temporary housing for one month, six months or longer. Often there is little or no cost to you because costs are paid by the landlord or management company. If you are not already working through a relocation service, contact one of the companies below:

Relocation Concepts (Individual)	Denver	303-695-0971
Relocation Resources (Corporate)	Denver	303-297-0500

New Kid In Town

RESOURCES

PHONE LISTS

Index of phone lists elsewhere in this book

	Page Number
Chambers of Commerce	176
Colorado Library & Information Network	173
Colorado State Parks	189
Colorado Wineries and Vineyards	197
Corporate and Private Libraries	74
County Clerks	97
Driver's License Offices	110
Government Departments / Agencies	26-49
Governor's Job Training Offices	175
Institutions of Higher Education	70
National Forests	187
National Monuments	187
School Districts	58
Ski Areas / Snow Reports	192
Small Business Development Centers	172
Work Force Centers	174

Area Codes and Prefixes

As with many other states, Colorado is rapidly adding new area codes and prefixes. Please consult a Qwest phone book or *www.qwestdex.com* for current information. Local numbers within the 303 and 720 prefix area require ten-digit dialing.

Fraternal Organizations

Colorado is home many chapters of fraternal organizations. The list below is arranged by organization name first, followed by the city and phone number.

AF & AM Hayden Valley Lodge	Hayden	970-276-3433
AF & AM Lodge	Lafayette	303-665-6876
Ahepa Denver Chapter 145	Denver	303-321-5715
Al Kaly Temple	Pueblo	719-544-0658
American Legion State HQ	Denver	303-477-1655
American Legion	Byers	303-822-9562
American Legion	Durango	970-247-1590
American Legion	Florence	719-784-6125
American Legion	Holyoke	970-854-3486
American Legion	Pagosa Springs	970-264-4884
Aurora Lodge # 156	Aurora	303-366-0402
Beta Theta Pi Fraternity	Golden	303-279-3081
Bethany Chapter 148 OES	Nucla	970-864-2195
B'nai B'rith Lodge 171	Denver	303-393-7358
Boys & Girls Club-Metro Denver	Ward	303-443-7394
Brighton K Of C Council	Brighton	303-659-0661
Carpenters Local No. 1068	Denver	303-355-4860
Civitan Club Colorado Springs	Colorado Springs	719-574-9004
Colorado Masons Benevolent Fnd	Englewood	303-290-8544
Colorado Springs Shrine Club	Colorado Springs	719-632-3881
Colorado State Grange Scholarship	Aurora	303-237-9655
Denver Consistory	Denver	303-861-4261
Denver Lodge 5 AF & AM	Denver	303-534-0939
Disabled American Veterans	Colorado Springs	719-392-7589
Eagle Lodge Inc.	Denver	303-393-7773
Eagle's Fraternal Order	Denver	303-820-2063
Edgewater Lodge AF & AM	Denver	303-233-0247

El Jebel Shrine Office	Denver	303-455-3470
Elks Lodge	Akron	970-345-2294
Elks Lodge	Alamosa	719-589-2362
Elks Lodge	Arvada	303-424-2278
Elks Lodge	Aspen	970-925-3516
Elks Lodge	Aurora	303-360-7204
Elks Lodge	Boulder	303-442-5003
Elks Lodge	Cañon City	719-275-1880
Elks Lodge	Central City	303-582-5181
Elks Lodge	Colorado Springs	719-633-1727
Elks Lodge	Cortez	970-565-3557
Elks Lodge	Craig	970-824-3557
Elks Lodge	Creede	719-658-2661
Elks Lodge	Cripple Creek	719-689-2625
Elks Lodge	Deer Trail	303-769-4480
Elks Lodge	Delta	970-874-3624
Elks Lodge	Denver	303-455-3557
Elks Lodge	Denver	303-238-1307
Elks Lodge	Durango	970-247-2296
Elks Lodge	Englewood	303-781-0257
Elks Lodge	Evergreen	303-674-5591
Elks Lodge	Florence	719-784-3892
Elks Lodge	Fort Collins	970-493-3777
Elks Lodge	Fort Morgan	970-867-6711
Elks Lodge	Glenwood Springs	970-945-2286
Elks Lodge	Grand Junction	970-243-0675
Elks Lodge	Gunnison	970-641-1527
Elks Lodge	Hotchkiss	970-872-3355
Elks Lodge	Idaho Springs	303-567-9996
Elks Lodge	Lamar	719-336-7886
Elks Lodge	Leadville	719-486-0236
Elks Lodge	Littleton	303-794-1811
Elks Lodge	Longmont	303-776-1055
Elks Lodge	Louisville	303-666-8600
Elks Lodge	Monte Vista	719-852-2456
Elks Lodge	Montrose	970-249-4852
Elks Lodge	Northglenn	303-452-1644
Elks Lodge	Ouray	970-325-4510

Fraternal Organizations

Elks Lodge	Pueblo	719-544-5922
Elks Lodge	Rangely	970-675-8533
Elks Lodge	Rifle	970-625-2195
Elks Lodge	Salida	719-539-6976
Elks Lodge	Silverthorne	970-468-2561
Elks Lodge	Sterling	970-522-0515
Elks Lodge	Telluride	970-728-6362
Elks Lodge	Trinidad	719-846-2980
Elks Lodge	Victor	719-689-2974
Elks Lodge	Walsenburg	719-738-1210
Elks Lodge	Westminster	303-429-2227
Elks Lodge	Wray	970-332-4907
Elks Lodge # 309	Colorado Springs	719-633-1727
Elks Lodge 1586	Brighton	303-659-2802
Elks Lodge 809	Greeley	970-330-3557
Englewood Shrine Club	Englewood	303-789-0272
Epsilon Sigma Alpha Intl.	Fort Collins	970-223-2824
Filipino-America Community	Edgewater	303-233-6817
Footprinters	Denver	303-806-9470
Fraternal Order Of Eagles	Arvada	303-433-8035
Fraternal Order Of Eagles	Aspen	970-925-9912
Fraternal Order Of Eagles	Aurora	303-695-0673
Fraternal Order Of Eagles	Broomfield	303-466-4928
Fraternal Order Of Eagles	Castle Rock	303-688-3947
Fraternal Order Of Eagles	Colorado Springs	719-596-2207
Fraternal Order Of Eagles	Commerce City	303-288-0861
Fraternal Order Of Eagles	Englewood	303-762-8107
Fraternal Order Of Eagles	Federal Heights	303-426-4665
Fraternal Order Of Eagles	Glenwood Springs	970-945-8333
Fraternal Order Of Eagles	Grand Junction	970-243-6454
Fraternal Order Of Eagles	La Salle	970-284-6880
Fraternal Order Of Eagles	Lamar	719-336-3780
Fraternal Order Of Eagles	Pueblo	719-564-3695
Fraternal Order Of Eagles	Pueblo	719-564-5715
Fraternal Order Of Eagles	Walsenburg	719-738-1900
Fraternal Order Of Eagles 179	Trinidad	719-846-3821
Fraternal Order Of Eagles 3226	Denver	303-427-2236
Fraternal Order Of Police	Arvada	303-940-9332

Fraternal Order Of Police	Brighton	303-450-1514
Fraternal Order Of Police	Colorado Springs	719-633-4889
Fraternal Order Of Police	Denver	303-477-1863
Fraternal Order Of Police	Fort Collins	970-204-0256
Fraternal Order Of Police	Loveland	970-669-3660
Friendship Lodge 185 AF & AM	Denver	303-934-9730
Garden Home Grange Hall	Denver	303-934-1372
George Washington Lodge 161	Denver	303-715-3712
Grand Chapter Of Colorado	Denver	303-759-5936
Grand Lodge	Colorado Springs	719-471-9587
Grandview Grange	Littleton	303-798-7433
Harmony Lodge 61 AF & AM	Denver	303-534-9918
Hop Sing Assoc	Denver	303-377-2265
Independent Order Of Foresters	Lakewood	303-988-2242
IOFF	Grand Junction	970-245-9576
IOFF Hall	Delta	970-874-4588
Jaycee's	Boulder	303-443-1030
Knights Of Columbus	Arvada	303-423-4603
Knights Of Columbus	Aurora	303-366-6314
Knights Of Columbus	Burlington	719-346-7600
Knights Of Columbus	Cañon City	719-275-1412
Knights Of Columbus	Cheyenne Wells	719-767-5353
Knights Of Columbus	Colorado Springs	719-392-9928
Knights Of Columbus	Colorado Springs	719-637-8052
Knights Of Columbus	Commerce City	303-287-0945
Knights Of Columbus	Denver	303-861-2419
Knights Of Columbus	Denver	303-934-9606
Knights Of Columbus	Englewood	303-789-0132
Knights Of Columbus	Fort Collins	970-484-1881
Knights Of Columbus	Grand Junction	970-242-9746
Knights Of Columbus	Greeley	970-352-9774
Knights Of Columbus	La Junta	719-384-2120
Knights Of Columbus	Lakewood	303-238-8740
Knights Of Columbus	Lamar	719-336-3591
Knights Of Columbus	Northglenn	303-460-8407
Knights Of Columbus	Pueblo	719-564-9620
Knights Of Columbus	Sterling	970-522-0857
Knights Of Columbus	Trinidad	719-846-0450

Fraternal Organizations

Knights Of Pythias Inc.	Denver	303-936-9771
Lambda Chi Alpha	Fort Collins	970-482-4096
Loyal Order Of Moose	Aurora	303-366-2061
Loyal Order Of Moose	Cañon City	719-275-1790
Loyal Order Of Moose	Colorado Springs	719-632-2914
Loyal Order Of Moose	Denver	303-936-6869
Loyal Order Of Moose	Evans	970-339-5715
Loyal Order Of Moose	Fort Collins	970-493-3056
Loyal Order Of Moose	Fort Lupton	303-857-4574
Loyal Order Of Moose	Grand Junction	970-242-4754
Loyal Order Of Moose	Longmont	303-776-4911
Loyal Order Of Moose	Loveland	970-667-2525
Loyal Order Of Moose	Northglenn	303-457-3391
Loyal Order Of Moose	Nucla	970-864-7610
Masonic Lodge	Akron	970-345-6522
Masonic Lodge	Alamosa	719-589-2361
Masonic Lodge	Arvada	303-424-9941
Masonic Lodge	Boulder	303-449-2711
Masonic Lodge	Brighton	303-659-3484
Masonic Lodge	Brush	970-842-2503
Masonic Lodge	Cañon City	719-275-3818
Masonic Lodge	Castle Rock	303-688-4131
Masonic Lodge	Cedaredge	970-856-3062
Masonic Lodge	Central City	303-582-5525
Masonic Lodge	Colorado Springs	719-632-8994
Masonic Lodge	Colorado Springs	719-635-1174
Masonic Lodge	Del Norte	719-657-3635
Masonic Lodge	Denver	303-778-1039
Masonic Lodge	Denver	303-778-9787
Masonic Lodge	Denver	303-534-7424
Masonic Lodge	Durango	970-259-5416
Masonic Lodge	Estes Park	970-586-8097
Masonic Lodge	Fort Collins	970-493-0888
Masonic Lodge	Fort Morgan	970-867-7534
Masonic Lodge	Georgetown	303-569-2811
Masonic Lodge	Glenwood Springs	970-945-5013
Masonic Lodge	Golden	303-279-9902
Masonic Lodge	Grand Junction	970-242-0120

Masonic Lodge	Greeley	970-353-1776
Masonic Lodge	Gunnison	970-641-1406
Masonic Lodge	Idaho Springs	303-567-2811
Masonic Lodge	La Junta	719-384-2271
Masonic Lodge	Lamar	719-336-5331
Masonic Lodge	Littleton	303-794-1771
Masonic Lodge	Longmont	303-776-3515
Masonic Lodge	Mancos	970-533-7721
Masonic Lodge	Manitou Springs	719-685-5304
Masonic Lodge	Monte Vista	719-852-3913
Masonic Lodge	Montrose	970-249-3943
Masonic Lodge	Monument	719-488-3785
Masonic Lodge	Pueblo	719-544-1056
Masonic Lodge	Rocky Ford	719-254-3861
Masonic Lodge	Salida	719-539-2708
Masonic Lodge	Springfield	719-523-6531
Masonic Lodge	Steamboat Spgs	970-879-0062
Masonic Lodge	Sterling	970-522-2366
Masonic Lodge	Woodland Park	719-687-2732
Masonic Lodge	Wray	970-332-4939
Masonic Temple	Leadville	719-486-1775
Montezuma Lodge	Dolores	970-882-7945
NCOA	Colorado Springs	719-576-0757
Odd Fellows	Boulder	303-442-5669
Odd Fellows 13	Golden	303-279-1272
Odd Fellows 145	Arvada	303-424-5815
Odd Fellows 48	Durango	970-247-8420
Odd Fellows Grand Lodge	Cañon City	719-275-1606
Odd Fellows Hall	Fort Lupton	303-857-2970
Odd Fellows Hall	Greeley	970-353-0061
Odd Fellows Hall	Sterling	970-522-3028
Odd Fellows Hall IOOF	Colorado Springs	719-633-4838
Odd Fellows Hall IOOF	Colorado Springs	719-633-2002
Odd Fellows Lodge	Longmont	303-776-4588
Odd Fellows Lodge	Loveland	970-667-4584
Odd Fellows Union Lodge 1	Arvada	303-427-0412
Phi Delta Theta Fraternity	Fort Collins	970-493-7511
Phi Kappa Tau Fraternity	Fort Collins	970-484-8266

Pueblo Shrine Club	Pueblo West	719-547-3184
Rebekah Lodge	Craig	970-824-4829
Rebekah's	Cedaredge	970-856-7558
Rosicrucian Order Amorc	Edgewater	303-985-8602
Schlaraffia Denvera	Denver	303-455-1783
Scottish Rite Bodies AAS	Grand Junction	970-245-2277
Scottish Rite Temple	Pueblo	719-544-5697
Silver State Lodge 95 AF & AM	Pueblo	719-545-1412
Sons Of Norway	Lakewood	303-232-1700
Sons Of Norway Fjellheim Lodge	Colorado Springs	719-574-3717
South Denver Lodge 93	Denver	303-777-9809
SPMDTU	Antonito	719-376-5470
Union Lodge 7 Af & Am	Denver	303-534-5051
Veterans Of Foreign Wars	Broomfield	303-460-9557
Veterans Of Foreign Wars	Colorado Springs	719-632-2776
Veterans Of Foreign Wars	Grand Junction	970-257-7745
Veterans Of Foreign Wars	Las Animas	719-456-2822
Veterans Of Foreign Wars	Ordway	719-267-4735
Veterans Of Foreign Wars	Platteville	970-785-9989
Veterans Of Foreign Wars	Steamboat Springs	970-879-9959
Westminster Grange Hall	Westminster	303-428-3191
Westminster Lodge 176	Westminster	303-429-9895

Daily/Weekly Newspapers

www.hometownnews.com/co.htm, www.n-net.com/co.

When my wife and I were looking for property in Colorado we always picked up a copy of the local paper. This offers the opportunity to get a feel for the area. Many of these publications will be happy to mail you a copy of their most recent issue. While I have tried to be as thorough as possible, there are several publications (bargain classifieds, thrifty shopping guides, etc.) that are not shown here.

Akron News Reporter	Akron	970-345-2296
Valley Courier *www.alamosanews.com*	Alamosa	719-589-2553
Allenspark Wind	Allenspark	303-747-0232
Arvada Sentinel Newspaper	Arvada	303-425-8755

Aspen Daily News www.*aspendailynews.com*	Aspen	970-925-2220
Aspen Times www.*aspentimes.com* www.*aspenalive.com*	Aspen	970-925-3414
Aurora Sentinel *aurorasentinel.com*	Aurora	303-750-7555
Vail Daily Ltd *www.vaildaily.com*	Avon	970-949-0555
Vail Valley Times	Avon	970-949-4402
Fairplay Flume *www.theflume.com*	Bailey	303-838-2108
Park County Republican *www.theflume.com*	Bailey	303-838-4423
Pine River Times Inc *www.pinerivertimes.com*	Bayfield	970-884-2331
Berthoud Recorder Newspaper	Berthoud	970-532-3715
Boulder County Business Report *www.bcbr.com*	Boulder	303-440-4952 or 4950
Boulder County Kids Newspaper	Boulder	303-939-8767
Boulder Weekly *www.boulderweekly.com*	Boulder	303-494-5511
Daily Camera *www.bouldernews.com*	Boulder	303-442-1202
Brush News Tribune	Brush	970-842-5516
Chaffee County Times *www.peaksnewsnet.com*	Buena Vista	719-395-8621
Burlington Record	Burlington	719-346-5381
Ranchland News	Calhan	719-347-2366
Daily Record & Marketplace www.*canoncitydailyrecord.com*	Cañon City	719-275-7565
Valley Journal Inc	Carbondale	970-963-3211
Castle Rock Chronicle	Castle Rock	303-841-5497
Douglas County News-Press *www.dcnewspress.com*	Castle Rock	303-688-3128

Douglas County Trail	Castle Rock	303-660-2360
Mountain Valley News	Cedaredge	970-856-7499
Greenhorn Valley News Inc	Colorado City	719-676-3304
Academy Spirit	Colorado Springs	719-333-2990
Cheyenne Edition	Colorado Springs	719-578-5112
Colorado Springs Business Journal www.csbj.com	Colorado Springs	719-634-5905
Gazette Telegraph www.gazette.com	Colorado Springs	719-632-5511
Independent News Weekly www.csindy.com	Colorado Springs	719-577-4545
Commerce City Beacon	Commerce City	303-289-4600
Commerce City Express	Commerce City	303-288-7987
Cortez Journal www.cortezjournal.com	Cortez	970-565-8527
Cortez Sentinel	Cortez	970-565-8574
Craig Daily Press www.craigdailypress.com	Craig	970-824-7031
Crested Butte Chronicle & Pilot	Crested Butte	970-349-6114
Tri-County Tribune	Deer Trail	303-769-4646
Del Norte Prospector	Del Norte	719-852-3531
Delta County Independent www.DCI-press.com	Delta	970-874-4421
Colorado Real Estate Journal	Denver	303-623-1148
Denver Business Journal http://denver.bcentral.com/denver	Denver	303-837-3500
Denver Post www.denverpost.com	Denver	303-820-1010
Denver Rocky Mountain News www.rockymountainnews.com	Denver	303-892-5000
Denver Weekly News	Denver	303-292-5158
Denver Daily News	Denver	303-443-1492
Newspapers & Technology www.newsandtech.com	Denver	303-575-9595

Northern Miner *www.northernminer.com*	Denver	303-607-0853
Wall Street Journal *www.wsj.com*	Denver	303-778-6615
Westword *www.westword.com*	Denver	303-296-7744
Woman's Business News	Denver	303-756-0780
Dolores Star	Dolores	970-882-4486
Dove Creek Press	Dove Creek	970-677-2214
Kiowa County Press *www.kiowacountypress.com*	Eads	719-438-5352
Eagle Valley Enterprise *www.searchcolorado.com/eagle*	Eagle	970-328-6656
North Weld Herald Newspaper	Eaton	970-454-3466
Estes Park Trail Gazette *www.eptrail.com*	Estes Park	970-586-3356
Canyon Courier *www.evergreenco.com/canyoncourier*	Evergreen	303-674-5534
Colorado Serenity	Evergreen	303-670-5448
Flagler News	Flagler	719-765-4466
Florence Citizen *www.angelfire.com/co2/florence*	Florence	719-784-6383
Fort Collins Coloradoan *www.coloradoan.com*	Fort Collins	970-493-6397
Fort Morgan Times	Fort Morgan	970-867-5651
El Paso County News	Fountain	719-382-5611
Fountain Valley News	Fountain	719-382-5611
Fowler Tribune	Fowler	719-263-5311
Summit Daily News *www.summitdaily.com*	Frisco	970-668-3998
Glenwood Post *www.postindependent.com*	Glenwood Springs	970-945-8515
Golden Transcript *www.goldentranscript.com*	Golden	303-279-5541
Daily Tribune *www.grandcountynews.com*	Granby	970-887-3334

Grand Lake Prospector *www.grandcountynews.com*	Granby	970-887-3334
Daily Sentinel *www.gjsentinel.com*	Grand Junction	970-242-5050
Grand Valley Business Times	Grand Junction	970-241-0177
Greeley Tribune *www.greeleytrib.com*	Greeley	970-352-0211
Rocky Mountain News	Greeley	970-353-0160
Gunnison-Country Times *www.gunnisontimes.com*	Gunnison	970-641-1414
Haxtun Herald *www.hfherald.com*	Haxtun	970-774-6118
Holyoke Enterprise *www.holyokecolorado.com*	Holyoke	970-854-2811
Clear Creek Courant *www.clearcreekcourant.com*	Idaho Springs	303-567-4491
Mountain Messenger	Idaho Springs	303-567-9623
Johnstown Breeze	Johnstown	970-587-4525
Julesburg Advocate	Julesburg	970-474-3388
Middle Park Times *www.grandcountynews.com/* *middleparktimes*	Kremmling	970-724-3350
Conejos County Citizen *www.conejoscountycitizen.com*	La Jara	719-274-4192
Ag Journal *www.agjournalonline.com*	La Junta	719-384-8121
La Junta Tribune-Democrat *www.zwire.com/news*	La Junta	719-384-4475
Lafayette News	Lafayette	303-665-6515
Louisville Times *www.coloradohometown.com/* *louisville/louisville.html*	Louisville	303-666-6576
Lake City Silver World	Lake City	970-944-2515
Lamar Daily News	Lamar	719-336-2266
North Forty News *www.northfortynews.com*	Laporte	970-221-0213

Herald Democrat *www.leadvilleherald.com*	Leadville	719-486-0641
Limon Leader	Limon	719-775-2064
Englewood Herald	Littleton	303-794-7877
Highlands Ranch Herald *www.southmetronews.com*	Littleton	303-794-7877
Littleton Independent *www.southmetronews.com*	Littleton	303-794-7877
The Voice	Littleton	303-794-7877
Longmont Daily Times-Call *www.longmontfyi.com*	Longmont	303-776-2244
Loveland Daily Reporter-Herald *www.lovelandfyi.com*	Loveland	970-669-5050
Rocky Mountain News Agency	Loveland	970-667-3416
Lyons Recorder *www.hometownusa.com/lyons*	Lyons	303-823-6625
Mancos Times Tribune	Mancos	970-533-7766
Pikes Peak Journal	Manitou Springs	719-685-0180
Meeker Herald	Meeker	970-878-4017
Monte Vista Journal *www.montevistajournal.com*	Monte Vista	719-852-3531
Daily Press *www.montrosepress.com*	Montrose	970-249-3444
Daily Sentinel News Bureau	Montrose	970-249-5573
Tri-Lakes Tribune	Monument	719-481-3423
Mountain Ear *www.mountainear.com*	Nederland	303-258-7075
Norwood Post *www.hometownusa.com/co/ news/norwood*	Norwood	970-327-4094
Ouray County Plain Dealer	Ouray	970-325-4412
Pagosa Springs Sun *www.websites.pagosasprings. net/pagosaspringssun/home*	Pagosa Springs	970-264-2101
Palisade Tribune	Palisade	970-464-5614

High Country News *www.hcn.org*	Paonia	970-527-4898
North Fork Times *www.paonia.com/news*	Paonia	970-527-4339
Weekly News Chronicle	Parker	303-841-5497
Chieftain & Star Journal *www.chieftain.com*	Pueblo	719-544-3520
Colorado Tribune	Pueblo	719-561-4008
Pueblo Business Journal	Pueblo	719-542-3616
Pueblo West Horizon	Pueblo	719-544-3834
Pueblo West View	Pueblo West	719-547-9606
Rangely Times	Rangely	970-675-8554
Citizen Telegram	Rifle	970-625-3628
Daily Sentinel	Rifle	970-625-9271
Daily Gazette	Rocky Ford	719-254-3351
Saguache Crescent	Saguache	719-655-2620
Mountain Mail Newspaper *www.themountainmail.com*	Salida	719-539-6691
Costilla County Free Press	San Luis	719-672-3764
Silverton Standard Newspaper	Silverton	970-387-5477
Ranchland News	Simla	719-541-2288
Snowmass Sun	Snowmass Village	970-923-5829
Baca Weekly *www.bacacountyline.com*	Springfield	719-523-6600
Plainsman-Herald *www.hometownusa.com/ co/news/springfield.html*	Springfield	719-523-6254
Journal Advocate *www.hometownusa.com/ co/news/sterling.html*	Sterling	970-522-1990
South Platte Sentinel	Sterling	970-522-8148
Eastern Colorado News	Strasburg	303-622-4417
Stratton Spotlight	Stratton	719-348-5913
Telluride Daily Planet *www.telluridegateway.com*	Telluride	970-728-9788
Jackson County Star	Walden	970-723-4404

Huerfano World	Walsenburg	719-738-1720
Wet Mountain Tribune *www.custerguide.com/tribune*	Westcliffe	719-783-2361
Northglenn-Thornton Sentinel	Westminster	303-426-6000
Wiggins Courier	Wiggins	970-483-7460
Ute Pass Courier	Woodland Park	719-687-3006
Wray Gazette *www.hometownusa.com/co/ news/wray.html*	Wray	970-332-4846
Yuma Pioneer *www.hometownusa.com/ co/news/yuma.html*	Yuma	970-848-2174

Employment Agencies

Mountain Temp Service	Aspen	970-920-3688
Absolute Staffing Solutions	Aurora	303-743-0222
Career 2000 Inc.	Aurora	303-696-2000
Express Temporary Service	Aurora	303-361-6894
Job Store	Aurora	303-755-6449
Labor Ready Inc.	Aurora	888-245-2261
Nesco Service Co. *www.nescoservice.com*	Aurora	303-360-0661
Peakload Temporary Service	Aurora	303-344-8300
Staffing Solutions	Aurora	303-360-9000
Star Personnel Service	Aurora	303-695-1161
Summit Staffing Inc.	Aurora	303-340-0440
Accountability	Boulder	303-444-3811
Accounting Solutions	Boulder	303-473-0600
ACT 1 Personnel Services *www.actpersonnel.com*	Boulder	303-545-2385
Addeco Employment Services	Boulder	303-442-2420
Bolder Staffing *www.bolderstaffing.com*	Boulder	303-444-1445
CoreStaff Services *www.corestaff.com*	Boulder	303-499-2800

First Choice Personnel Network	Boulder	303-444-7939
Staffing Solutions *www.staffingsolutions.com*	Boulder	303-443-1700
Westaff *www.westaff.com*	Boulder	303-444-5982
Bolder Temporaries Inc.	Broomfield	303-444-1445
Pro Staff Personnel Service	Broomfield	303-465-3888
Douglas County Temp Service	Castle Rock	303-688-6795
Miller-Denver	Castle Rock	303-688-6630
Accounting Solutions Inc	Colorado Springs	719-531-6600
Add Staff Inc *www.addstaffinc.com*	Colorado Springs	719-528-8888
Apple One Employment Service	Colorado Springs	719-391-1117
Colorado Career Consultants	Colorado Springs	719-590-9199
CoreStaff Services	Colorado Springs	719-599-4100
Express Personnel Service	Colorado Springs	719-520-9100
G T Employment Service	Colorado Springs	719-380-8998
Geo Search Inc.	Colorado Springs	719-260-7087
High Tech Enterprises	Colorado Springs	719-328-1660
Interim Personnel	Colorado Springs	719-636-1606
Job Search	Colorado Springs	719-475-9755
Kelly Services	Colorado Springs	719-528-5811
Labor Finders Of Colorado Inc *www.laborfinders.com*	Colorado Springs	719-630-1982
Labor Ready Inc	Colorado Springs	719-632-1883
Med-Temp	Colorado Springs	719-578-5819
Nelson Coulson & Associates	Colorado Springs	719-883-6612
Office Team	Colorado Springs	719-532-9300
Spencer Services	Colorado Springs	719-522-1077
Staffing Solutions	Colorado Springs	719-599-7400
Volt Services Group *www.volt.com*	Colorado Springs	719-277-7260
WSI Personnel Services *www.wsijobs.com*	Colorado Springs	719-630-7500
Action Employment Services	Conifer	303-838-9118

Accountability	Denver	303-297-2929	
Accountants On Call *aocnet.com*	Denver	303-291-1212	
Accounting Solutions Inc. *www.accountingsolutions.com*	Denver	303-534-1950	
Act 1 Personnel Service	Denver	303-756-7200	
ADECCO *www.adecomcom*	Denver	303-399-7706	
Appleone Employment Services *www.appleone.com*	Denver	303.698.1466	
Bank Temps Inc. *www.banktempsinc.com*	Denver	303-861-4115	
Careers Limited	Denver	303-832-5200	
CoreStaff Services	Denver	303-446-0700	
Creative Assets *www.creativeassets.com*	Denver	303-296-9777	
Denver Staffing Services	Denver	303-534-5344	
Employment Connection	Denver	303-756-1316	
Execustaff Inc. *www.execu-staff.com*	Denver	303-696-6868	
First Choice Nannies Inc.	Denver	303-333-9669	
First Choice Personnel	Denver	303-297-2020	
Ford Personnel Inc	Denver	303-322-2317	
Genesis Jobs Inc	Denver	303-860-8904	
Gibson Arnold & Assoc.	Denver	303-595-3655	
Goodwin Personnel Inc.	Denver	303-863-1500	
Hospitality Personnel Service	Denver	303-830-6868	
Hunter Group	Denver	303-861-0405	
Initial Staffing Services	Denver	303-296-1700	
J Kent *www.j.kentstaffingservices*	Denver	303-777-7734	
Job Store Staffing	Denver	303-757-7686	
Manpower	Denver	303-297-9802	
Mary Smith Assoc., Inc. *www.marysmith.com*	Denver	303-221-4750	

Employment Agencies

Mathews & Ball Inc.	Denver	303-759-8130
MEDIRECT Staffing & Consulting *www.medirectstaffing.com*	Denver	303-850-9080
Mile High Employment	Denver	303-650-0332
Office Team *www.officeteam.com*	Denver	303-296-4900
Phillips Personnel-Search *www.phillipspersonnel.com*	Denver	303-893-1850
Preferred Staffing	Denver	303-757-6335
Printers Personnel	Denver	303-454-9199
Quik Temps Inc.	Denver	303-825-8367
Real Estate Personnel	Denver	303-832-2380
Resources In Food *www.rifood.com*	Denver	303-863-7858
Robert Half Intl.	Denver	303-296-1010
Rocky Mountain Recruiters Inc.	Denver	303-296-2000
Scheer & Assoc *scheerandassociates.com*	Denver	303-757-7357
Search Network	Denver	303-846-3055
Senior Skills	Denver	303-756-4510
Snap Staffing Services	Denver	303-329-6693
Snelling Personnel Service *www.snellingpersonnel.net*	Denver	303-964-8200
Spherion	Denver	303-830-1030
Stand-By Temporaries	Denver	303-454-9199
Sunny Side Inc./Temp Side *www.sunnysidetemps.com*	Denver	303-320-5361
Techies.com *www.techies.com*	Denver	303-433-3416
Tech Minds, Inc. *www.techmindsinc.com*	Denver	303-357-6463
Ultimate Staffing Services *www.ultimatestaffing.com*	Denver	303-221-3131
Urban League Of Metro Denver	Denver	303-388-5861

Volt Temporary Service *www.volt.com*	Denver	303-373-5525
Volt Temporary Service *www.volt.com*	Denver	303-436-1822
SOS Staffing Services	Durango	970-259-3131
Aquent Partners	Englewood	303-721-6360
Casey Services *www.caseystaffing.com*	Englewood	303-721-9211
Command Technologies *www.cmotech.com*	Englewood	303-770-1200
Denver Staffing Service	Englewood	303-694-6661
Dunn & Nelson	Englewood	303-694-1998
Edp Recruiting Service Inc.	Englewood	303-694-2222
Lakeshore Staffing	Englewood	303-483-1100
Medical Personnel Resources *www.medicaljobs-co.com*	Englewood	303-762-0806
National Executive Resources	Englewood	303-721-7672
Personnel Plus	Englewood	303-694-6233
Pro Staff Personnel Service	Englewood	303-268-2888
Remedy Intelligent Staffing	Englewood	303-770-9675
Resumes On-Line	Englewood	303-781-0055
Sales Consultants	Englewood	303-706-0123
Snelling Personnel Service *www.snelling.com/dtc*	Englewood	303-779-3060
Tempstaff Inc.	Englewood	303-220-1094
Triad Consultants	Englewood	303-220-8516
Trish & Assoc.	Englewood	303-220-0700
United Personnel Of Colorado	Englewood	303-741-6983
Volt Temporary Service *www.volt.com*	Englewood	303-721-8400
Wow Employment Inc.	Englewood	303-674-5504
Colorado Division-Employment	Fort Collins	970-223-2470
Creative Career Connections *www.careerdesign.com*	Fort Collins	970-221-3511

Express Personnel Service	Fort Collins	970-226-4300
Fits Services	Fort Collins	970-225-0085
Mountain States Personnel	Fort Collins	970-484-5590
Olsten Staffing Service	Fort Collins	970-223-2000
Snelling Personnel Services	Fort Collins	970-225-9292
Synergy Technical www.synergytechnical.com	Fort Collins	970-484-4000
Westaff	Fort Collins	970-223-3434
SOS Staffing Services www.sosstaffing.com	Frisco	970-668-8991
Career Forum Inc	Golden	303-279-9200
Mesa Employment	Grand Junction	970-245-6372
Quick Temps Inc	Grand Junction	970-241-6007
SOS Staffing Services	Grand Junction	970-243-9950
Western Temporary Service	Grand Junction	970-243-6505
Insurance Professional	Highlands Ranch	303-470-7811
Labor Finders Of Colorado Inc.	Lakewood	303-238-4120
RoeGand Co	Lakewood	303-986-1112
Professional Search & Placement	Littleton	303-779-8004
Recruiting Resources	Littleton	303-797-2575
Snelling Personnel Service www.snellingpersonnel.net	Littleton	303-794-4331
Apple One Employment Service	Longmont	303-651-6251
Aspen Personnel Services	Longmont	303-776-9661
Staff Exchange	Longmont	303-651-3444
Dunn & Nelson Inc	Northglenn	303-280-9757
G T Global Staffing	Northglenn	303-451-5662
Summit Staffing Temporary	Northglenn	303-255-3009
Express Personnel Service	Pueblo	719-545-9120
Interim Personnel	Pueblo	719-544-8955
Kelly Services	Pueblo	719-545-9300
Western Temporary Service	Pueblo	719-543-8196
Colorado Technical Staffing	Wheat Ridge	303-421-9735

Television Stations

Aspen Snowmass Video Magazine	Aspen	970-920-9292
Aspen Video Guide-Channel 11	Aspen	970-925-2251
CTVA	Aurora	303-671-0938
KACT *www.kact.com*	Aurora	303-739-6588
KPXC (PAX)	Aurora	303-751-5959
Universal Broadcasting	Aurora	303-671-9722
Vail Valley Community TV	Avon	970-949-5657
K43CG-TV	Colorado Springs	719-574-7777
KKTV *www.kktv.com*	Colorado Springs	719-634-2844
KMGH Southern News Bureau *www.kmgh.com*	Colorado Springs	719-633-7777
KOAA *www.koaa.com*	Colorado Springs	719-632-5030
KRDO *www.krdotv.com*	Colorado Springs	719-632-1515
KXRM *www.kxrm.com*	Colorado Springs	719-596-2100
K27FA	Craig	970-824-7265
CB TV-28	Crested Butte	970-349-5844
Five Points Media Ctr. Corp	Denver	303-295-1357
Fox Sports *foxsports.com*	Denver	720-855-9300
KBDI Public TV-12 *www.kbdi.org*	Denver	303-296-1212
KCEC Channel 50	Denver	303-832-0050
KCNC *www.kcncnews4.com*	Denver	303-861-4444
KDEN	Denver	303-282-7499
KDVR Fox 31 *www.kdvr.com*	Denver	303-595-3131

KMGH *www.thedenverchannel.com* *www.kmgh.com*	Denver	303-832-7777
KRMA (Rocky Mtn. PBS) *rmpbs.com*	Denver	303-892-6666
KTVJ TV	Denver	303-832-1414
KUSA Channel 9 *www.9news.com*	Denver	303-871-9999
Vacation Channel	Dillon	970-262-6388
KREZ	Durango	970-259-6666
AT&T Cable Services	Englewood	303-930-2000
KTVD *www.ktvd.com*	Englewood	303-792-2020
KWGN TV WB2 *www.wb2.com*	Englewood	303-740-2222
KWHD *www.kwhd.com*	Englewood	303-799-8853
Time Warner Cable	Englewood	303-792-9061
Channel 8 Estes Park	Estes Park	970-586-6045
KCNC Northern Bureau *www.kcnc.com*	Fort Collins	970-244-4444
KUSA Northern Newsroom *www.9news.com*	Fort Collins	970-484-5332
Optical Audio Productions	Fort Collins	970-484-5535
News 4 Mountain Bureau	Frisco	970-668-0444
KUSA West Slope Bureau	Glenwood Springs	970-945-9999
KFQX	Grand Junction	970-242-5285
KJCT TV 8 *www.cjct8.com*	Grand Junction	970-245-8880
KKCO *www.nbc11news.com*	Grand Junction	970-243-1111
KREX *www.krextv.com*	Grand Junction	970-242-5000
KRMJ TV *www.rmpbs.org*	Grand Junction	970-245-1818

Gunnison County Metro Recreation	Gunnison	970-641-9148
Rocky Mountain Television *www.rmtv.net*	Gunnison	970-641-0197
Mountain View Engineering	Leadville	719-486-2085
Jones Intercable Inc.	Littleton	303-933-1981
Channel 3-The Longmont Channel *www.channel3.org*	Longmont	303-776-1424
KREY *www.montrose-colo.com/krey*	Montrose	970-249-9601
Professional Antenna Tower Svc	Montrose	970-249-5926
KKTV *www.kktv.com*	Pueblo	719-542-6247
KOAA *www.koaa.com/pueblo*	Pueblo	719-544-5781
KRDO *www.krdotv.com*	Pueblo	719-543-0033
KTSC-TV *www.rmpbs.org*	Pueblo	719-543-8800
KSBS	Steamboat Springs	970-870-6110
KTVS	Sterling	970-522-2729
TCTV Telluride Community TV	Telluride	970-728-3838
KVBA TV 8	Vail	970-479-0800
Trinity Broadcasting Of Denver	Westminster	303-650-5515

Internet Service

Colorado DSL.com Inc. *www.coloradodsl.com*	Arvada	303-432-7777
Warp 8 Inc. *www.warp8.com*	Arvada	303-421-5140
Last Mile Communications Inc.	Aurora	303-745-1930
Colorado Internet Coop *www.coop.net*	Boulder	303-443-3786
CSD Internet Services	Boulder	303-444-1671
Earthnet *www.earthnet.net*	Boulder	303-546-6362

Experience Internet www.*xpi.net*	Boulder	303-447-3106
Indra's Net *www.indra.com*	Boulder	303-546-9151
Fone.net	Byers	303-822-9207
Royal Internet Services *www.ris.net*	Cañon City	719-275-6858
Alcatel USA	Colorado Springs	719-277-8700
Colorado Info. Technologies *www.coinfotech.com*	Colorado Springs	719-473-2800
Corbett Systems Development	Colorado Springs	800-416-9843
DataWest Internet *www.datawest.net*	Colorado Springs	719-635-9999
High Plains Internet *www.hpi.net*	Colorado Springs	719-471-0117
MDI *www.mdione.net*	Colorado Springs	719-457-6414
NetBeam *www.netbeam.net*	Colorado Springs	970-453-5699
North American Internet Ltd. *www.nais.com*	Colorado Springs	719-635-6245
PCI Systems, Inc. *www.pcisys.net*	Colorado Springs	719-572-5704
Peak to Peak Internet *www.peakpeak.com*	Colorado Springs	719-227-9335
RMI.NET *www.rmi.net*	Colorado Springs	800-864-4344
Southern Colorado Internet/ High Plains *www.scip.net*	Colorado Springs	719-632-8481
Business Technology Consultant	Denver	303-639-6010
BBN Planet *www.bbnplanet.net*	Denver	303-672-1885
Colorado Legal Network Inc.	Denver	303-436-9500
Comfluent *www.comfluent.net*	Denver	303-376-1600
Computer Avenue	Denver	303-733-4508

Denver On Line *www.denveronline.net*	Denver	303-691-8200
E Central *www.ecentral.com*	Denver	303-377-7045
Front Range Internet *www.frii.com*	Denver	303-448-5599 800-935-6527
LDR	Denver	303-393-7300
Mindspring Enterprises *www.mindspring.net*	Denver	888-677-7464
Odyssey Technologies *www.odyssey.com*	Denver	303-861-4270
Online Systems Integration *www.olsi.com*	Denver	303-692-0233
Qwest Communications Intl. *www.qwest.com*	Denver	877-660-6342
Rocky Mountain Internet	Denver	303-672-0700
Rockynet.com *www.rockynet.com*	Denver	303-623-2263
Touch America Colorado *www.tacolorado.com*	Denver	720-371-2437
Ultrasys.net *www.ultrasys.net*	Denver	303-761-3100
ViaWest Internet Services *www.viawest.net*	Denver	720-891-1000
Frontier Internet *www.frontiernet.com*	Durango	800-205-8074 970-385-4177
Eazy.net *www.eazy.net*	Englewood	303-770-5747
4DV.net *www/4division.com*	Englewood	303-843-9400
ID Communications *www.idcomm.com*	Englewood	303-790-4343
Prodigy Internet *www.prodigy.com*	Englewood	800-776-3449
United Online Inc. *www.uoli.com*	Englewood	303-267-0038
Office On Web	Evergreen	303-674-6900

Internet Service

EZ Link Internet Access *www.ezlinkusb.com*	Fort Collins	970-482-0807
Fone.net *www.fone.net*	Fort Collins	970-897-2200
Front Range Internet Inc. *www.frii.com*	Fort Collins	970-224-3668 800-935-6527
Image Net Inc.	Fort Collins	970-203-9200
INFRA's Net	Fort Collins	970-407-9151
Info 2000 *www.info2000.net*	Fort Collins	970-416-1211
NetBeam *www.netbeam.net*	Colorado Springs	970-453-5699
Northern Colorado Online	Fort Collins	970-221-4508
Peak to Peak Internet *www.peakpeak.com*	Fort Collins	970-225-9911
Qwest Internet Services *www.qwest.com*	Fort Collins	877-660-6342
Web Access	Fort Collins	970-221-2555
Frontier Internet *www.frontier.net*	Grand Junction	970-245-6366
Grand Valley Internet *www.gvii.net*	Grand Junction	970-257-9045
Rural Net *www.ruralnet.org*	Grand Junction	970-385-9700
Western Frontier Internet *www.wic.net*	Grand Junction	970-245-6366
Clark & Thompson Online Svc.	Greeley	970-353-8126
Front Range Internet	Greeley	970-346-6888 800-935-6527
Internet Communications Corp. *www.incc.net*	Greenwood Village	303-414-7000
Peak Computer Resource Center *www.youndminds.com*	Gunnison	970-641-3702
Autometric Inc. *www.autometric.com*	Lakewood	303-986-5311
Mile High Internet *www.milehigh.net*	Littleton	303-730-8191

Micro Computer World	Loveland	970-667-6606
Frontier Internet *www.frontier.net*	Montrose	800-205-8074
Western Frontier Internet *www.wic.net*	Montrose	970-249-7054
Coyotenet *www.cnip.net*	Pueblo	719-583-0358
Peak to Peak Internet *peakpeak.com*	Pueblo	719-253-2753
Independence Network Corp. *www.plains.net*	Ridgway	970-626-4400
Yipes	Wheat Ridge	303-572-0948
Premier Systems	Yuma	970-848-0475

Storage Facilities

The phone numbers shown below represent a small sample of storage facilities in the major cities of Colorado. With respect to space allotted, this list has been condensed greatly. Please consult your local Yellow Pages for a complete list.

Adams County Self Storage *www.selfstoragecolorado.com*	Arvada	303-477-3844
Storage Center	Arvada	303-477-5998
Aspen Mini Storage	Aspen	970-920-3333
Aspen Secure Storage	Aspen	970-920-4298
Aspen Self Storage Warehouses	Aspen	970-925-8333
Columbine Moving & Storage	Aspen	970-925-2201
A And A Moving & Storage	Aurora	303-364-4275
A-Aaakey Mini Storage	Aurora	303-341-2365
Abco Mini Storage	Aurora	303-341-0277
Affordable Moving & Storage *www.affordablemoving.net*	Aurora	303-693-7077
All American Moving Services	Aurora	303-373-5101
Altura Self Storage	Aurora	303-343-4020
Aurora Mini-Storage	Aurora	303-343-3389

Chambers East Mini-Storage	Aurora	303-340-4144
Harbor Plaza Mini & Outdoor	Aurora	303-690-2759
Lock-Ur-Own Storage Inc	Aurora	303-364-6032
Public Storage	Aurora	303-366-3588
Security Self Storage	Aurora	303-338-0800
Self Storage	Aurora	303-344-2429
U S Storage Inc	Aurora	303-341-0122
U-Haul Co	Aurora	303-344-9771
U-Stor	Aurora	303-368-0334
Wolf's Mini Storage	Aurora	303-341-0223
Ace Self Storage	Boulder	303-444-7870
Arapahoe Self Storage	Boulder	303-449-5851
Boulder Bins	Boulder	303-443-2002
Boulder SSI Storage Center	Boulder	303-449-6597
North Broadway Self Storage	Boulder	303-449-6900
SecurCare Self Storage	Boulder	303-444-7867
Storage Containers *www.selfstoragecolorado.com*	Boulder	303-938-8286
Western Disposal Service	Boulder	303-444-2037
Breckenridge Mini Storage	Breckenridge	970-453-6669
Castle Rock Mini-Storage Inc	Castle Rock	303-688-3883
Castle Rock RV& Boat Storage	Castle Rock	303-688-4280
Haulaway Storage Containers	Castle Rock	303-688-0344
Jerry Street Self Storage	Castle Rock	303-688-0693
Park Street Storage	Castle Rock	303-688-2242
Triple N	Castle Rock	303-688-9757
8th Street Self Storage	Colorado Springs	719-633-1820
A A Mobile Storage	Colorado Springs	719-473-0433
A Better Self Storage	Colorado Springs	719-471-8800
A Low Cost Self Storage	Colorado Springs	719-574-2065
A-1 Self Storage Warehouses	Colorado Springs	719-591-8900
AAA Self-Store-All Warehouse	Colorado Springs	719-392-5954
Able Movers Inc.	Colorado Springs	719-591-9330

Academy Moving *www.academymoving. uswestdex.com*	Colorado Springs	719-531-7553
Academy Place Storage	Colorado Springs	719-574-7111
Academy South Mini-Storage	Colorado Springs	719-391-0222
All American Moving Service	Colorado Springs	719-390-8080
Amick North American	Colorado Springs	719-597-8850
Arrow Moving & Storage Co.	Colorado Springs	719-527-0616
Astro/Securcare Self Storage	Colorado Springs	719-390-4677
Astrozon Self Storage	Colorado Springs	719-390-4288
Bekins Moving & Storage	Colorado Springs	719-520-5700
Central Self-Storage	Colorado Springs	719-591-1957
Chapel Hills Mini Storage	Colorado Springs	719-532-0479
Chapel Hills Self Storage	Colorado Springs	719-590-7135
City Center Self Storage	Colorado Springs	719-633-1331
Colorado Springs Moving & Storage Inc.	Colorado Springs	719-636-8987
Commercial Self Storage	Colorado Springs	719-535-2782
Downtown Mini Warehouse	Colorado Springs	719-630-1575
El Paso Mini Storage	Colorado Springs	719-635-3405
Goeson Moving & Storage	Colorado Springs	719-596-3306
Interstate Secure Storage	Colorado Springs	719-633-0222
Knob Hill Storage	Colorado Springs	719-630-1575
Mobile Mini-Warehousing *www.mobilemini warehouseing.com*	Colorado Springs	719-390-1900
Motor City Mini-Storage	Colorado Springs	719-633-6952
North Nevada Self Storage	Colorado Springs	719-633-8923
Northside U-Store-It	Colorado Springs	719-635-0488
Old Mill Self Storage	Colorado Springs	719-634-6332
Peakview Self Storage	Colorado Springs	719-473-7445
Pikes Peak Moving & Storage	Colorado Springs	719-475-2806
Public Storage	Colorado Springs	719-390-8580
Rampart Self-Storage	Colorado Springs	719-592-0662

Rite Place Self Storage	Colorado Springs	719-633-7652
Rockrimmon Self Storage	Colorado Springs	719-532-1880
www.rockrimmonselfstorage.com		
Rocky Mt. Moving And Storage	Colorado Springs	719-634-0908
Self Storage	Colorado Springs	719-599-8717
Storage Trust	Colorado Springs	719-570-1300
Stor-N-Lok	Colorado Springs	719-576-0800
STX Truck & Equipment Sales	Colorado Springs	719-599-3575
Sun Self Storage	Colorado Springs	719-633-6058
U-Haul Co.	Colorado Springs	719-574-6500
Westwind Storage	Colorado Springs	719-447-0452
A Design Mover	Commerce City	303-853-8151
64th and Clay Storage	Denver	303-427-6123
70th & Washington Self Storage	Denver	303-288-1111
A & R Transfer Co	Denver	303-320-9092
A Bargain Evans/Holly Storage	Denver	303-756-4154
A Business Storage Inc	Denver	303-893-1414
Able Movers Inc	Denver	303-333-1090
Alameda Storage	Denver	303-363-0939
All American Mini Storage Inc.	Denver	303-573-6464
American Worldwide International	Denver	303-321-7716
Amick Great Plains	Denver	303-333-8212
Atlantic Relocation Systems	Denver	303-373-5383
Benedict Warehouse & Transfer	Denver	303-292-5077
Berkeley Moving & Storage Co	Denver	303-399-1815
Big City Storage	Denver	303-573-3863
Buehler Moving & Storage	Denver	303-388-4000
Certified Discount Mini Storage	Denver	303-296-9955
Complete Container Services	Denver	303-428-6800
Devonshire Mini Warehouse	Denver	303-288-1119
Downtown Denver Storage Inc.	Denver	303-298-0176
Downtown Self Storage	Denver	303-292-9816
Indoor Storage Center	Denver	303-295-2446

Lowell Mini Storage	Denver	303-657-3661
Mini U-Storage	Denver	303-321-3055
Movemasters	Denver	303-777-2290
Nationwide Self Storage	Denver	303-751-9702
Nationwide Storage Center	Denver	303-296-2933
Private Self Storage	Denver	303-371-0063
Public Storage	Denver	303-294-9055
Santa Fe Self Storage	Denver	303-534-8342
Shurgard Storage Center	Denver	303-770-3211
U-Haul Co.	Denver	303-298-1971
USA Central Denver	Denver	303-333-5741
U-Stor	Denver	303-761-2277
U-Stor-All	Denver	303-722-0370
Wagner Rents	Denver	303-433-2727
West Evans Mini-Storage	Denver	303-922-1555
Almost Anything Stored	Englewood	303-761-5511
Arapahoe & Holly Self Storage	Englewood	303-694-9400
SecureCare Self Storage	Englewood	303-793-3789
Self Storage	Englewood	303-789-9585
Warehouse Mini-Storage	Englewood	303-789-0686
A A Wholesale Outside Storage	Erie	303-449-0088
Mountain Mini Storage Inc.	Evergreen	303-674-8400
Old Mine Mini Storage	Evergreen	303-674-6431
A Big A Self Storage	Fort Collins	970-224-2424
A Low Cost Self Storage	Fort Collins	970-223-1443
A Plus Mini's Self Storage	Fort Collins	970-226-5625
A-1 U Store-It Warehouses	Fort Collins	970-493-8313
ABC Storage	Fort Collins	970-482-9921
All Storage-Mini Self Storage	Fort Collins	970-484-2090
Colonial Self Storage Co.	Fort Collins	970-482-0894
Dandelion Moving & Storage *www.dandelionmoving.com*	Fort Collins	970-484-1717
G & P Mini-Storage	Fort Collins	970-493-6277

U Stuff It	Fort Collins	970-493-3895
Nationwide Self Storage	Golden	303-277-1658
Shut & Lock Self Storage	Golden	303-233-5627
Lakewood Self Storage	Lakewood	303-989-6330
Public Storage	Littleton	303-623-4030
Self Storage	Littleton	303-798-8078
City Moving & Storage Inc.	Louisville	303-666-2121
A Discount Storage	Sheridan	303-761-1099
Cowen Moving & Storage	Wheat Ridge	303-433-0200

Appendix A

RECOMMENDED READING FROM COLORADO PUBLISHERS

The following Colorado publishers contributed materials for this book. They have numerous titles about different aspects of Colorado and many have their own catalogs. Please check with your favorite bookstore for the titles listed or you can order directly from the publisher. Please note the prices indicated may have changed and they do not include shipping & handling, which varies with each order.

Bradford Publishing Company
www.bradfordpublishing.com
1743 Wazee Street
Denver, CO 80202
303-292-2590

> *Behind the Wheel in Colorado:*
> *Rules, Tickets and Traffic Court* $9.95
> By Theresa Leming
> ISBN 1-883726-63-9, 476 p.
>
> *Friendly Divorce Guidebook for Colorado, 4th Edition* $44.95
> By M. Arden Hauer and S. M. Whicher
> ISBN 1-883726-51-4, 366 p.
>
> *Landlord & Tenant Guide to Colorado Evictions* $18.50
> By Victor M. Grimm, Esq.
> ISBN 1-883726-03-4, 182 p.
>
> *Winning Big in Colorado Small Claims Court* $17.95
> By Charles P. Brackney, Esq.
> ISBN 1-883726-04-2, 198 p.
>
> *Vehicles and Traffic: Title 42 and Common Code* 14.95

Publishing Colorado legal forms and supplemental materials on topics including divorce, child support, wills and probate, liens, garnishment, evictions, real estate, small business start-up, and more.

C & C Publications
The Junior League of Denver, Inc.
www.jld.org/cookbooks.cfm
6300 East Yale Avenue, Suite 110
Denver, CO 80222
303-692-0270

> *Colorado Cache Cookbook* $15.95
> ISBN 0-96039-4656, 430 p
>
> *Crème de Colorado Cookbook* $21.95
> ISBN 0-96039-4621
>
> *Colorado Collage* $24.95
> ISBN 0-96039-4648

Communications Creativity

www.spannet.org
PO Box 909
425 Cedar Street
Buena Vista, CO 81211
800-331-8355 or 719-395-4790

> *Big Ideas for Small Service Businesses: How to*
> *Successfully Advertise, Publicize, and Maximize*
> *Your Business or Professional Practice, Revised Edition* $15.95
> By Marilyn and Tom Ross
> ISBN 0-918880-16-5, 224 p.
>
> *Country Bound: Trade Your Business Suit*
> *Blues for Blue Jean Dreams, Revised Edition* $19.95
> By Marilyn and Tom Ross
> ISBN 0-918880-30-0, 432 p.
>
> *Discover the Good Life In Rural America:*
> *The City Slicker's Guide to Buying Country*
> *Real Estate Without Losing Your Shirt* $12.95
> By Bob Bone
> ISBN 0-918880-36-X, 159 p.

Fulcrum Publishing

www.fulcrum-books.com
16100 Table Mountain Parkway, Ste. 300
Golden, CO 80403
303-277-1623 or 800-992-2908

> *Ancient Walls: Indian Ruins of the Southwest* $19.95
> Text by Susan Labb; Photos by Chuck Place
> ISBN 1-55591-126-9, Paperback, 112 p.
>
> *Canine Colorado: Where to Go and*
> *What to Do with Your Dog* $17.95
> By Cindy Hirschfeld
> ISBN 1-55591-239-7, 2nd Edition, May 2001, 224 p.
> ISBN 1-55591-375-X, 1st Edition, 224 p.
>
> *Colorado's Fourteeners: From Hikes to Climbs,*
> *2nd Edition* $18.95
> By Gerry Roach
> ISBN 1-55591-412-8, 336 p.

Rocky Mountain National Park:
Classic Hikes & Climbs $14.95
By Gerry Roach
ISBN 1-55591-412-8, 336 p.

Rocky Mountain Skiing $21.95
By Claire Walter
ISBN 1-55591-330-X, 544 p.

Rocky Mountain Walks $15.95
By Gary Ferguson
ISBN 1-55591-120-X, 304 p.

Seasonal Guide to the Natural Year:
Colorado, New Mexico, Arizona, and Utah $15.95
By Ben Guterson
ISBN 1-55591-153-6, 360 p.

Snowshoeing Colorado $18.95
By Claire Walter
ISBN 1-55591-053-X

The Colorado Guide, 5th Edition $24.95
By Bruce Caughey and Dan Winstanley
ISBN 1-55591-006-8

Gylantic Publishing Company

PO Box 2792
Littleton, CO 80161-2792
303-797-6093 or 800-828-0113

Moving With Children: A Parent's
Guide To Moving With Children $12.95
By Thomas T. Olkowski, Ph.D.,
and Lynn Parker, L.C.S.W.
ISBN 1-55591-006-8

Eight titles in print. Many other self-help/recovery titles.

Ice Castle Editions

PO Box 280166
Lakewood, CO 80228-0116
303-988-6424

Leadville's Ice Palace: A Colossus
in the Colorado Rockies $16.95
By Darlene Weir
ISBN 0-9637431-0-4, 391 p.

Johnson Publishing
www.jpcolorado.com
1880 South 57th Court
Boulder, CO 80301
303-443-9766 or 800-258-5830

Roadside History of Colorado, Revised Edition $13.95
By James McTighe
ISBN 1-55566-054-1

Tales, Trails and Tommyknockers:
Stories From Colorado's Past $8.95
By Myriam Friggens
ISBN 1-93347-201-3, 144 p.

The Archaeology of Colorado $19.00
By E. Steve Cassells
ISBN 1-55566-193-9, 144 p.

The Four Corners Anasazi:
A Guide to Archaeological Sites $17.95
By Rose Houk

The Xeriscape Flower Gardener: A Waterwise Guide
for the Rocky Mountain Region $19.00
By Jim Knopf
ISBN 1-55566-077-0, 182 p.

Many, many other Colorado titles!

Magnolia Street Press
2600 Magnolia
Denver, CO 80207
303-322-2822

Colorado Private Elementary
and Secondary Schools, 1999-2000 .... $11.50
ISBN 1-89094-302-9

The Guide to Metro Denver Public Schools,
1999-2000 Edition $14.50
ISBN 1-89094-301-0

Child Care and Preschools in Metro Denver $15.95
ISBN 1-890943-03-7

Please contact the publisher for the most current information.

Outdoor Books & Maps
www.outdoorcolorado.com
PO Box 417
Denver, CO 80201-0147
1-800-352-5342

Best of Northern Colorado Hiking Trails $12.95
ISBN 0-93065-71-87, 112 p.

Colorado Lakes & Reservoirs:
Fishing & Boating Guide, 7th Edition $14.95
ISBN 0-93065-7-00-4, 16 p.

The Best of Colorado Bike Trails $9.95
ISBN 0-93065-7-28-4, 96 p.

The Complete Colorado Campground Guide $14.95
ISBN 0-93065-7-23-3, 160 p.

Pruett Publishing Company
www.gorp.com/pruett
7464 Arapahoe Road, Suite A-9
Boulder, CO 80303-1500
303-449-4919 or 800-247-8224

A Climbing Guide to Colorado's
Fourteeners, 20th Anniversary Edition $16.95
By Walter Borneman and Lyndon Lampert
ISBN 0-87108-850-9, 255 p.

A Colorado History, 8th Edition $25.00
By Carl Ubbelohoe, Maxine Benson
and Diane Smith
ISBN 0-87108-923-8, 480 p.

*Tomboy Bride: A Woman's Personal Account
of Life in the Mining Camps of the West* $16.95
By Harriet Fish Backus
Foreword by Pam Houston
ISBN 0-87108-512-7, 318 p.

*Boulder Hijing Trails: The Best of the
Plains, Foothills, and Mountains* $18.50
By Ruth Carol Cushman and Glenn Cushman
ISBN 0-87108-907-6, 225 p.

Many, many other similar Colorado titles!

Roberts Rinehart Publishers
c/o National Book Network
15200 NBN Way
Blue Ridge Summit, PA 17214
800-462-6420

*Alpine Flower Finder: The Key to
Wildflowers FoundAbove Treeline
in the Rocky Mountains* $5.95
By Loraine Yeats
ISBN 1-57098-026-8

Chronicles of Colorado $14.95
By Carol Ann Moorhead
ISBN 1-87937-365-3

Colorado's Backyard Wildlife $10.95
ISBN 1-87937-308-4

*Handbook of Rocky MountainPlants,
4th Edition* $19.95
ISBN 1-91179-796-3

*Rocky Mountain National Park
Natural History Handbook* $14.95
By John C. Emericks
ISBN 1-87937-380-7

Rocky Mountain Safari: A Wildlife
Discovery Guide $9.95
By Cathy Ille
ISBN 1-87937-379-3, full color

Many, many other Colorado/nature titles
including several for children!

The Colorado Directory, Inc.
www.coloradodirectory.com
5101 Pennsylvania Ave., Suite #5
Boulder, CO 80303-2799
303-499-9343 or 800-886-9343

The Colorado Directory .... Free
By Hilton and Jenny Fitt-Peaster

Available online or contact their Boulder office
for a free copy.

University Press of Colorado
www.upcolorado.com
5589 Arapahoe Ave.
Boulder, CO 80303
720-406-8849 or 800-627-7377

Colorado: A History of The Centennial State,
3rd Edition $29.95
By Carl Abbott, Steve Leonard, David McComb
ISBN 0-87081-344-7

Denver Landmarks and Historic Districts:
A Pictorial Guide $42.50
By Thomas J. Norl
ISBN 0-87081-427-3

Denver: Mining Camp to Metropolis $34.95
By Steve Leonard, Thomas J. Noel
ISBN 0-87081-240-8

Exploring Colorado State Parks, 2nd Edition $19.95
By Martin Kleinsorge
ISBN 0-87081-442-7

Rocky Mountain Flora, 5th Edition $23.95
By William A. Weber
ISBN 0-87081-068-5

The Colorado General Assembly, 2nd Edition $24.95
By John A. Straayer
ISBN 0-87081-542-3

Westcliffe Publishers
www.westcliffepublishers.com
PO Box 1261
Englewood, CO 80150-1261
800-523-3692

Colorado 1870–2000 . . . . $95.00
By John Fielder
ISBN 1-56579-347-1, hardcover, coffee-table book, 224 p.

*Colorado Hut to Hut: A Guide to Skiing
and Biking Colorado's Backcountry*
By Brian Litz

   Vol. 1: *Northern and Central Regions*
   ISBN 1-56579-384-6, full color, 312 p. $24.95

   Vol. 2: *Southern Region*
   ISBN 1-56579-385-4, full color, 232 p. $19.95

Cooking with Colorado's Greatest Chefs $14.98
By Marilynn A. Booth
ISBN 1-56579-127-4, hardbound, full color

Explore Colorado: A Naturalists Notebook $19.95
By Frances A. Kruger and
Carron A. Meaney
ISBN 1-56579-124-X, full color, 128 p.

Guide to Colorado Wildflowers $24.95
By G.K. Guenner

   Vol. 1: *Plains and Foothills*
   ISBN 1-56579-118-5, full color, 336 p.

   Vol. 2: *The Mountains*
   ISBN 1-56579-119-3, full color, 352 p.

*Places around the Bases: A Historic Tour of the
Coors Field Neighborhood* $16.95
By Diane Bakke and
Jackie Davis
ISBN 1-56579-117-7, 160 p.

Along the Colorado Trail
Photos by John Fielder
Text by M. John Fayhee
ISBN 1-56579-010-3, paperback $25.00

ISBN 0-92996-987-1, hardcover $35.00

The Complete Guide to Colorado's Wilderness Areas $24.95
By John Fielder and Mark Pearson
ISBN 1-56579-052-9, full color, 340 p.

*Many, many other Colorado titles
and full color calendars,
including the works of John Fielder!*

Appendix B

MAPS

Colorado Counties

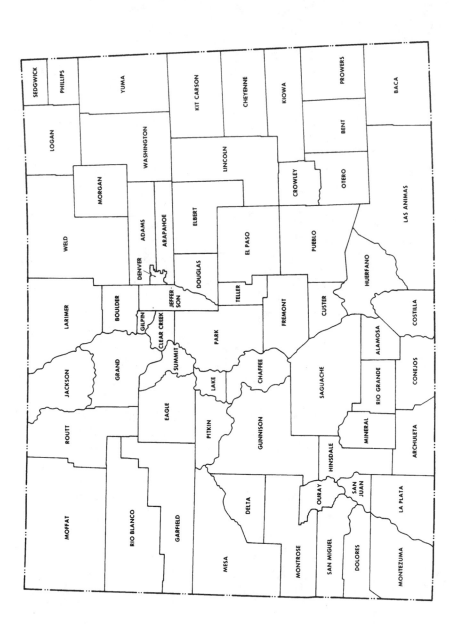

Colorado Sub-state Regions

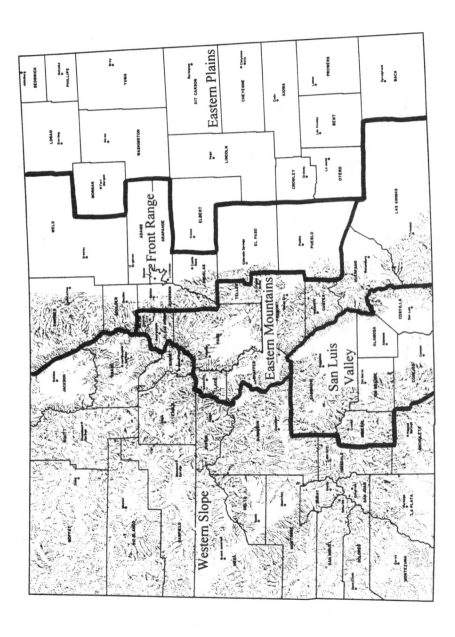

Colorado State Parks

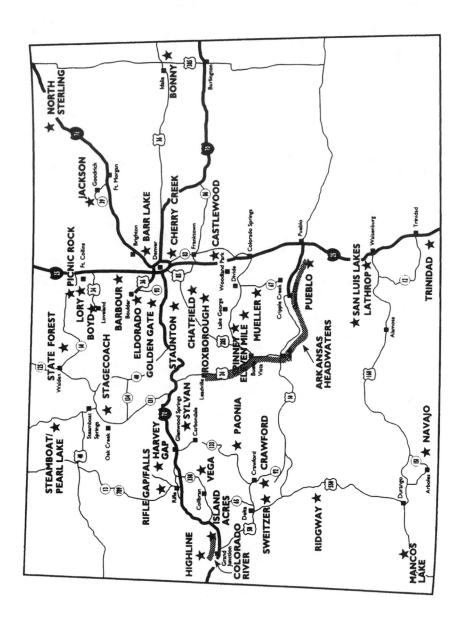

Appendix C

REGIONAL TRANSPORTATION

Denver International Airport

www.flydenver.com

Denver International Airport moves people and cargo more efficiently than any other major airport. DIA passenger and cargo traffic robustly increased in 1996 as airlines and passengers discovered how well Denver's airport works. The high-performance airfield elevated Denver to one of the very best airports for on-time arrivals and fewest delays.

DIA's operational excellence has also helped create a fertile environment for surrounding business development. Plans for the airline-related business and long-term commercial development became reality in 1996 and the area around Denver International Airport is experiencing potent growth.

Opened:	February 28, 1995
Location:	23 miles northeast of downtown Denver
Size:	34,000 acres; 53 square miles
Average number of per day:	104,000 in 1999 passengers
Number of airlines:	22 offering non-stop service to 105 domestic cities and 11 international destinations

Major/national
America West
American
American Trans Air
Continental
Delta
Frontier
Midwest Express
Northwest
Trans World
United
USAir
Vanguard

Foreign flag
Air BC
Air Canada
British Airways
Lufthansa
Mexicana

Regional/Commuter
Air Wisconsin (United Express)
Big Sky
Great Lakes Aviation (United
    Express)
Mesa (United Express)

Average number of daily flights:	1,371 in 1999
Runways:	Five; each 12,000 feet long
Concourses:	Three airside concourses—A, B, and C
Gates:	94 (including access gates to commuter facilities)
Terminal building:	Elrey B. Jeppesen Terminal (dual-sided)
Elevation:	5,431 feet

Other facts (*www.flydenver.com*)

• DIA is the 6th busiest airport in the U.S.

• Served 39 million passengers in 2000

• *Wall Street Journal* recently named DIA one of the five best airports in U.S. *International Business Traveler* magazine rated DIA the second best airport in the Americas in a recent survey.

Number of parking spaces: For a breakdown on parking in or near the terminal, go to *www.flydenver.com* and click on the parking option.

Rates

Close-in:	$2.00/hour or $12.00 each 24 hours in garage
Long-term:	$1.00/hour or $6.00 each 24 hours in economy

Parking Lots

U.S. Airport Parking:	303-371-7575 or 303-866-PARKING *www.usairportparking.com*
Airport Parking:	303-373-4892
Allright Parking Garages	303-343-3933
Pikes Peak Shuttle Lot:	303-DIA-PARK

Parking for the disabled is available on all levels of the Terminal Parking Garage (excluding Level 3) and in the Long Term (Economy) Parking lots. Additional spaces for the disabled have been added to level 1 of the parking garage.

Parking Information: General parking information menu and suggestion line, please call 303-342-4165. For where to park call 303-DIA-PARK (303-342-7275).

Vehicle Assistance: Emergency car starts, tire inflations, lock outs, lost vehicles and more than 30-day stays. 24 hours a day/7 days a week, please call 303-342-4645.

RTD Skyride

www.RTD-Denver.com

SkyRide buses operate between DIA and metro Denver Park-n-Rides. They generally run between 4:00 A.M.–midnight. Route and schedule information is available by calling 303-299-6000.

Rates

$4.00, $6.00, or $8.00 to DIA. More than 28 Skyride stops throughout the Denver Metro area. Skyride buses depart from each stop at least one per hour (every 15–20 minutes, 7 days a week, 365 days a year).

Fun Facts About DIA

- 2.5 million cubic yards of concrete were used to construct five runways, taxiways and aprons.

- DIA has 1,200 flight and baggage information display monitors.

- A quarry in Marble, Colorado supplied the white marble used on the terminal walls. This stone is from the same quarry that supplied marble for the Tomb of the Unknown Soldier and the Lincoln Memorial.

- The total area of DIA is 53 square miles, twice the size of Manhattan Island and larger than the city boundaries of Boston, Miami, or San Francisco.

- DIA has a fiber optic communications spine with 5,300 miles of cable. That is enough cable to run from New York City to Buenos Aires, Argentina. That length is longer than the Nile River. Its 11,365 miles of copper cable would be enough to run from Los Angeles to Paris and back.

Driving

www.trexproject.com

In October 2001 massive highway construction will begin on the central and south portions of Interstate 25 through Denver. Nicknamed T-Rex, the project will take at least five years and will add two lanes in each direction and a Light Rail line. About 17 miles of highway improvements is planned. The website is full of helpful tips about schedules, delays, and alternate routes. For project information call 303-786-TREX (8739).

RTD

www.rtd_denver.com/fastfacts

The Regional Transportation District is a public agency created in 1969 by the Colorado General Assembly to develop, operate and maintain a mass transportation system for the benefit of the people in RTD's six-county service area. The service area includes all of

Boulder, Denver and Jefferson Counties and parts of Adams, Arapahoe and Douglas Counties. A 15-member board of directors elected for four-year terms governs the District.

- Service area population: 2.2 million
- Cities and towns served: 41 municipalities in 6 counties
- Square miles in service area: 2,406
- Bus stops: 10,719
- Park-n-Ride facilities: 59
- Light Rail Service: 31 vehicles, 14 miles of track, 20 stations
- Total number of routes: 179
    Local: 65
    Express: 44
    Regional: 20
    Limited: 15

  Boulder City Local: 14
  Boulder City Limited: 3
  Longmont City Local: 6
  SkyRide: 5
  Miscellaneous: 7 (Mall Shuttle, Light Rail, Goodwill, etc.)

  For more information, please call 303-299-6000, 800-366-7433, or visit www.rtd-denver.com.

- Other bus fleet
    Total 976 buses
    Using compressed natural gas: 8
    Wheelchair and lift equipped buses: 965
    RTD owned and operated: 772
    RTD owned and leased to private carriers: 204
    Average age of fleet: 7 years
- RTD Ridership
    1999 annual boardings: 74,241,221
    1999 weekday boardings: 248,729
- Total Operating Budget
    2000 amended: $231,839,000

- Staff
  Number of total RTD employees: 2,711
    Salaried: 521
    Represented: 2,190
    Private bus operators/mechanics: 360
- RTD Fares
  RTD fares vary for bus and Light Rail service according to the time (peak or off-peak) and are or distance travelled. Discounts for seniors, disabled, students, and monthly passes. Complete fare information is available online at *www.rtd-denver.com/FaresandPasses*

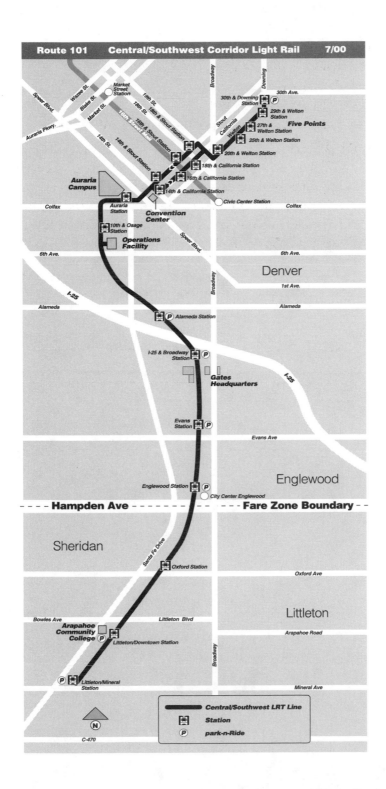

Bibliography

1993 Local Government Financial Compendium
  Colorado Division of Local Government, 1995

1994 Annual Report
  Colorado Department of Revenue, 1994

1994-1995 Colorado Education and Library Directory
  Colorado Department of Education, 1994

1994-95 Tuition and Fee Report
  Colorado Commission on Higher Education, 1994

1994/95 Official Denver Visitors Guide
  Denver Convention & Visitors Bureau, 1994

A Climbing Guide to Colorado's Fourteeners, Third Edition
  Walter Borneman & Lyndon Lampert, Pruett Publishing, Boulder, CO, 1994

A Colorado History, Seventh Edition
  Ubbelohde/Benson/Smith, Pruett Publishing, Boulder, CO, 1995

A Roadside Guide to Rocky Mountain National Park
  B. Willard & S. Foster, Johnson Books, Boulder, CO, 1990

Absolutely Every Bed & Breakfast in Colorado, Third Edition
  Toni Knapp, Travis Ilse Publishers, Niwot CO, 1994

Ancient Walls, Indian Ruins of the Southwest
  Chuck Place, Fulcrum Publishing, Golden, CO, 1992

Best of Northern Colorado Hiking Trails
  Jack O. Olofson, Outdoor Books & Maps, Denver, CO, 1995

Big Ideas for Small Service Businesses
  Marilyn & Tom Ross, Communication Creativity, Buena Vista, CO, 1994

Bike With a View
  Mark Dowling, Concepts in Writing, Denver, CO, 1994

Colorado: A History of the Centennial State, 3rd Edition
  Abbott/Leonard/McComb, University Press of Colorado, Niwot, CO, 1994

Colorado's Fourteeners, From Hikes to Climbs
  Gerry Roach, Fulcrum Publishing, Golden, CO, 1992

Colorado at a Glance
  Department of Local Affairs, 1994

Colorado Business Start-Up Kit
  Colorado Business Assistance Center

Colorado Cabins, Cottages & Lodges
Hilton and Jenny Fitt-Peaster, Rocky Mountain Vacation Publishing,
Boulder, CO, 1993

Colorado Cache Cookbook
The Junior League of Denver, Inc., C & C Publications, Denver, CO, 1978

Colorado Child Support Handbook
Charles P. Brackney, Bradford Publishing, Denver, CO, 1997 (Out of Print)

Colorado Cycling Guide,
Jean and Hartley Alley, Pruett Publishing, Boulder, CO, 1990

Colorado Department of Regulatory Agencies
Department of Regulatory Agencies, 1993

Colorado Driver's License Handbook
Colorado Department of Motor Vehicles, 1995

Colorado Fact Booklet
Department of Local Affairs

Colorado Factbook, Vol. V, No. 1
Pyramid Publications, 1994

Colorado Hut to Hut
Brian Litz, Westcliffe Publishers, Englewood, CO, 1992

Colorado Lakes & Reservoirs
Jack O. Olofson, Outdoor Books & Maps, Denver, CO, 1994

Colorado Occupational Employment Outlook 1994-1999
Colorado Department of Labor and Employment, 1994

Colorado Private Elementary and Secondary Schools, 1995-96
Margorie Hicks, Magnolia Street Press, 1995

Colorado Revised Statutes 1997, Vehicles and Traffic
Bradford Publishing, Denver, CO, 1997

Colorado RV Parks
Hilton and Jenny Fitt-Peaster, Rocky Mountain Vacation Publishing,
Boulder, CO, 1995

Colorado Ski Country USA, Ski Guide 1997/98
Colorado Ski Country USA, 1997

Colorado, The State We're In
League of Women Voters of Colorado, 1995

Country Bound, Trade Your Business Suit Blues for Blue Jean Dreams
Marilyn and Tom Ross, Communication Creativity, Buena Vista, CO, 1992

Creme de Colorado Cookbook
The Junior League of Denver, Inc., C & C Publications, Denver, CO, 1987

Denver, Mining Camps to Metropolis
S. Leonard & T. Noel, University Press of Colorado, Niwot, CO, 1990

Discover the Good Life in Rural America
Bob Bone, Communication Creativity, Buena Vista, CO, 1994

Exploring Colorado State Parks
Martin Kleinsorge, University Press of Colorado, Niwot, CO, 1992

Friendly Divorce Guidebook for Colorado, 4th Edition
M.A. Hauer, J.D. and S.W. Whicher, Bradford Publishing, Denver, CO, 2001

Get Out of Town, A Comprehensive Guide to Outdoor Activities in the Boulder Area
M. Harding & F. Snalam, All Points Publishing, Boulder, CO, 1994

Governor's Advocate Corps. A Citizen's Handbook to Colorado State Departments
Governor's Advocate Corps, 1995

Handbook of Rocky Mountain Plants
Ruth Ashton Nelson, Roberts Rinehart Publishing, Niwot, CO, 1992

Landlord & Tenant Guide to Colorado Evictions
Victor M. Grimm, Esq., Bradford Publishing, Denver, CO, 1995

Leadville's Ice Palace
Darlene Weir, Ice Castle Productions, Lakewood, CO, 1994

Mountain Bike Rides in The Colorado Front Range
William L. Stoehr, Pruett Publishing, Boulder, CO, 1988

Moving With Children: A Parent's Guide to Moving with Children
T. Olkowski & L. Parker, Gylantic Publishing, Littleton, CO, 1993

Newcomers' Packet
Colorado Department of Education, 1995

Places Around The Bases
Diane Bakke and Jackie Davis, Westcliffe Publishers, Englewood, CO, 1995

Reports from the Colorado Economic and Demographic Information System
Colorado Division of Local Government, 1995

Roadside History of Colorado
James McTighe, Johnson Books, Boulder, CO, 1984

Rocky Mountain National Park Classic Hikes & Climbs
Gerry Roach, Fulcrum Publishing, Golden, CO, 1988

Rocky Mountain National Park Natural History Handbook
John C. Emerick, Roberts Rinehart Publishing, Niwot, CO, 1995

Rocky Mountain Safari: A Wildlife Discovery Guide
Cathy and Gordon Illg, Roberts Rinehart Publishing, Niwot, CO, 1994

Rocky Mountain Skiing
Claire Walter, Fulcrum Publishing, Golden, CO, 1992

Rocky Mountain Walks
Gary Ferguson, Fulcrum Publishing, Golden, CO, 1993

Rocky Mountain Wineries
L. Collison & B. Russell, Pruett Publishing, Boulder, CO, 1994

Seasonal Guide to The Natural Year
Ben Guterson, Fulcrum Publishing, Golden, CO, 1994

State Report Card 1994
Colorado Department of Education, 1994

Tales, Trails and Tommyknockers
Myriam Friggens, Johnson Books, Boulder, CO, 1979

The Archaeology of Colorado
E. Steve Cassells, Johnson Books, Boulder, CO, 1983

The Best of Colorado Biking Trails
Jack O. Olofson, Outdoor Books & Maps, Denver, CO, 1994

The Colorado General Assembly
John A. Straayer, University Press of Colorado, Niwot, CO, 1990

The Colorado Guide, 4th Edition
B. Caughey & D. Winstanley, Fulcrum Publishing, Golden, CO, 1997

The Colorado Trail
Randy Jacobs, Westcliffe Publishers, Englewood, CO, 1994

The Complete Colorado Campground Guide
Jack O. Olofson, Outdoor Books & Maps, Denver, CO, 1992

The Complete Guide to Colorado's Wilderness Areas
John Fielder & Mark Pearson, Westcliffe Publishers, Englewood, CO, 1994

The Entrepreneur's Resource for Success
The Colorado Small Business Development Center

The Four Corners Anasazi
Rose Houk, San Juan National Forest Association, 1994

The Guide to Metro Denver Public Schools, 1995-96 Edition
Margorie Hicks, Magnolia Street Press, 1995

The Mountain Bike Guide to Summit County, Colorado
Laura Rossetter, Sage Creek Press, Silverthorne, CO, 1993

The Mover's Guide
Targeted Marketing Solutions, Inc, 1993

The Practical Steps to Successful Business Ownership
U.S. Small Business Administration, 1995

The Xeriscape Flower Gardener for the Rocky Mountain Region
Jim Knopf, Johnson Books, Boulder, CO, 1991

US West Guide to Home Office Success
  US West, 1995

Winning Big in Colorado Small Claims Court
  Charles P. Brackney, Bradford Publishing, Denver, CO, 1996

Index

A

Accreditation 54

ACLIN 172, 173

Altitude Sickness 208-210

Anasazi 6

Artifacts 6

Attorney General 20

Avalanche Hotline 191

B

Bad Checks 114

Ballooning 194

Bed and Breakfast
  Accommodations 195

Bicycling 193, 194

Bighorn Sheep 4

Blue Spruce 4

Board of Education 53

Brewpubs 198

Brown Cloud 101, 208

Business Insurance 167

C

Cabins, Cottages 195

Centennial State 8

Chambers of Commerce 175-179

Charter Schools 54

Chinooks 12

Cliff Dwellings 6

Colleges 70, 71

Colorado Consumer Protection
  Act 156

Colorado ID Card 109

Colorado Plateau 11

Colorado Territory 11

Columbine 4

Commission on Indian Affairs 20

Common Law Marriage 117

Community Colleges 70, 172

Concerts 201

Continental Divide 9, 10

Corporation 157, 168

County Clerk 97

Courts
  Appeals 22
  County 21
  District 22
  Municipal 11
  Small Claims 11
  Supreme 22
  Water 27

Cripple Creek 8

Cross-Country Skiing 191

CSAP 53

D

Dance 206

Denver International Airport 85

Dinosaurs 6, 206

Divorce 116, 117

Drivers Licenses   103-107, 110

Dude and Guest Ranches   196

DUI   108, 113

DWI   113

E

Economic Development Offices   175

Economic Statistics   5

Education Demographics   4

Elections   16-17

Emissions Testing   101-103

Employee Classifications   162-165

Employment   86

Evictions   114-115

Executive Branch   19

Eye Irritation   209

F

Festivals   201

Financial Aid, Student   67-69

Four Corners Area   6

Four-Wheel-Drive Tours   196

Front Range   10, 84, 85

G

Gambling   201

General Assembly   18, 24

Geography   3

Golf   202

Government
  Branches of   19
  State   4

Governor   19

Great Plains   10, 11

Growing Season   218

H

Hang Gliding   194-195

Healthcare   89

High Altitude Cooking   210-216

Higher Education   66

Highways
  Road Conditions   34
  Statistics   5

Historical Tours   196

History   5

Hot Springs   202

House of Representatives   24

I

Initiatives   17

J

Job Service Centers   174

Job Training Office   175

Judicial Branch   21

Jury Duty   21

Jury Summons   21

L

Lark Bunting   4

Leadville   8, 9

League of Women Voters   17

Legislative Committees   25

Legislative Council   18, 24

Legislators   24

Libraries   72-74

License Plates   98

Licenses
  Drivers   103-107, 110
  Sales Tax   159

Lieutenant Governor   20

Limited Liability Company   158

Limited Liability Partnership   158

Limited Partnership   158

Liquor   114

Little Dry Creek   7

Lottery   119, 120

M

Magnet Schools   54

Mail-In Ballot   16

Marriage   115, 116

Mesa Verde National Park   6

Micro-Climates   219

Mine Tours   197

Minority Business Office   171

Motion Picture & Television
  Commission   30

Motorcycle Endorsement   105, 106

Moving Tips   221

Mt. Elbert   9, 207

Mt. Evans   10

Museums   203, 204

N

Narrow Gauge Trains   202

National Forests, Monuments,
  Parks   186, 187

Navajo   7

Nomadic Tribes   6

Non-Profit Corporation   158

Nosebleeds   208

O

Office of Business Development   171

Opera   205

P

Para Gliding   195

Parole Board   27

Pikes Peak Gold Rush   7, 8

Planetariums   204

Polling Places   17

Pollution Information   12

Population Demographics   2

Population Growth   2

Private Colleges   71

Proof of Insurance   100

Property Taxes   170

R

Referendum   17, 18

Rocky Mountain National
  Park   10, 141, 186

RV Parks   193

S

S Corporation   157

San Juan Mountains   10

Sangre de Cristo Mountains   10

Sawatch Mountain Range   10

Schools
  Choice   54
  Districts   51
  Entrance Age   52
  Enrollment Requirements   52
  Exceptional   52
  Information   124
  Private   66

Secretary of State   18, 20

Senate   24

Ski Areas   191, 192

Small Business   151

Small Business Administration   173

Small Business Development
  Centers   171-172

State Departments   26-49

State Flag   4

State Park Regulations   185

State Parks Pass   189

State Sales Tax   90
  Collecting   161

State Seal   4

State Symbols   4

Stegosaurus   6

Storage Tips   222

Substate Regions   10

T

Temperature Fluctuations   218

Tennis   202-203

Theater   203

Topography   9

Tornado   13

Traffic Violations   107, 108

Trail Ridge Road   10

Train Rides   202

Treasurer   20

V

Vehicle
  Classes of   99
  Insurance   100
  Registration   95
  Title   95

Voting   16, 17

W

Weather   10-13

Western Slope   9, 84

Wilderness Areas   188

Winery Tours   196

X

Xeriscape   219, 220

Z

Zoos   204, 205